Learning Torah

A Self-Guided Journey through the Layers of Jewish Learning

Joel Lurie Grishaver

UAHC Press

New York, New York

Library of Congress Cataloging-in-Publication Data

Grishaver, Joel Lurie.

Learning Torah

Summary: A study guide for the Torah which can be used as a classroom text or as a self-study resource and which has pre- and post-tests, discovery activities and worksheets.

1. Bible. O.T. Pentateuch—Juvenile literature. 2. Bible O.T. Pentateuch—Criticism, interpretation, etc. Jewish—Juvenile literature. [1. Bible. O.T. Pentateuch—Criticism, interpretation, etc.] I. Title BS 1227.G75 1990 222'.106   86-7127

ISBN 0-8075-0322-9

1 2 3 4 5 6 7 8 9 0

Publication of this volume

was made possible by a grant from the

Memphis-Plough Charitable Trust

in memory of

Moses and Julia Plough

ועשו לי מקדש ושכנתי בתוכם

And they shall make Me a Dwelling-Place,
and I shall dwell in them.

My father, Ira Lester Grishaver ז״ל, once taught me this verse, explaining,

"It is the act of building and creating together
which brings God into the community.
It is the act of building, not the building itself."

My father was an electrical engineer. He built buildings for a living. This piece of Torah came from his experience.

ACKNOWLEDGMENTS

This book has taken more than twelve years, more than one-third of my life. Through it all, Danny Syme had faith. No one else ever believed that it would be complete, but Danny would regularly remind me: "I have faith in you." His coaching and support made this book possible. One never wants to weaken Danny's sense of faith.

The staff at the UAHC, Stuart L. Benick, Aron Hirt-Manheimer, and all of the behind-the-scenes people in the editorial department, helped to shepherd this project through its many gyrations and manifestations. Thank you.

The editorial readers—Rabbi Bernard Zlotowitz in particular, as well as my own teachers Dr. William Cutter and Dr. Michael Signer—helped to guide and shape this attempt. They helped to release this work from the stone which contained it originally.

My own production department at Alef Type & Design was incredibly supportive and patient. My business partners, Alan Rowe and Jane Golub, kept the project alive at every turn. Their sweat joins mine on every page. Ira J. Wise, my HUC-JIR intern, and Linda Shulkin, our administrator, did yeomen's jobs ten years later, tracking down and clearing all of the sources which had been woven into the book's growth and development. And Lisa Rauchwerger, our staff artist, provided many of the renderings of my drawings used in this book. Her patience and skill literally make my work look good—in fact, better.

This work is dedicated to the memory of my father, Ira Lester Grishaver. In Rashi's first comment on the Torah, there is a citation attributed to "Rabbi Isaac." It is assumed by many Rashi scholars that this Rabbi Isaac is the Rabbi Isaac who was Rashi's father. This is an echo of two rabbinic principles: a parent should teach his own child Torah, and one who teaches anyone Torah has the status of a parent. I would like to thank my many teachers and parents who helped to shape the understandings and insights which became this book. First, Earl Auerbach, whose Shabbat afternoons with Rashi and the Red Sox built my connection with the text. Shlomo Carlebach, who let me play lead guitar poorly, taught me that stories have many lives. Dr. David Weiss showed me in one week of sessions that Torah can be a relationship. Dr. Ben Hollander demonstrated how study becomes *mentshlechkeit*. And Dr. Stanley Gevirtz ז״ל, despite my best efforts to resist, forced me to recognize that interpretation is only one part artistry and nine parts technical skill. Finally, I want to thank Dr. Stanford Levy for creating the environment where I clarified my own calling as Jewish teacher.

This book came into being through the confusion and enlightenment of my students (not necessarily in that order). It took form on the page through both their support and their challenges. I thank all of those who taught me, by providing me with the opportunity to learn with them. And I want to thank Rashi, Cassuto, Robert Alter, Nehama Leibowitz, Everett Fox—and many other friends and teachers whom I have met over the Torah's text—friends whose insight and support constantly change and renew my life.

Joel Lurie Grishaver
Los Angeles, California
Kislev 5751

CREDITS

TO THE LEARNER

This is a book about *learning*. It is probably different from most books you have used before. It is halfway between a workbook and a textbook. It provides both information for your background and the opportunity for you to discover and master many insights on your own. It is also designed to help you measure your own progress. Starting with Module Two, you will find a prescription and a pre-test at the beginning of each module. Each module will end with a post-test. Using these tools, you will be able to monitor your own progress with this material. At the end of each module you'll find the answers to each of the worksheets.

By combining both discovery activities and form book we've made this work impossible to just read your way through. To work your way through this book, you'll need to do a combination of things: reading, filling out worksheets, hunting, problem-solving, and thinking, as well as a great deal of research.

In writing this book, we imagined two different ways it could be used. One was as a classroom text; the other was as a self-study resource. Regardless of the setting, to work your way through this book, you will regularly need to use a copy of the Bible. Also, you will probably want access to a good Jewish library, to the *Encyclopaedia Judaica*, and to a teacher who can answer at least your basic questions.

CONTENTS

THE INTRODUCTION: FROM TEXTBOOK TO TEXT

This book is about ways of learning Torah. American English usually talks about *studying*, but Jewish English uses *learning*; by the end of this book, you'll understand the difference.

Today, getting a Jewish education usually means classrooms, lectures, quizzes, and textbooks. It may also mean camps, discussions, youth groups, videos, games, and even computers. We usually assume that it is the content which we are studying rather than the way we are learning which is Jewish. As products of "modern" schools, we are used to applying the ways we have been trained to learn to master every new subject. We know how to outline, take notes, use a card catalogue, and how to annotate a bibliography. Judaism seems to be just another subject to which we can apply our good study skills.

But, some Jewish subjects have their own unique study skills. Jews have developed ways of learning which differ from "normal" school skills.

This book is more than a collection of new Jewish information; it examines the texts and books through which Judaism has evolved and introduces the reader to the skills and methods needed to comprehend these texts. In other words, it presents a chance to learn new ways of reading and learning.

List those qualities which you believe are needed by good students.

1. literacy
2. no procrastinators
3. insomniacs
4. reading
5. writing
6. patience
7. good study habits
8. serious
9. mature
10. respect
11. want to learn
12. hard work

Pirke Avot 6:6

The Talmud says that a good student must do, have, and be these things:

1. Study out loud
2. Clear pronunciation
3. Understanding
4. Understanding of the heart
5. Awe
6. Reverence
7. Meekness
8. Cheerfulness
9. Serving scholars
10. Good friendship with other students
11. Discussions with other students
12. Sedateness
13. Knowledge of the Bible and the Mishnah
14. Moderation in business
15. Moderation in outside interests
16. Moderation in pleasure
17. Moderation in sleep
18. Moderation in conversation
19. Moderation in laughter
20. Self-discipline
21. A good heart
22. Faith in the wise
23. Accept criticism
24. Understand one's place
25. Rejoice in one's portion
26. Guard one's words
27. Claim no self-merit
28. Being loved
29. Loving God
30. Loving people
31. Loving justice
32. Double-check
33. Avoiding honor
34. Not boastful of knowledge
35. Not enjoy making judgments
36. Share others' burdens
37. Judge fairly
38. Show others truth
39. Showing others to peace
40. Be organized
41. Ask
42. Answer
43. Hear and adding onto
44. Learn in order to teach
45. Learn in order to do
46. Make one's teacher wise
47. Pay attention
48. Cite the source of a quotation

Compare your list with the talmudic list:

1. Underline the items on the talmudic list which are also on your list.
2. Circle the number of any items on the talmudic list which you find strange or confusing.
3. How are the lists different?

_____

4. How do the talmudic images of a good student differ from yours?

_____

To understand something of what is meant by a "Jewish way of learning," let's look at four clues.

The Alphabet:
For Jews, the Hebrew alphabet has been more than a way to communicate. Letters have a power of their own.

The Book:
Not only the Torah, but many Jewish books have special styles and traditions.

The Classroom:
Jews have learned in many kinds of settings, and many of these learning places generate special feelings.

The Student and the Teacher:
Jewish education has always stressed a very special relationship between teachers and students.

Back when God was thinking about creating the world, the twenty-two letters of the א־ב/*Alef-Bet* (the Hebrew alphabet) surrounded God, and each one begged to be the first letter of the word God would use to create the world:

"Hey, God," said the letter TAV, "create the world with me. תּוֹרָה */TORAH would be a good word to start with."*

But God said: "You are forgetting that TAV finishes the word מָוֶת */MAVET (death) and so you bring death into the world."*

Clue #1

The Alphabet:

For the Jewish tradition, letters and words are holy. God creates the world through words. The Torah describes creation as happening through God's speech—**"And God said: Let there be light...."** (Gen. 1:3), and we will see over the next few pages how even letters have a special role in creation.

The following legend is found in both the Midrash and the Zohar. (Midrash Hagadol 1:12-13, Aseret Hadibrot 62, Midrash R. Akiva 23-24, Zohar 1: 2b-3a, and 205b.)

"What about שָׁלוֹם *SHALOM (peace)?" said SHIN.*

"What about שֶׁקֶר */SHEKER (lie)?" said God.*

"KOF can stand for קָדוֹשׁ *KADOSH (holy)," said KOF. But God said, "KOF can also stand for* קְלָלָה */KELALAH (curse)."*

REISH thought that רַחֲמִים */RACHAMIM (mercy) would be a good way to create the world, but God reminded REISH of* רַע */RA (evil).*

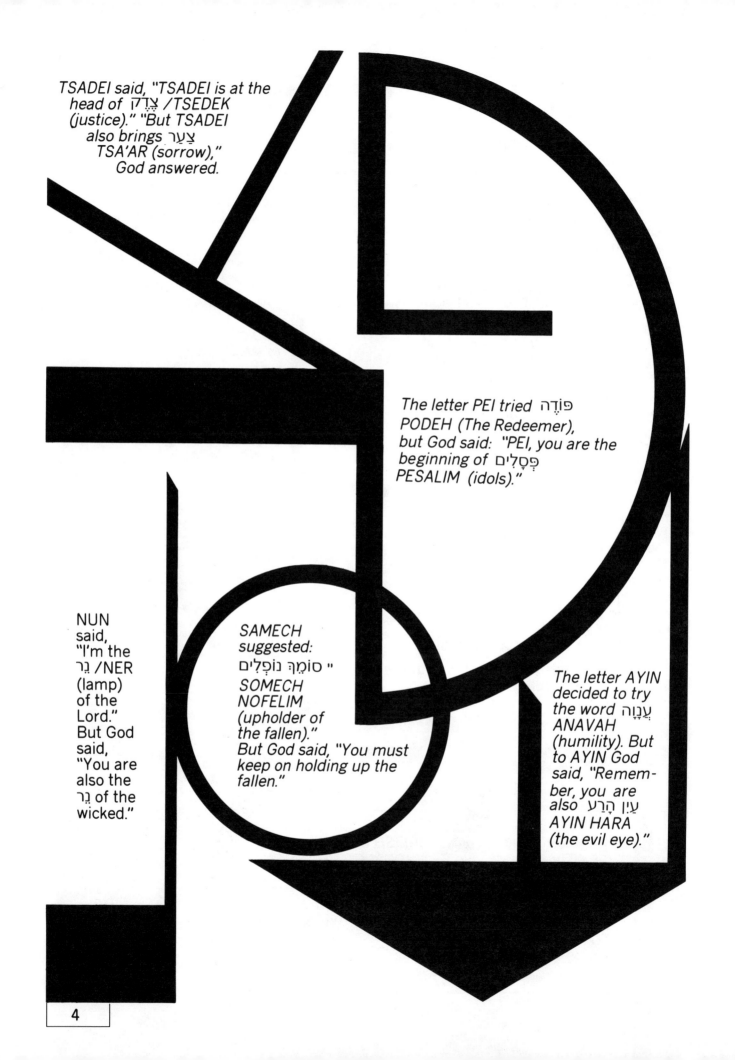

TSADEI said, "TSADEI is at the head of צֶדֶק /TSEDEK (justice)." "But TSADEI also brings צַעַר TSA'AR (sorrow)," God answered.

The letter PEI tried פּוֹדֶה PODEH (The Redeemer), but God said: "PEI, you are the beginning of פְּסָלִים PESALIM (idols)."

NUN said, "I'm the נֵר /NER (lamp) of the Lord." But God said, "You are also the נֵר of the wicked."

SAMECH suggested: " סוֹמֵךְ נוֹפְלִים SOMECH NOFELIM (upholder of the fallen)." But God said, "You must keep on holding up the fallen."

The letter AYIN decided to try the word עֲנָוָה ANAVAH (humility). But to AYIN God said, "Remember, you are also עַיִן הָרַע AYIN HARA (the evil eye)."

When the letter BET stood up to speak, the other letters stepped back. BET said: "I begin the word בָּרוּךְ / BARUCH (blessed), the first word of every blessing that Jews use to praise Your name." And God said, "Yes, through the BET in בְּרֵאשִׁית /BERESHIT will the world be created."

After God had already promised BET, God saw ALEF. "Oh, ALEF," God said, "why didn't you speak up?" (ALEF was always silent.) "Why didn't you suggest אָנֹכִי /ANOCHI (I am) as a way to create the world? I could not have refused you. But now I've already promised BET. But, we'll make you the first letter of the Ten Commandments."

Kermit, Big Bird, and all their friends have taught us the importance of the alphabet. But, no matter how excited our first grade teachers got over the ABC's, they couldn't make the English alphabet feel "holy." For the Jewish tradition, the world was created out of letters. These letters are not only part of words but part of the mystery of our existence.

If letters can be holy, so can words. Words combine to form books.

Clue #2
The Book:

Let's compare Jewish sacred books with everyday books. Take the *Talmud*, the *commentaries*, the *Midrash*, etc. Every one of these books follows more or less the same format. Somewhere on the page in large type is the major text and then around it in smaller type are all kinds of commentaries and explanations.

- Jewish sacred books tend to give you "working answers" and then have you work out the question. We are used to books that ask questions and make us find the answers.

- Today, when people come up with new ideas or theories, they write a new book or article. In the traditional Jewish approach, the writer publishes his/her theories as a new commentary added to older commentaries around the major text. The new commentary combined with the older commentaries constitute an ongoing dialogue.

- None of us would ever kiss a copy of the Constitution or an encyclopedia if it fell on the floor. None of us would ever worry about whether it is proper to stack a thesaurus on top of an almanac. But Jews kiss copies of their sacred books when they fall to the floor and have rules about whether you have to place a volume of the Talmud on a copy of the Bible or put the copy of the Bible on top of the Talmud.

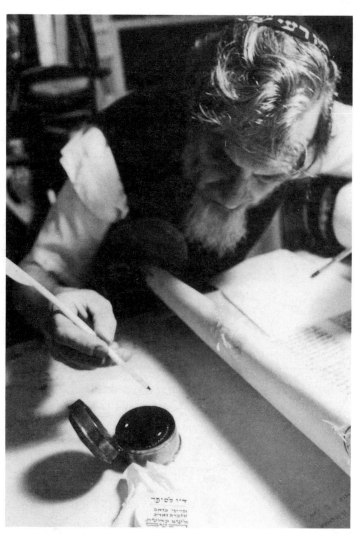

The beauty of the form bespeaks the worth of the scribe.   Ibn Tibbon

The Torah is the most special of all Jewish books. Let's take a look at what is involved in producing a סֵפֶר תּוֹרָה / *Sefer Torah* (Torah Scroll).

Every Jew is commanded to write a *Sefer Torah* for his* own use. Even if he has inherited a *Sefer Torah*, it is a *mitzvah* to write one at his own expense. If he writes it with his own hand, it is as if he has received it himself at Mt. Sinai. If he does not know how, he should have others write it for him. Anyone who corrects a single letter in a *Sefer Torah* is credited with writing all of it.

Rambam, **Mishneh Torah, Laws of the Sefer Torah, 7:1**

When Rambam (Rabbi Moses Ben Maimon/a.k.a. Maimonides, 1135-1204) wrote the **Mishneh Torah, women didn't participate in much of Jewish ritual life. Changing this text to a nonsexist understanding would change its meaning. However, Rambam's understanding of Jewish ritual need not be ours.*

The rabbis based the *mitzvah* which obligates every Jew to write a *Sefer Torah* on this biblical verse:

וְעַתָּה כִּתְבוּ לָכֶם אֶת הַשִּׁירָה הַזֹּאת

Therefore, write down this song for yourself. (Deut. 31:19)

Even today, a סֵפֶר תּוֹרָה / *Sefer Torah* is handwritten by a סוֹפֵר /*sofer* (scribe). Writing it is a long, hard process. It takes between nine months and a year of work to finish a Torah. It has to be written with the best permanent black ink, on parchment made from the skins of "clean" (*kosher*) animals. For a pen, the *sofer* must use a quill or a reed. Metal, which is used to make weapons, cannot be used for making a Torah. All of the separate parchments must be sewn together with sinews from *kosher* animals, and the *sofer* must use a thorn for a needle.

The *sofer* cannot write a single letter from memory. The *sofer* must read from a correct text, pronounce every word out loud, and only then copy it. Every letter and every word must be perfectly spaced. Every letter must be clearly drawn so that a child can recognize it. In addition, the *sofer* has to add crowns to thirteen letters. The letters ש ע ט נ ז ג צ have three-stroke crowns and the letters ב ד ק ח י ה have one-stroke crowns.

Here is a passage handwritten by a *sofer*. Add the crowns on your own.

וְעַתָּה כִּתְבוּ לָכֶם אֶת הַשִּׁירָה הַזֹּאת

Every letter is a whole world.

The Maggid of Mezhirich

There is not a single letter in the Torah on which a thousand secrets do not hang.

Menashe Ben Israel

Every single letter has a soul.

Moses Cordovero

To understand how hard it is to write a *Sefer Torah*, look at this list of conditions which can make it un-*kosher* (and therefore unusable).

If it was written on the skin of an unclean animal.
If a clean skin was not made into parchment.
If the parchment was not made specifically for a *Sefer Torah*.
If it was written on the wrong side of the parchment.
If just one section was written on the wrong side of the parchment.
If it was written without traced lines.
If it was not written with indelible ink.
If it was written in any language but Hebrew.
If the *sofer* was a heretic or impure.
If the *sofer* wrote the name of God without *kavanah* (devotion).
If one letter was omitted.
If one letter was added.
If two letters touch.
If one letter can be misread as another.
If a letter can't be read.
If one word looks like two.
If two words look like one.
If the *sofer* changed the form of any section.
If it is not sewn together with the dry tendons of clean animals.

Rambam, **Mishneh Torah**, *Laws of the Sefer Torah, 10:1*

One chasidic rabbi took the laws for writing a *Sefer Torah* and explained them this way:

The many letters in the Torah represent the many souls of the Jewish people. If one single letter is left out of the Torah, it is unfit for use. If one single soul is left out of the union of the Jewish people, the Divine Presence will not join them. Like the letters, the soul must join together in a union. Then why is it forbidden for one letter to touch another? Because every soul must have its own unique relationship with its Creator.

Rabbi Uri of Strelisk, from **Tales of the Hasidim: Later Masters**, *Buber, p. 147*

We even learn from the ways the letters are written. When we find the שְׁמַע /Shema in the Torah, it looks like this.

שְׁמַע יִשְׂרָאֵל יְהוָה אֱלֹהֵינוּ יְהוָה אֶחָד

The letters ד and ע are larger to help us read them carefully. The word שְׁמַע /shema could be misread as שֶׁמָּא /she-ma, which means "perhaps." The Shema would then proclaim: "(O) Israel, perhaps, the Lord is our God."

Rambam, **Mishneh Torah**, *Laws of Reading Shema*, 2:9

The ע and ד form the word עֵד /ed, which means witness. Saying the Shema makes us witnesses to God's unity.

From the Midrash

The last word in the Torah is יִשְׂרָאֵל / Yisrael. The last letter is ל /lamed. The first word in the Torah is בְּרֵאשִׁית / Bereshit. The first letter is ב /bet. Whenever we finish the Torah, we go right back to the beginning. We join ל to ב and we have לֵב /lev (heart).

Folk teaching

Clue #3
The Classroom:

There have been many different kinds of Jewish classrooms and schools, most of them reflecting the surrounding culture. In our experience, Jewish classrooms usually have desks, wall clocks, and blackboards. The Midrash suggests that Mt. Sinai, where Moses learned Torah directly with God, was the first Jewish classroom.

The great Sanhedrin was the congress of Israel in the rabbinic period. Members won their membership not through election but through knowledge of the Torah. It was both a court and a law-making body; but most of all it was a school.

In ancient Israel, the Torah was read outdoors in the marketplace on both Mondays and Thursdays. Torah was brought to the people wherever they gathered, so the marketplace was transformed into a classroom.

Also, the *Bet Din*, the Jewish courtroom, serves as a classroom. In a *Bet Din*, three rabbis who are ordained as both judges and teachers hand down verdicts. Here, they used the Torah's laws to judge between the people and, while doing so, teach its practice to all who are gathered. Every Jewish courtroom is a place of Torah.

In Yemen, where printed copies of books were scarce, students learned how to read sideways or upside down, depending on which side of the shared book they sat.

While each of these settings reflected the culture around them, each of these schools was a uniquely Jewish place where learning was not just a way to acquire information but a way to live.

The בֵּית מִדְרָשׁ / *Bet Midrash* is probably the best example of a unique Jewish classroom. It is a place where Torah in all forms, but especially Talmud, is learned.

The front wall has an אֲרוֹן הַקֹּדֶשׁ / *Aron Hakodesh* (Holy Ark) and the back wall is full of סְפָרִים / *sefarim* (books). The learners work at tables and sit on benches or, sometimes, they stand at high bookstands. The teacher has no fixed place.

The *Bet Midrash* was not a school for children; it was (and still is) a place for adults. Often, a guild or another business association would have its own *Bet Midrash*—a place where its members could meet and learn after work.

1 When the class begins a text, the teacher introduces it, showing the students how to read the text correctly and helping them to begin understanding the passage.

2 Then the students would work in pairs called a *chevrusa* and go over the text. Together they would master the passage and try to discover its deeper meaning.

3 The students would also spend time alone with the passage, often rocking and chanting the passage in an attempt to put themselves back into the world and experience of the text's origin.

4 Finally, the students would regather as a class, share what they had learned, and see what other insights their teacher could bring to the text. This was done with every passage studied.

In the *Bet Midrash*:

- Learning is a team process. A student masters a text through the help of a partner.

- The place of study is both a classroom and a synagogue. With the Torah in the Ark at the front of the room, with the Eternal Light burning over the Ark— both teacher and student know the source of the final answers.

- Learning is a holy act.

Jewish classrooms can be special places.

Clue #4
Students and Teachers:

In Judaism, like in many cultures, children are seen as the bearers of the tradition—of the future; but, in the Jewish tradition, the future is also rooted in the Torah.

Look at these three rabbinic passages:

The world exists only because of the innocent breath of schoolchildren.

Talmud, Shabbat 119b

Jerusalem was destroyed only because the children did not attend school and loitered in the streets.

Talmud, Shabbat 119b

When the Sanhedrin went into captivity, the *Shechinah* (Divine Presence) did not go with them. The priests went into captivity and the *Shechinah* did not join them. But when the schoolchildren went into captivity, the *Shechinah* went with them.

Lam. Rabbah 1:3 on 1:6

In the same way, the Talmud regards a Jewish teacher as someone special.

One who teaches a child is as if she/he created that child.

Talmud, Sanhedrin 19b

Rabbi Chiyya, Rabbi Assi, and Rabbi Judah were sent to visit the cities in the land of Israel in order to appoint teachers of Bible and Mishnah. When they came to a city and found no teachers, they said, "Bring us the guardians of the town." When the people brought the armed guards, the rabbis said, "These are not the guardians, these are the destroyers." "Who then?" the people asked. The rabbis answered, "The teachers."

Yerushalmi, Hagigah 1, 7f, 76c

SO WHAT HAVE WE GOT?

Clue #1 **THE ALPHABET** The alphabet is God's building blocks
Words are powerful
Letters are HOLY

Clue #2 **THE BOOK** Books create dialogue between generations
Books let you work out both the question and the answer
Books are special
Books of traditional texts are HOLY

Clue #3 **THE CLASSROOM** Learning is communal
Learning is a spiritual process
Learning is HOLY

Clue #4 **STUDENTS AND TEACHERS** Students and teachers save the world
Studying is HOLY

We're often taught that education is important. We understand that schooling can lead us to secure a good job, learn how to better ourselves, and teach us about the ways of the world. We often assume that learning is valuable when it produces tangible results.

Make books your companions. Let your shelves be your treasure grounds.

Ibn Tibbon

As Jews, it is also important to understand that learning is a spiritual process. It is a way of bonding deep friendships with others, it is a method of coming to understand ourselves, and it is a path towards God. For the Jew, learning is also a process of world change, a way of directing humanity towards its potential. For Jews, Jewish learning (Torah learning) is a holy process.

The heart of Torah learning is a kind of special dialogue. The text is read slowly, word by word. As we read, questions emerge. We struggle to solve these questions. Along the way, other voices, other Jews who have looked at these words before, join the discussion with their commentaries. They point out

To an extent unequaled among other sections of humanity, Jews have been interested in books....A book was not to him as to his neighbor an object of veneration, of mystery, of distrust. It was a sheer necessity of everyday life.

Cecil Roth, **Essays on Jewish Booklore**

problems, they share their personal solutions. The conversation continues. Between students, between teachers and students, the perceptions differ, the inferred meanings conflict, and the quest continues. In the end, the learner is left staring in his/her own text, the voices and insights of many others are heard, but for each learner the passage has yielded a personal understanding. Jewish text study is a wondrous combination of learning from others and finding out about yourself.

Learning requires a talent for sitting.

Yiddish folk saying

The Torah speaks in a language all people understand.
Talmud

There is no subject not mentioned in the Torah.
Talmud

The Torah has seventy faces.
Midrash

It is a Tree of Life.
Proverbs 3:18

The Torah is Light.
Proverbs 6:23

ENCYCLOPEDIA TORATICA

עץ חיים

תורה אורא

THE MORE TORAH THE MORE LIFE

Pirke Avot

The Torah is like a good friend.
Talmud, Yevamot

The Torah sheds its grace on those who study it.
Midrash

MODULE ONE: PRESENTING THE TORAH

The Torah cannot be learned unless it is learned among friends.

Talmud

The Torah is deeper than the sea.

Midrash

The Torah is like water coming down drop by drop and becoming a great river.   Midrash

The Torah is a deep sea, and people can draw water from it.

Yosef Hurwitz

Its measure is longer than the measure of the earth. Job 11:9

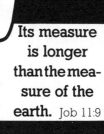

A BEFORE WORD

This is a book about TORAH. Torah is a word we use a lot, and it is a word which has many meanings.

Torah can be a PROCESS—a way of studying, learning, and growing. That is, Torah can be something a JEW DOES.

Torah means LAW. We use it to mean the codes, rules, and values which guide the way we live. We use it to mean the principles which shape the way we act. That is, Torah can be the way a JEW LIVES.

Torah can mean all the LITERATURE the Jewish people consider HOLY. Torah can mean the whole Bible, the commentaries, the Talmud—the huge body of material a JEW LEARNS.

So, we can DO **Torah**
by LEARNING **Torah**
in order to LIVE **Torah.**
(It can get confusing.)

Torah also means the Five Books of Moses, that is the סֵפֶר תּוֹרָה / *Sefer Torah*, the scroll we keep inside the ark.

The Maggid of Mezhirich, a great chasidic teacher, tried to weave all these meanings together when he told his students:

Don't say words of Torah—BE Torah.

In other words, Torah seems to have two meanings.

Torah can be a symbol. We can dance with the Torah, stand up for it, and kiss it with our *talit* or prayer book as it is carried by. We can talk about the Torah as being "a light" or as being the "length of our days." Torah can be a **symbol** for our Judaism.

Torah can be a book. The Torah is a body of literature filled with history, stories, poems, laws, and other sacred information. The Torah is a collection of names, places, events, and codes. Written in Hebrew, the Torah is a **book** we struggle to fully understand.

Sometimes, it is hard for us to find all the beauty of the **symbol** when we wrestle with the **book**.

PRESENTING THE TORAH

The Torah is:
5 Books
187 Chapters
54 *Sidrot*
(Torah portions)
5,846 Verses

It tells a story which begins with God creating the universe and ends with the death of Moses. In between, people discover God, and God makes a covenant with Israel.
B'nai Yisrael (the Children of Israel) enter and leave Egypt, and the Law is given. In between, we have lots of laws and stories.

It stars (in order of appearance):
God, Adam & Eve, Cain & Abel, Noah, Abraham, Sarah, Eliezer, Hagar, Ishmael, Lot, Lot's wife, Isaac, Rebekah, Laban, Esau, Jacob, Abimelech, Rachel, Leah, Reuben, Simeon, Levi, Judah, Issachar, Zebulun, Joseph, Dan, Naphtali, Gad, Asher, & Benjamin, Dinah, Potiphar, Potiphar's wife, Pharaoh, Manasseh & Ephraim, a new pharaoh, his daughter, Moses, Zipporah, Miriam, Jethro, Aaron, Nadab & Abihu, Bezalel, Korach, Balaam, Balaam's ass, & Joshua.

Featuring:
The goring ox, the red heifer, angels, the stranger in your midst, the corners of your fields, holy convocations, and a wandering Aramean.

With a cast of thousands.

The Torah is the central source book for Judaism. No matter how we define our being Jewish, no matter what we talk about Jewishly, it all comes down to Torah.

Christianity and Islam both have Jewish roots. Both are rooted in Torah.

Do you really want to know what the Torah is all about?

Exercise 1.1

Clue #1: Look for the following hidden message. Take a copy of the Torah or a Bible and write down the last word of each of the five books of the Torah.

_____   _____   _____   _____   _____

Genesis   Exodus   Leviticus   Numbers   Deuteronomy

What story do they tell? _____

Exercise 1.2

Clue #2: A second place to look for what the Torah is really all about is the first comment Rashi, the leading medieval Bible commentator, made on Genesis. Here, he tries to explain why the Torah begins with the Book of Genesis.

תּוֹרָה	TORAH (law, teaching)
מוֹרָה/מוֹרֶה	MORAH/MOREH (teacher)
הוֹרָאָה	HORA'AH (instructing)
חוּמָשׁ	CHUMASH (Torah)
חָמֵשׁ	CHAMESH (five)
	PENTATEUCH (Greek for Chumash)

Rabbi Isaac said: The Torah really should have begun at Exodus 12:2, **This month shall mark for you the beginning of months....**

This is the first MITZVAH that the Jewish people were commanded to perform. Since the major purpose of the Torah is to teach MITZVOT, it should have begun with the first major MITZVAH.

The Torah begins with the Book of GENESIS in order to show that God created the world, and, being the Creator, God had the right to give the LAND OF ISRAEL to the Jewish people.

To find out more about Rashi, look at **Module Eight.**

1. What does Rashi mean by MITZVAH? _____

2. What does Rashi see as the major purpose of the Torah? _____

3. What does Rashi understand as the secondary purpose? _____

4. How does the Book of Genesis link the Land of Israel to the Jewish people? _____

5. What do you think is the major purpose of the Torah? _____

The Torah is made up of five books. In English, the names come from the major theme of each book. In Hebrew, the names are taken from the first important word in each book.

GENESIS means origin. בְּרֵאשִׁית / BERESHIT means "In the beginning."

BERESHIT starts with the creation of the world and tells us the story of the Patriarchs and Matriarchs. It focuses on ABRAHAM, SARAH, ISAAC, REBEKAH, JACOB, RACHEL, and LEAH and their evolving relationship with God. The last part of the book is JOSEPH's story, and it ends with the Children of Israel and their life in **EGYPT.**

EXODUS means leaving. שְׁמוֹת / SHEMOT means "names."

SHEMOT starts with the list of names of the Children of Israel (now the twelve tribes). It tells the story of their struggle to leave EGYPT, and it introduces MOSES as a leader who aids God in redeeming them from EGYPT. The new nation of ISRAEL is brought to MT. SINAI and there in the wilderness receives the TORAH and builds the TABERNACLE, its first place of worship. The book ends with God promising to be with them in all their **JOURNEYS.**

LEVITICUS comes from LEVI, the name of the tribe of priests and Levites. וַיִּקְרָא / VAYIKRA means "And He called."

VAYIKRA is the book of the priests. Sometimes it is even called תּוֹרַת כֹּהֲנִים / TORAT KOHANIM (the Torah of the Priests). It is a rule book which talks about how to offer sacrifices, how to observe holidays, and how to lead a good life. It ends by summing up all the MITZVOT God gave to Israel at **MT. SINAI.**

NUMBERS comes from the census Moses takes at the start of this book. בְּמִדְבַּר / BEMIDBAR means "In the wilderness."

BEMIDBAR is the further adventures of ISRAEL in the WILDERNESS. It describes various portions of daily life and sundry incidents, battles, Korach's rebellion, and other laws which came to them as they wandered. It ends with the laws of inheritance, stating these were the commandments which Moses taught to the people near **JERICHO.**

DEUTERONOMY means the second "telling." דְּבָרִים / DEVARIM means "things."

DEVARIM is a collection of the things that MOSES retells the Children of Israel while they are camped on the far side of the Jordan River. MOSES retells their experiences in the wilderness, including the laws they received. At the end of the book MOSES dies, and the Children of Israel are ready to move into the Land of **ISRAEL.**

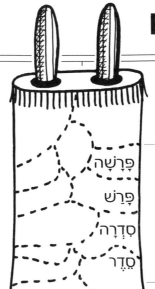

פָּרָשָׁה PARASHAH (Torah portion)

פָּרַשׁ PARASH (separate)

סִדְרָה SIDRAH (Torah portion)

סֵדֶר SEDER (order, sequence)

בְּרֵאשִׁית בָּרָא אֱלֹהִים אֵת הַשָּׁמַיִם וְאֵת הָאָרֶץ
וְהָאָרֶץ הָיְתָה תֹהוּ וָבֹהוּ וְחֹשֶׁךְ עַל פְּנֵי תְהוֹם וְרוּחַ
אֱלֹהִים מְרַחֶפֶת עַל פְּנֵי הַמָּיִם וַיֹּאמֶר אֱלֹהִים יְהִי
אוֹר וַיְהִי אוֹר וַיַּרְא אֱלֹהִים אֶת הָאוֹר כִּי טוֹב
וַיַּבְדֵּל אֱלֹהִים בֵּין הָאוֹר וּבֵין הַחֹשֶׁךְ וַיִּקְרָא
אֱלֹהִים לָאוֹר יוֹם וְלַחֹשֶׁךְ קָרָא לָיְלָה וַיְהִי עֶרֶב
וַיְהִי בֹקֶר יוֹם אֶחָד
וַיֹּאמֶר אֱלֹהִים יְהִי רָקִיעַ בְּתוֹךְ הַמָּיִם וִיהִי מַבְדִּיל
בֵּין מַיִם לָמָיִם וַיַּעַשׂ אֱלֹהִים אֶת הָרָקִיעַ וַיַּבְדֵּל
בֵּין הַמַּיִם אֲשֶׁר מִתַּחַת לָרָקִיעַ וּבֵין הַמַּיִם אֲשֶׁר
מֵעַל לָרָקִיעַ וַיְהִי כֵן וַיִּקְרָא אֱלֹהִים לָרָקִיעַ שָׁמָיִם
וַיְהִי עֶרֶב וַיְהִי בֹקֶר יוֹם שֵׁנִי
וַיֹּאמֶר אֱלֹהִים יִקָּווּ הַמַּיִם מִתַּחַת הַשָּׁמַיִם אֶל
מָקוֹם אֶחָד וְתֵרָאֶה הַיַּבָּשָׁה וַיְהִי כֵן וַיִּקְרָא אֱלֹהִים
לַיַּבָּשָׁה אֶרֶץ וּלְמִקְוֵה הַמַּיִם קָרָא יַמִּים וַיַּרְא
אֱלֹהִים כִּי טוֹב וַיֹּאמֶר אֱלֹהִים תַּדְשֵׁא הָאָרֶץ
דֶּשֶׁא עֵשֶׂב מַזְרִיעַ זֶרַע עֵץ פְּרִי עֹשֶׂה פְּרִי לְמִינוֹ
אֲשֶׁר זַרְעוֹ בוֹ עַל הָאָרֶץ וַיְהִי כֵן וַתּוֹצֵא הָאָרֶץ
דֶּשֶׁא עֵשֶׂב מַזְרִיעַ זֶרַע לְמִינֵהוּ וְעֵץ עֹשֶׂה פְּרִי
אֲשֶׁר זַרְעוֹ בוֹ לְמִינֵהוּ וַיַּרְא אֱלֹהִים כִּי טוֹב וַיְהִי
עֶרֶב וַיְהִי בֹקֶר יוֹם שְׁלִישִׁי
וַיֹּאמֶר אֱלֹהִים יְהִי מְאֹרֹת בִּרְקִיעַ הַשָּׁמַיִם לְהַבְדִּיל
בֵּין הַיּוֹם וּבֵין הַלָּיְלָה וְהָיוּ לְאֹתֹת וּלְמוֹעֲדִים וּלְיָמִים
וְשָׁנִים וְהָיוּ לִמְאוֹרֹת בִּרְקִיעַ הַשָּׁמַיִם לְהָאִיר עַל
הָאָרֶץ וַיְהִי כֵן וַיַּעַשׂ אֱלֹהִים אֶת שְׁנֵי הַמְּאֹרֹת
הַגְּדֹלִים אֶת הַמָּאוֹר הַגָּדֹל לְמֶמְשֶׁלֶת הַיּוֹם וְאֶת
הַמָּאוֹר הַקָּטֹן לְמֶמְשֶׁלֶת הַלַּיְלָה וְאֵת הַכּוֹכָבִים
וַיִּתֵּן אֹתָם אֱלֹהִים בִּרְקִיעַ הַשָּׁמַיִם לְהָאִיר עַל
הָאָרֶץ וְלִמְשֹׁל בַּיּוֹם וּבַלַּיְלָה וּלְהַבְדִּיל בֵּין הָאוֹר
וּבֵין הַחֹשֶׁךְ וַיַּרְא אֱלֹהִים כִּי טוֹב וַיְהִי עֶרֶב וַיְהִי
בֹקֶר יוֹם רְבִיעִי

When we open up the Torah, we find it divided into chapters and verses. But a SEFER TORAH (Torah Scroll) has no verses, no punctuation, and few real separations.

The idea of dividing the Torah into chapters and verses is relatively new, an innovation of Christian Bible scholars during the 1300s and the 1400s.

Traditionally, Jews read Torah three days a week: Mondays, Thursdays, and Shabbat morning and afternoon. Mondays and Thursdays were market days and people came into the city; Shabbat was Shabbat.

We read one SIDRAH a week and finish the Torah every year on SIMCHAT TORAH, when we read the first and last PARASHAH.

Each PARASHAH is named after the first important Hebrew word(s) in the portion. The Hebrew names of the five books of the Torah come from the first SIDRAH in each book.

Try to find the word(s) each of these PARASHIYOT is named for. (Circle them.)

וַיִּהְיוּ חַיֵּי שָׂרָה
מֵאָה שָׁנָה
וְעֶשְׂרִים שָׁנָה
וְשֶׁבַע שָׁנִים
שְׁנֵי חַיֵּי שָׂרָה

1. Sarah's lifetime (came to)
   one hundred years
   and twenty years
   and seven years—
   (This was) the span of Sarah's life.
   (Gen. 23:1)

וְאֵלֶּה הַמִּשְׁפָּטִים
אֲשֶׁר תָּשִׂים לִפְנֵיהֶם

2. These are the rules
   that you shall set before them.
   (Exod. 21:1)

וַיְדַבֵּר יהוה אֶל־מֹשֶׁה לֵּאמֹר
דַּבֵּר אֶל־כָּל־עֲדַת בְּנֵי־יִשְׂרָאֵל
וְאָמַרְתָּ אֲלֵהֶם
קְדֹשִׁים תִּהְיוּ
כִּי קָדוֹשׁ אֲנִי יהוה אֱלֹהֵיכֶם

3. The LORD spoke to Moses saying:
   Speak to the whole Israelite community
   and say to them:
   You shall be holy,
   for I, the Lord your God, am holy.
   (Lev. 19:1-2)

אֵלֶּה הַדְּבָרִים
אֲשֶׁר דִּבֶּר מֹשֶׁה
אֶל־כָּל־יִשְׂרָאֵל
בְּעֵבֶר הַיַּרְדֵּן

4. These are the words
   that Moses spoke
   to all Israel
   on the other side of the Jordan....
   (Deut. 1:1)

וַיַּקְהֵל מֹשֶׁה
אֶת־כָּל־עֲדַת בְּנֵי יִשְׂרָאֵל
וַיֹּאמֶר אֲלֵהֶם

5. Moses gathered
   the whole Israelite community
   and said to them....
   (Exod. 35:1)

וַיִּשְׁמַע יִתְרוֹ
כֹהֵן מִדְיָן
חֹתֵן מֹשֶׁה
אֵת כָּל־אֲשֶׁר עָשָׂה אֱלֹהִים
לְמֹשֶׁה וּלְיִשְׂרָאֵל עַמּוֹ
כִּי־הוֹצִיא יהוה אֶת־יִשְׂרָאֵל מִמִּצְרָיִם

6. Jethro heard—
   (He was the priest of Midian,
   Moses' father-in-law)
   —all that God had done
   for Moses and for Israel His people,
   That God had brought Israel out from
   Egypt.
   (Exod. 18:1)

וַיְדַבֵּר יהוה אֶל־מֹשֶׁה
בְּמִדְבַּר סִינַי
בְּאֹהֶל מוֹעֵד
בְּאֶחָד לַחֹדֶשׁ הַשֵּׁנִי
בַּשָּׁנָה הַשֵּׁנִית
לְצֵאתָם מֵאֶרֶץ מִצְרַיִם
לֵאמֹר

7. God spoke to Moses
   in the wilderness of Sinai,
   in the Tent of Meeting,
   on the first day of the second month,
   in the second year following
   the exodus from Egypt,
   saying:
   (Num. 1:1)

REVIEW

The Torah can be both a SYMBOL and a BOOK. We can use it as a RITUAL OBJECT, we can study it as a DOCUMENT.

As a symbol, the Torah is the communications-link between God and the Jewish people. It is the guide-book which God gave us to help us discover the Divine. This makes Torah a way of life. It is the source of the mitzvot, the core of the Jewish tradition.

We stand up for this Torah, keep it in a Holy Ark, kiss it, decorate it, and we even dance with it.

The book Torah presents different images. The symbol Torah is filled with truth and meaning, with a path towards holiness. The DOCUMENT we find when we open up the Torah and begin to learn doesn't automatically seem to fulfill the Torah's symbolic image. We find lists of names, rules that seem hard to apply to our lives, and passages which confuse us. While we can celebrate the SYMBOL Torah, it is a lifelong task to decode and understand the DOCUMENT.

Concretely, the Torah is made up of five books, so it is called "The Five" חוּמָשׁ /CHUMASH (in Hebrew), PENTATEUCH (in Greek).

בְּרֵאשִׁית —GENESIS
The story of the Patriarchs and Matriarchs, going from creation to the death of Joseph.

שְׁמוֹת —EXODUS
The story of leaving Egypt, coming to Mt. Sinai, being given the first *mitzvot*, and then building the Tabernacle.

וַיִּקְרָא —LEVITICUS
The "Torah of the Priests" is a code of law.

בְּמִדְבַּר —NUMBERS
The further wilderness adventures of the Children of Israel.

דְּבָרִים —DEUTERONOMY
Moses retells all that has happened to the Children of Israel.

There are two ways of dividing these five books. Jews have traditionally separated the Torah into PARASHIYOT/SIDROT (weekly Torah portions). Since the fourteenth century, we have also adopted the use of chapters and verses from Christian Bible scholars.

ANSWERS

Exercise 1.1

בְּמִצְרַיִם	(in) EGYPT
מַסְעֵיהֶם	(their) JOURNEYS
סִינַי	SINAI
יְרֵחוֹ	JERICHO
יִשְׂרָאֵל	ISRAEL

These words tell a shorthand version of the Exodus. In one sense, this is the overall story of the Torah. This is also the story of Abram who goes down to Egypt and returns, of Jacob who has an "Egypt-like" experience with Laban, and of Joseph. In a greater sense, it is the ongoing story of the Jewish people, and the long historical cycle of oppression and redemption. It is the story of coming home.

Exercise 1.2

1. For Rashi, a mitzvah is a "commandment," an order, something which God has told the Jewish people they **must** do.

2. For Rashi, the major purpose of the Torah is to teach the Jewish people about mitzvot. For him, the Torah is the way Jews learn how to live a good Jewish life; it is the tool God has given us to learn how to live by the laws and practices which improve and perfect the world, and which lead people towards peace.

3. For Rashi, the second major purpose of the Torah is to show that the Jewish people belong in the Promised Land because God has given it to them as a homeland.

4. The Book of Genesis is the story of an evolving covenant. It starts with a relationship between God and all people. Adam, Cain, and Noah each defined portions of this relationship. Then, with Abram, God makes a specific and formal covenant. This *berit* obligates the Jewish people to follow God's laws; in return God promises to be our God, to make us many, and to give us the Land of Israel. There are five statements of the covenant made to Abraham. It is then renewed with Isaac, and again restated to Jacob. The Book of Genesis is the story of this evolving relationship, and the Land of Israel is continually promised as a homeland.

Exercise 1.3

1. חַיֵּי שָׂרָה / *Chaye Sarah* (Sarah's lifetime)
2. מִשְׁפָּטִים / *Mishpatim* (Rules)
3. קְדשִׁים / *Kedoshim* (Holy)
4. דְּבָרִים / *Devarim* (Things/words)
5. וַיַּקְהֵל / *Vayak'hel* (Gathered)
6. יִתְרוֹ / *Yitro* (Jethro)
7. בְּמִדְבַּר / *Bemidbar* (In the wilderness).

Attempt to go through all of our sacred books in the course of your lifetime. You will then have visited every place in the Torah.

Rich people often travel from land to land, spending huge amounts of money so that they can boast of their far-flung journeys.

You should likewise travel everywhere through the Torah. In the future, you will be able to boast that you have visited every place in the Torah.

Rabbi Nachman of Bratzlav

PRESCRIPTION

In this module, we are going to work on one skill: improving your ability to open up an English copy of the Torah and find a particular story or section. The more you get involved in learning Torah, the more you'll need to be able to find particular sections. One important technique of learning you'll be using has you compare one passage to similar passages you can find.

When you've finished this module, you should be able to:

2.1 Name the five books of the Torah in their right order and describe the basic content of each book.

2.2 Know how to use standard abbreviations to find specific passages in the Torah.

2.3 Identify which book contains given events or sections and give the order of events and sections within each of the five books.

2.4 Find these major events and sections by flipping through a Torah.

2.5 Tell the approximate locations of major events and sections.

A Pre-Test Story

Rabbi Nachman once asked: "Why do people often forget the Torah they have learned?"

He answered: "Because, when they restudy the subject for a second time, it can become as new and as special for them as it was the first time."

A group of workers were once asked to fill punctured barrels with water. As they worked, all that they poured in spilled out. Most of the workers asked why they should continue to work since the barrels could never be filled.

But, one wise man said: "What difference does it make to me since I'm getting paid for each day's work. If the boss had wanted the barrels full, he would have given us barrels without holes."

Rabbi Nachman explained the story this way: So, too, God can be trusted to pay us for the Torah study we have forgotten....We are rewarded for effort and not achievement.

PRE-TEST—EXERCISE 2.0

I. List the five books of the Torah in the right order.

_____
_____
_____
_____
_____

Score 2 points per name and 2 points per right order (Total 20 points)

2. In which of the five books would you find each of the following?

_____ Moses' death
_____ Tower of Babel
_____ Holiness Code
_____ Balaam's ass
_____ Burning Bush
_____ Golden Calf
_____ Census of tribes
_____ Binding of Isaac
_____ Blessings and curses
_____ The Shema
_____ Red heifer
_____ The holidays (the first time)
_____ Joseph's coat of many colors
_____ Moses kills an Egyptian
_____ The Ten Commandments
                    (the first time)
_____ The Ten Commandments
                    (the second time)
_____ The Tabernacle
_____ Moses reviews history

Score I point per right answer (Total 18 points)

3. Explain the following abbreviations:

Deut. 5:23 _____
Exod. 2:4 _____
Lev. 7:23_____
Gen. 48:22 _____
Num. II:I5_____

Score 4 points per item (Total 20 points)

4. For each of the following series of items mark I, 2, or 3 to show their order of appearance in the Torah.

A. ____ Abram leaves home
   ____ Jacob's dream
   ____ The Binding of Isaac

B. ____ Joshua takes over
   ____ The Flood
   ____ Mt. Sinai

C. ____ Golden Calf
   ____ Red Sea divides
   ____ Ten Commandments

D. ____ A new pharaoh
   ____ Cain and Abel
   ____ Moses dies

E. ____ Census of tribes
   ____ Holiness Code
   ____ The spies

F. ____ Cain and Abel
   ____ Adam and Eve
   ____ The Flood

G. ____ Moses reviews history
   ____ Moses kills the Egyptian
   ____ Moses strikes the rock

H. ____ Holiness Code
   ____ The Exodus
   ____ The Creation

I. ____ Moses
   ____ Joseph
   ____ Balaam

J. ____ Rachel
   ____ Sarah
   ____ Miriam

K. ____ Rebekah
   ____ Eve
   ____ Leah

Score 2 points per correct series (Total 22 points)

5. Where in the Torah would you find the following? In the first third, in the middle, or in the last third?

_____ Binding of Isaac
_____ Moses' farewell
_____ Rules for Yom Kippur
_____ Cain and Abel
_____ The plagues
_____ Jacob wrestling with the angel
_____ The Shema
_____ Rules for priests
_____ Holiness Code
_____ Setting up the Tabernacle

Score 2 points per item (Total 20 points)

POST PRE-TEST STORIES

(To score your test, use answers on page _37._)

Your total score: _____*(100 points possible)*

A man came to see Rabbi Hillel (a famous scholar during the first century B.C.E. and founder of the school known as the "House of Hillel"). The man asked Hillel to teach him the entire Torah while standing on one foot. Hillel said: "What you hate—don't do that to your neighbor." Then he added, "The rest is all commentary (to learn how to apply this)— *So go and learn it.*"

Talmud, Shabbat 31a

Even if you did very well on the pre-test, you have more to learn, so go and learn.

WEIGHTLIFTING

The first ark for the Ten Commandments was built while the Children of Israel were wandering in the desert. It was made of acacia wood covered with gold. A midrash says that it was so heavy that it took the strength of many men even to budge it. But, then the midrash explained, once they lifted it, it carried its carriers.

David Moshe of Tchortkov was a chasidic rabbi. Once, during the dedication of a new *Sefer Torah*, he had to hold a large heavy scroll for a long time. One of his students offered to help him, but he said: "Once you've picked it up, it is no longer heavy."

For the rest of this chapter, we'll be involved in the lifting of Torah. There is hard work to do, learning the order and structure of the text. In the chapters that follow, you'll find insights in the text that can uplift you.

NOTATION	GENESIS

NOTATION

When we work with biblical sources, there is a special access code we use.

Gen. = Genesis
Exod. = Exodus
Lev. = Leviticus
Num. = Numbers
Deut. = Deuteronomy

Each of these books is divided into chapters which are numbered. Then each of the sentences (which are called "verses") is also numbered. Every verse in the Bible can be identified through (a) the **name** of the book, (b) the **number** of the chapter, and (c) the **number** of the verse.

Gen. 1:1 = Genesis, chapter 1, verse 1
Lev. 19:3 = Leviticus, chapter 19, verse 3.

Exercise 2.1

Now, let's apply this coding. Take out a copy of the Torah (or a Bible) and look up the following sources. Write down the first words of each verse you find.

1. Gen. 22:2 _____
2. Exod. 20:13 _____
3. Deut. 5:17 _____
4. Lev. 23:27 _____
5. Gen. 37:3 _____
6. Lev. 19:18 _____
7. Num. 24:5 _____
8. Deut. 6:4 _____
9. Exod. 1:8 _____
10. Num. 6:24 _____

Match the sources you have found with the following "labels."

_____ The Shema
_____ The source for Yom Kippur
_____ *Mah Tovu* (How Goodly)
_____ The Holiness Code
_____ Ten Commandments
_____ Ten Commandments
_____ The Binding of Isaac
_____ The Joseph story
_____ The priestly benediction
_____ The beginning of anti-Semitism

GENESIS

Genesis, the first book of the Torah, is made up of twelve *parashiyot* and fifty chapters. It tells the history of the world from Creation through the deaths of Jacob and Joseph. It can really be divided into five sections.

1 **Pre-history**—Creation, Adam and Eve, Cain and Abel, Noah and the Flood, and the Tower of Babel. This fills chapters 1 to 11 and the first two *sidrot*: בְּרֵאשִׁית / *Bereshit* and נֹחַ / *Noach*.

2 **Abraham**—From his leaving Haran, through his trips to Canaan and Egypt, we watch his family and his relationship with God evolve and grow. These adventures take up chapters 12 to 12-22, לֶךְ־לְךָ / *Lech-Lecha* and וַיֵּרָא / *Vayera*.

3 **Isaac**—He is born in chapter 21 and almost sacrificed in chapter 22, but his marriage to Rebekah and his adventures continue beyond chapter 25 (verse 10), where he buries his parents. חַיֵּי שָׂרָה / *Chaye Sarah* is the central *sidrah*.

4 **Jacob**—His struggles and adventures take place between chapters 25 and 36. He lies, cheats, steals, wrestles—moving from a young *Yaakov*, "the heel-grabber," into a mature *Yisrael*, "the God-wrestler." Jacob's transformation and the evolution of his holy family can be found in תּוֹלְדֹת / *Toledot*, וַיֵּצֵא / *Vayetze*, and וַיִּשְׁלַח / *Vayishlach*.

5 **Joseph**—His epic concludes the Book of Genesis. In it, the dreamer transports his family to Egypt, saving them from starvation, and thus beginning the next phase of their evolution. Joseph's tale goes from chapters 37 to 50 and fills וַיֵּשֶׁב / *Vayeshev*, מִקֵּץ / *Miketz*, וַיִּגַּשׁ / *Vayigash*, and וַיְחִי / *Vayechi*.

EXERCISE 2.2

Below you will find twenty-eight events in Genesis. To make it easy, we've left them in the correct order. Take a Bible (or a copy of the Torah) and find them. Write down the number of the chapter which begins the listed event.

1. Adam and Eve _____
2. Cain and Abel_____
3. Noah and the Flood _____
4. The Tower of Babel _____
5. Abram comes to Canaan _____
6. Abram and Lot separate _____
7. Ishmael's birth _____
8. Abraham's circumcision _____
9. Three angels visit Abraham _____
10. Sodom and Gomorrah destroyed
_____
11. Isaac's birth _____
12. Binding of Isaac _____
13. Sarah's death _____
14. Isaac and Rebekah _____
15. Esau and Jacob are born _____
16. Stolen birthright _____
17. Stolen blessing _____
18. Jacob's dream _____
19. Jacob's marriages _____
20. Jacob wrestles _____
21. Joseph gets coat _____
22. Joseph sold into slavery _____
23. Joseph goes to jail _____
24. Joseph explains Pharaoh's dreams
_____
25. The brothers come to Egypt _____
26. The family moves to Egypt _____
27. Jacob's blessings _____
28. The deaths of Jacob and Joseph
_____

Bereshit Gen. 1:1—6:8

- God **creates** the world in seven days.
- **Adam** and **Eve** are placed in the **Garden of Eden**, eat the forbidden fruit, and are driven out.
- **Cain** kills his **brother**, Abel.
- List of **ten generations** from Adam to Noah.

Noach Gen. 6.9—11.32

- All of creation turns evil, so God destroys it with a **flood.**
- Noah, his family, and a limited number of animals are saved. God uses a rainbow to make a **covenant** with them.
- Noah gets drunk.
- People start to build the **Tower of Babel**, and God babbles their language.
- List of **ten generations** from Noah to Abram.

Lech Lecha Gen. 12.1—17.27

- **Abram, Sarai,** and **Lot** move to **Canaan.**
- There is a famine, so the family moves to Egypt.
- Pharaoh mistakes Sarai, Abram's **wife**, for Abram's sister.
- The family returns to Canaan where **Abram and Lot split up** and go their separate ways.
- Abraham is the hero of a **war** fought among nine **kings.**
- God and Abraham make **The Covenant of the Pieces.**
- **Ishmael** is born.
- God and Abraham make **The Covenant of Circumcision.**

Vayera Gen. 18.1—22.24

- Abraham welcomes **three visitors**. They announce the birth of Isaac.
- God and Abraham **debate** the destruction of **Sodom and Gomorrah.** Lot's family is saved. The cities are **destroyed.**
- Abimelech mistakes Abraham's **wife** for his **sister.**
- **Isaac** is born. **Hagar** and her son, **Ishmael,** are **sent away.** An angel saves their lives.
- Abraham is **tested** when God asks him to **sacrifice Isaac.**

Chaye Sarah Gen. 23.1—25.18

- **Sarah dies.** Abraham buys the **Cave of Machpelah** for a burial place.
- Abraham **sends a servant** to find a bride for Isaac. He plans a test. **Rebekah** passes the test and is chosen. Isaac and Rebekah are married.
- **Abraham dies.** Isaac and Ishmael bury him in the Cave of Machpelah.

Toledot Gen. 25.19—28.9

- Rebekah gets **pregnant. Twins** are in her womb. They **fight** in her belly. **Esau** is born first. **Jacob** is pulling at his heel.
- Esau **sells** Jacob his **birthright.**
- Abimelech thinks that Isaac's **wife** is really his **sister.**
- Isaac plans to bless Esau. Rebekah and Jacob **trick** him.
- **Isaac blesses Jacob.** Jacob leaves to go to Paddan-aram.

Vayetze Gen. 28.10—32.3

- **Jacob** has a **dream** of angels going up and down. God promises to be with him. Jacob names the place Beth El.
- Jacob **meets Rachel** at the well. He works seven years to marry her. Laban **tricks** Jacob into marrying **Leah**. He then also marries Rachel and promises to work seven more years.
- Rachel and Leah have children. There are two sons and one daughter. Jacob and his family **leave Laban's** household. Laban chases him. They make peace.

Vayishlach Gen. 32.4—36.43

- Jacob prepares to meet Esau. He **wrestles** with a stranger who **changes his name to Israel.**
- Jacob and Esau meet.
- **Dinah** gets involved with a man from Shechem.
- God blesses Jacob and changes his name to Israel.
- Rachel dies giving birth and is buried. Jacob names his twelfth son **Benjamin.**

Vayeshev Gen. 37.1—40.23

- Joseph is Israel's **favorite son.** He makes him a **coat of many colors.**
- Joseph has **two dreams** in which his family bows down to him.
- Israel sends Joseph to join his brothers in the field.
- Judah, Tamar, and Onan have a subplot.
- Joseph is **sold into slavery** and taken to Potiphar's house. He **succeeds** and becomes **head of the household.**
- Joseph is **thrown in jail.** Again, he succeeds and becomes the **head prisoner.** Here, he interprets **two dreams.**

Miketz Gen. 41.1—44.17

- Joseph interprets Pharaoh's **two dreams,** and predicts a famine.
- Pharaoh puts Joseph in charge of famine control.
- Joseph has a family. **Seven years of plenty** are followed by **famine.**
- Jacob sends **ten sons** to buy food in Egypt. Joseph's brothers **do not recognize** him. He tricks them and returns their gold. He demands that they **bring Benjamin** next time.
- Later, they return and Joseph throws Benjamin in jail.

Vayigash Gen. 44.18—47.27

- **Judah pleads** for Benjamin.
- **Joseph reveals himself** to his brothers.
- Pharaoh welcomes Joseph's family.
- Jacob moves the family to Egypt. They settle in the land of **Goshen.**

Vayechi Gen. 47.28—50.26

- Joseph **promises** Jacob that he will not bury him in Egypt.
- Jacob **blesses** Joseph's sons and his own twelve sons.
- Jacob **dies** and is taken to the Cave of Machpelah and is buried.
- Joseph **dies** and is buried in Egypt. The Children of Israel **promise** to move him to **Canaan.**

EXODUS

Exodus is the second book of the Torah. It is made up of eleven *parashiyot* and forty chapters. *Shemot* seems to be a combination of two different kinds of material.

From chapter 1 through chapter 19 we have an adventure story where we watch the Jewish people become slaves, become liberated under Moses' leadership, and then encounter God at the foot of Mt. Sinai. This story is told in five *sidrot*: שְׁמוֹת / *Shemot*, וָאֵרָא /*Va'era*, בֹּא / *Bo*, בְּשַׁלַּח / *Beshalach*, and יִתְרוֹ / *Yitro*.

In chapter 20, the Jewish people receive the Ten Commandments and, from then on, Exodus turns into a law book, beginning with civil codes and moving into long descriptions of how to build the Tabernacle. These laws fill six *parashiyot*: מִשְׁפָּטִים /*Mishpatim*, תְּרוּמָה / *Terumah*, תְּצַוֶּה / *Tetzaveh*, כִּי תִשָּׂא / *Ki Tisa*, וַיַּקְהֵל / *Vayak'hel*, and פְּקוּדֵי / *Pekude*.

> **The book of Genesis intends to relate *toledot*, generations. It is concerned with deriving the *toledot* of the nation of Israel from the *toledot* of the human race; and these, from the generations of the heavens and the earth. The cosmogony, the origin of the world, is related for the sake of ethnology, the origin of the people. We are to trace the meaning of the people's origin back to the meaning of the origin of the world, and back to the intention of the Creator for creation.**
>
> Martin Buber, **Abraham the Seer**

Exercise 2.3

Here is the list of sixteen things you should be able to locate in the Book of Exodus. Look them up in your copy of the Torah and then write down the number of the chapter in which each is found.

1. A new pharaoh _____
2. Moses is hidden and found _____
3. Moses kills and runs _____
4. The Burning Bush _____
5. The ten plagues _____
6. Pharaoh lets Israel go _____
7. The Red Sea _____
8. Amalek attacks _____
9. Jethro visits _____
10. The Ten Commandments _____
11. Basic law code (damages, slaves, etc.)
    _____
12. Moses ascends the mountain
    _____
13. Instructions for Tabernacle _____
14. The Golden Calf _____
15. The second tablets _____
16. Dedication of Tabernacle _____

Exercise 2.4

The rabbis had a principle אֵין מֻקְדָּם וּמְאוּחָר בַּתּוֹרָה / En mukdam u'me'uchar batorah —there's no before or after in the Torah—meaning that the order in which the Torah tells us about events is not necessarily the order in which they happened historically. (Pesachim 6b, Rashi Num. 9:1)

Look at these three events. Look at what comes between each one.

THE TEN COMMANDMENTS

_____

MOSES RECEIVES THE TABLETS
(the first time) _____
MOSES ASCENDS THE MOUNTAIN

_____

1 What is the "problem" with the order in which the Torah tells this story?

_____ _____

2 Why might the author of Exodus have chosen to interrupt the telling of the history of the giving of the Ten Commandments with laws and instructions?

_____
_____
_____

Biblical religion revolves around two themes, Creation and Exodus. The former asserts God's sovereignty over nature, the latter God's absolute hegemony over history....God is vitally concerned with the welfare of God's creatures, intensely involved in their fate and fortune. An unqualified moral Being, who insistently demands human imitation of God's moral attributes. God imposes divine law on the human race, and judges the world in righteousness. History, therefore, is the arena of divine activity. ...It is no wonder that the Exodus is the pivotal event in the Bible.... The slavery of the Israelites, the liberation from Egypt, the covenant between God and Israel at Sinai, and the journey in the wilderness toward the Promised Land—all constitute the dominant motif of the scriptures....

Nahum M. Sarna, **Exploring Exodus**

Shemot Exod. 1.1—6.1

- A new generation of the Children of Israel grows into a **nation**.
- A **new pharaoh** comes to rule.
- The Jewish people are turned into **slaves**.
- Moses is born, hidden, found floating in a basket, raised in Pharaoh's house, turned into an outlaw when he kills to defend a Hebrew slave, and married to the daughter of the High Priest of Midian.
- God talks to him from inside a **Burning Bush**.

Va'era Exod. 6.2—9.35

- **Moses and Aaron** visit **Pharaoh** and do the staff-into-snake trick. They tell him: **"Let my people go."**
- The first seven plagues:
- **Blood, frogs, lice, insect swarms, cattle blight, boils, and hail.**

Bo Exod. 10.1—13.16

- God sends the last three plagues:
- **Locusts, darkness**, and the **death of the firstborn.**
- God teaches the mitzvah of the **new month**.
- The Jews **celebrate Passover** while still slaves in Egypt.

Beshalach Exod. 13.17—17.16

- The Children of Israel flee from Egypt.
- Pharaoh and his army chase them.
- The Children of Israel cross the **Sea of Reeds** while Pharaoh and company drown.
- The **Song of the Sea** is sung.
- The people complain about the water. Moses **hits a rock** and brings water.
- Israel fights a **battle with Amalek**.

Yitro Exod. 18.1—20.23

- Yitro brings Zipporah, Gershom, and Eliezer to Moses.
- Moses follows Yitro's advice and **appoints judges**.
- The Children of Israel prepare and God gives them the **Ten Commandments.**
- The Children of Israel ask Moses to serve as a go-between for God and the people.

Mishpatim Exod. 21.1—24.18

- God has Moses teach the Jewish people a basic law code. It includes:
- Rules of owning slaves.
- A list of capital crimes.
- Rules of damages.
- Assorted rules including social codes and fair courts.
- Then the Children of Israel accept the law.

Terumah Exod. 25.1—27.19

- Moses asks the Children of Israel to donate gifts and materials for the Tabernacle.
- Thirteen specific kinds of material gifts are described.
- The **aron**, the **shulchan**, and the **menorah** are each described in detail.

Tetzaveh Exod. 27.20—30.10

- The Children of Israel are instructed to bring pure olive oil for the menorah.

- Aaron and his sons, Nadab, Abihu, Eleazar, and Itamar, are chosen to serve as priests.
- God instructs Moses to make special clothes for the priests including **tunic, breeches, belt, hat, mantle, apron, breastplate,** and **headplate**.
- We are given a description of the sacrifices to consecrate the priests.

Ki Tisa Exod. 30.11—34.35

- God instructs Moses in the taking of a census.
- Description of the **kiyor**—a basin for washing.
- The formulas for **incense** and **anointing oil**.
- God restates rules of **Shabbat**.
- God gives Moses the first tablets of the **Ten Commandments.**
- Moses breaks the tablets when he sees the **Golden Calf**.
- Moses goes up to get a second set of tablets after punishing the Children of Israel.

Vayak'hel Exod. 35.1—38.20

- Moses again teaches the rules of **Shabbat** and the **building of the Mishkan**.
- The actual work of building the Mishkan is described.
- Moses refuses more donations since there have been too many.
- Description of the *kiyor,* which was made of copper mirrors.

Pekude Exod. 38.21—40.38

- Moses reports how the donations were given and how they were used.
- Moses sets up the Mishkan and the priests are established therein.
- A description is given of a **cloud** that covers the Mishkan **by day** and a **fire that burns by night**, indicating God's presence therein.

LEVITICUS

Leviticus is the third book of the Torah. In Hebrew it is labeled as *Vayikra*, but it is also called *Torat Kohanim* — Torah of the Priests. It is filled with laws (centering on those for priests).

In the book we have twenty-seven chapters and ten *parashiyot*. It is almost all law codes.

The first eight chapters and two *sidrot* (וַיִּקְרָא / *Vayikra and* צַו /*Tzav*) present the laws of sacrifice.

Chapters 9 and 10 (שְׁמִינִי / *Shemini*) describe the initiation of sacrifices and the deaths of Aaron's two sons, Nadab and Abihu.

Most of the rest of the book, chapters 11 through 25, deals with laws of purity and holiness. Topics include acceptable foods to eat, leprosy, sexual conduct, interpersonal relations, priestly conduct, and holidays. It takes seven *parashiyot* to cover this material: שְׁמִינִי / *Shemini*, תַזְרִיעַ / *Tazria*, מְצֹרָע / *Metzora*, אַחֲרֵי מוֹת / *Achare Mot*, קְדֹשִׁים /*Kedoshim*, אֱמֹר / *Emor*, and בְּהַר / *Behar*.

The last *sidrah*, בְּחֻקֹּתַי / *Bechukotai*, is a collection of blessings Israel will receive if they obey the Torah and the curses which will fall upon them if they don't.

Exercise 2.5

As we have done for Genesis and Exodus, here is a list of a few things in Leviticus. Find the chapter where each one begins.

1. Laws of sacrifice_____
2. Deaths of Nadab and Abihu_____
3. Laws of kashrut_____
4. Laws of leprosy_____
5. The Holiness Code_____
6. Laws of the sabbatical year_____
7. Blessings and curses_____

While you may not know the exact order of the laws in Leviticus, you will still want to know something about these laws. While you are looking things up, answer these questions.

1. List the five basic kinds of sacrifices.

_____
_____
_____
_____
_____

2. What happened to Nadab and Abihu?_
_____

3. How does the Torah connect priests and leprosy?_____
_____

4. Why is Leviticus 19 called the "Holiness Code"?_____
_____

Leviticus is the shortest of the Five Books of Moses. It is also the middle book, and its centrality in the Pentateuch is more than a mere matter of position. (It was typically the first text of the traditional *cheder*.) For all its apparent attention to archaic and obsolete priestly concerns, a far different focus emerges when the book is set against the Torah as a whole and against the literature of the surrounding Near East. Then we see that its real concern is with consumption of food and with the related requirements of purification and sanctification. These three broad topics provide, as it were, the warp of the book, while the woof is based on another triad: **God, priests, and laity.**

William W. Hallo, Leviticus and Ancient Near Eastern Literature, in **The Torah: A Modern Commentary,** edited by W. Gunther Plaut

Vayikra Lev. 1.1—5.26

- The introduction of sacrifices:
- The *Olah*—regular **daily offering**.
- The *Minchah*—**meal offering** of flour and oil.
- The *Shelamim*—**peace offering**.
- The *Chatat*—**sin offering**.
- The *Asham*—**guilt offering**.

Tzav Lev. 6.1—8.36

- There is a description of what the Kohanim have to do in the Mishkan.
- Then the Kohanim are taught how to offer the sacrifices.
- Finally, we are given the rules for eating meat.

Shemini Lev. 9.1—11.47

- The Mishkan is dedicated and sacrifices are offered.
- **Nadab and Abihu die** after offering a strange fire before God.
- God warns Aaron that priests should not drink before doing priestly service.
- **Rules** are given about which **animals, birds, fish**, and **insects can be eaten.**

Tazria Lev. 12.1—13.59

- We are taught more laws:
- Laws of the **impurity** of women after giving birth.
- Laws of **skin disease.**
- List of conditions which are considered **leprosy.**
- Then we are taught procedures for dealing with leprosy.

Metzora Lev. 14.1—15.33

- Leprosy Part II:
- The priests' duties in curing leprosy.
- Procedures for curing leprosy.
- Laws concerning house leprosy.
- Laws of discharges from the body which require acts of purification.

Achare Mot Lev. 16.1—18.30

- God gives additional laws and duties for the Kohanim.
- The responsibilities of the **Head Kohen** on **Yom Kippur.**
- Laws for fasting and atonement on Yom Kippur.
- Laws about blood.
- Laws of eating meat.
- Prohibitions of nakedness.

Kedoshim Lev. 19.1—20.27

- **The Holiness Code.**
- These laws include: respecting parents, not worshiping idols, observing Shabbat, eating sacrifices right away, leaving the corners of fields, not stealing, not taking advantage of handicaps, judging cases fairly, not hating people, and loving your neighbor as yourself.

Emor Lev. 21.1—24.23

- We are taught more rules about Kohanim:
- Rules about a Kohen coming in contact with the dead.
- Rules about serving as a Kohen.
- Rules about how to celebrate holidays:
- **Shabbat, Passover**, the **Omer, Shavuot, Rosh Hashanah, Yom Kippur**, and **Sukot** are described.

- Also, there is the story of a man who cursed God.

Behar Lev. 25.1—26.2

- And the rules go on:
- Rules for **Sabbatical years**.
- Rules for **Jubilee years**.
- Rules of **owning property** in the **Land of Israel**.
- A rule about **not lending money at interest**.

Bechukotai Lev. 26.3—27.34

- God promises **five blessings** to the Children of Israel if they follow the law.
- Then God warns about **thirty-two curses if the promises are not kept**.
- Also, we get some more laws:
- Laws about **vows, tithes, things promised to God**, and **things which need to be redeemed**.

Numbers

Numbers is the fourth book in the Torah. Its ten *parashiyot* and thirty-six chapters divide into four parts. (No, it is not an even division.)

The first part of the book, 1:1 to 10:10, describes the preparations for the generation-long journey through the wilderness. Including the first two *sidrot*, בְּמִדְבַּר /Bemidbar and נְשֹׁא /Naso, as well as most of the third *sidrah*, בְּהַעֲלֹתְךָ /Beha'alotecha , Numbers gives the results of a detailed census, marriage laws, Nazarite Laws, and laws for the Levites. These include the famous Priestly Benediction.

In Numbers 10:11, the Torah tells us: "In the second year, on the twentieth day of the second month, the cloud lifted from the Tabernacle of the Pact and the Israelites set out on their journeys from the wilderness of Sinai." This begins thirty-eight years of wandering; it also begins the second part of the Book of Numbers. These thirty-eight years lead us through four *parashiyot*, the remainder of בְּהַעֲלֹתְךָ/Beha'alotecha , שְׁלַח־לְךָ /Shelach-Lecha—the story of the spies, קֹרַח /Korach—the history of a rebellion, and into part of חֻקַּת /Chukat--a bunch, more rules.

In Numbers 20, we meet Moses the rock-basher. This begins the third section of the book. It is the beginning of the fortieth year in the wilderness. In two *parashiyot*, the rest of חֻקַּת /Chukat, and בָּלָק /Balak, we cover the first ten months of this fortieth year. We fight battles with Edom, the Amorites, Bashan, and Moab. The focus is the story of Balaam the magician.

In chapter 25, the very end of חֻקַּת/Chukat, we enter the last part of the book with a case of Israelites violating God's rules. In three *parashiyot*, פִּינְחָס /Pinchas, מַטּוֹת/Matot, and מַסְעֵי/Mas'ei, the final preparations are made for entering the Promised Land.

Exercise 2.6

Find the answers to each of these questions about the Book of Numbers. Write down the chapter and verse where you found the answer. (It is about time we upped the stakes a little bit. No, this time they are not in order.)

1. How did Balaam's blessing of Israel begin?

_____

2. How many men were in the Tribe of Judah (First Census)?

_____

3. Which spy disagreed with the general report?

_____

The Book of Numbers narrates Israel's departure from Mount Sinai and its journey in the wilderness for an entire generation until reaching the border of the Promised Land...the work provides at least one set of answers to questions faced by the Jewish community in exile....

The need to enter the Promised Land has the same desperate urgency. The temptation to "return to Egypt" (settle in the lands of the Diaspora) was strong, as was the threat of assimilation by foreigners and their gods. Many will succumb to that temptation and turn aside; but this is a test, a purging. The way back to Egypt leads to sure destruction. The only hope is to press on to Canaan; and although the giants controlling the land make the goal seem impossible, divine guidance is available to the faithful. How do we learn the divine will? Prophets may arise claiming charismatic authority, but as our ancestors were nurtured by the bread from heaven and given God's instruction through Moses, we still have that word. Through that word we are nurtured and led. If we adhere to it, we will survive the ordeal; the bitter waters of divine testing will become the "many waters flowing from our buckets."

James S. Ackerman, **The Literary Guide to the Bible**, 78, 90

4. What words were said when the ark was moved? (Clue at the beginning of the march.)

_____

5. What was the City of Refuge?

_____

Bemidbar Num. 1.1—4.20
- A census is taken of men over twenty.
- Instructions are given for where each tribe should camp.
- Aaron's family is listed and other clans are identified.

Naso Num. 4.21—7.89
- There are still more rules for the Kohanim.
- The clans of Levi are assigned to moving the Mishkan.
- Next come the rules of **Sota** and the **Nazir**.
- The Kohanim are taught the words of **Birkat Kohanim**.
- The chieftains bring gifts.
- Moses talks to God in the Tent of Meeting.

Beha'alotecha Num. 8.1—12.16
- The menorah is described.
- The tribe of Levi become assistants to the priests.
- We are taught the laws of the firstborn and of Passover.
- The Children of Israel again complain about food and a fire breaks out.
- The council of seventy elders is established.
- Moses marries a Cushite woman. Miriam complains and she gets leprosy.

Shelach-Lecha Num. 13.1—15.41
- **Twelve spies** are sent to the Land of Israel and they make a report.
- The Children of Israel become afraid and **rebel**.
- God threatens to wipe out the Children of Israel but relents when Moses intercedes.
- God then decides that **all who knew Egypt would not enter the Land of Israel**.
- And we are taught the laws of _tzitzit_.

Korach Num. 16.1—18.32
- **Korach and his followers rebel** against Moses and Aaron.
- God ends the rebellion.
- Then we are taught more laws:
- Duties of the Kohanim and the Levites.
- Laws of the firstborn which should go to the priests.
- Laws of tithing.

Chukat Num. 19.1—22.1
- There are still more laws to teach:
- Laws of the **red heifer**.
- Rituals and laws of **purification**.
- Miriam and Aaron die.
- The people complain again and **Moses strikes the rock** for water.
- The King of Edom refuses to let the Children of Israel pass through his land.
- They fight battles with the Canaanites; Amorites; and Og, King of Bashan.

Balak Num. 22.2—25.9
- **Balak**, king of Moab, **sends for Bil'am** to curse the Children of Israel.
- Bil'am gets in a fight with **his ass**.
- Bil'am **blesses** the Children of Israel rather than **cursing** them.
- Bil'am prophesies that the foes of the Children of Israel will be conquered.
- The Children of Israel take part in the sacrifices to Baal-Peor.

Pinchas Num. 25.10—30.1
- Pinchas is rewarded for killing the people who cursed God.
- Israel fights a war against the Midianites.
- A census is taken.
- The **daughters of Zelophechad force a change in the laws of property inheritance.**
- **Joshua** is chosen to be Moses' successor.
- Another list of sacrifices is presented.

Matot Num. 30.2—32.42
- The laws of vows are given.
- Israel fights against the Midianites. This provides the opportunity to teach some new laws:
- Rules for dividing the spoils of war.
- Rules for purifying warriors.
- Two tribes ask to stay on the east bank of the Jordan River. Their rights and responsibilities are clarified.

Mas'ei Num. 33.1—36.13
- We are on the eve of entering the Promised Land.
- Israel's **journey** from Egypt to the Jordan is **reviewed**.
- We are taught **laws** concerning the **settlement** of Canaan.
- The **boundaries** of the Land of Israel are defined and along with the **Priestly Cities** and the **Cities of Refuge** are described.
- A careful distinction between **murder** and **manslaughter** is taught.
- Also, we are introduced to laws of inheritance for women who marry men of other tribes.

Deuteronomy

The Book of Deuteronomy, the last book in the Torah, is made up of four elements : three speeches, and a portrait of Moses' final days. It includes eleven *parashiyot* and thirty-four chapters.

Deuteronomy 1.5-4.40, דְּבָרִים /Devarim and half of וָאֶתְחַנַּן /Va'etchanan, is Moses' first farewell address. The people of Israel are gathered on the far side of the Jordan River. Moses begins by reviewing their history.

Moses' second speech begins at 4.44 and goes through chapter 26. This address deals with law. It includes the Ten Commandments, the Shema, and a lot of other codes. It runs from the second half of וָאֶתְחַנַּן /Va'etchanan, through עֵקֶב /Ekev, רְאֵה /Re'eh, שֹׁפְטִים /Shofetim, כִּי-תֵצֵא /Ki Tetze, and part of כִּי-תָבוֹא /Ki Tavo.

The final speech to the people begins in chapter 27 and runs through chapter 30. It includes the rest of כִּי-תָבוֹא /Ki Tavo, as well as all of נִצָּבִים /Nitzavim. This speech deals with the covenant, explaining how the laws form a relationship between Israel and God.

The last three *sidrot*, וַיֵּלֶךְ /Vayelech, הַאֲזִינוּ /Ha'azinu, and וְזֹאת הַבְּרָכָה /Vezot Ha-Berachah, bring Moses' story and the Exodus to a close. The leadership is passed to Joshua, a final blessing is given, and Moses dies.

Exercise 2.7

For your last exercise in this module, here is something completely different. We'll make it a treasure hunt. Find the chapter and verse of each of these quotations.

1. Hear, O Israel, the Lord our God, the Lord is one.

2. Never again did there arise in Israel a prophet like Moses, whom the Lord singled out, face to face....

3. See, this day I set before you blessing and curse: blessing if you obey the commandments of the Lord your God....

4. These are the words that Moses addressed to all Israel on the other side of the Jordan.

5. Honor your father and your mother, as the Lord your God has commanded you, that you may long endure....

Deuteronomy may be described as a story told by an anonymous narrator who directly quotes only two persons, for the most part Moses, and occasionally God...nothing is more clearly shown in the book than the fact that Israel, already destined for disobedience, is going to receive a land it does not deserve. God's central decision...to give Israel, despite the people's initial and immediate disobedience, is a prelude to the entire Deuteronomic history...God is nothing if not partial to Israel.... What Deuteronomy shows...is a God continually mindful of the promise He made to the fathers....

Robert Polzin, **The Literary Guide to the Bible**, pp. 91, 100

Devarim Deut. 1.1—3.22
- Moses begins his review:
- The review of the **journey from Sinai to Kadesh.**
- The **appointment of assistants** for Moses.
- The **journey to Horeb,** and then to **Kadesh-barnea.**
- The people's **refusal to enter** the Land of Canaan.
- The allotment of conquered land.

Va'etchanan Deut. 3.23—7.11
- Moses prays to be allowed to enter the Land of Israel and is again refused by God.
- Moses warns against **idolatry.**
- Moses assigns three **Cities of Refuge.**
- We review the Sinai experience and the commandments.
- We are taught the **Shema** and **V'ahavta.**

Ekev Deut. 7.12—11.25
Moses reviews some important ideas:
- That **following God's laws will bring blessings** of prosperity and health.
- That we should not be **self-righteous.**
- That we must learn the lessons of our **history.**

Re'eh Deut. 11.26—16.17
- God sets before the Children of Israel the choice of doing right rather than wrong, of choosing **the blessing** rather than **the curse.**
- We also receive warnings against eating and pouring **blood** and warnings against **false prophets.**
- Laws are also reviewed: **shemita** and **yovel,** and the **pilgrimage festivals.**

Shofetim Deut. 16.18—21.9
More laws are reviewed:
- The appointment of **judges.**
- Laws against worshiping **idols.**
- Laws concerning the **High Court,** a **king,** and the **priests** and **Levites.**
- **Criminal laws** and the **laws of warfare.**

Ki Tetze Deut. 21.10—25.19
Still more laws are reviewed:
- **Family laws** including marriage, rights of a firstborn, and the disobedient child.
- **Laws of kindness.**
- **Laws** of restoring **lost property.**
- **Miscellaneous laws:** distinction of sex in apparel; sparing a mother bird; parapets on rooftops; against mixing seeds, unlike animals working together, and sha'atnez; and laws of *tzitzit.*

Ki Tavo Deut. 26.1—29.8
Even more laws are reviewed:
- Rituals of presenting **first fruits** and **tithing.**
- Descriptions of the **three tithes**—to the Levites; to the owner of Jerusalem; and to the poor and dependent.
- Procedure for crossing the Jordan River.
- The command to build an altar immediately after the crossing.

Nitzavim Deut. 29.9—30.20
- Moses speaks to all who have and will enter into the **covenant.**
- Moses explains that God does not want to punish the Children of Israel—**if they seek God,** God will show mercy.
- Moses explains that God's commandments are not hard and distant, but practical to follow.

Vayelech Deut. 31.1—31.30
- Moses announces that **Joshua** will soon take over as the leader, but makes the Children of Israel realize that God will still be with them.
- Moses gives Joshua public recognition that he has confidence in him as a leader.
- Moses hands the law to the Levites to be deposited in the *Aron.*

Ha'azinu Deut. 32.1—32.52
- Moses sings "**The Song of Moses,**" a farewell to the people.
- Moses is ordered to ascend Mt. Nebo.

Vezot Ha-Berachah Deut. 33.1—34.12
- Moses **blesses** the Children of Israel before his death—he blesses each tribe individually.
- Moses goes up to **Mt. Nebo** to the **top of Pisgah** to die. Before he closes his eyes, he gets a chance to see the **Land of Israel**.

POST-TEST

If you've worked your way through this module, feel good; it has been a lot of work. When you pass this post-test, you'll prove to yourself that you have mastered our five objectives.

2.1 Naming the five books of the Torah

2.2 Decoding the standard abbreviation format

2.3 Identifying the content of given books

2.4 Finding major events in the Torah

2.5 Knowing approximate locations of passages

Exercise 2.8

1. For 10 points, name the five books of the Torah.

_____

_____

_____

_____

_____

2. For 5 points each (a total of 10 points), decode these two abbreviations.
Lev. 19.1
Num. 8.13

3. Name the book which contains each of these incidents and mark 1,2,3, or 4 to show their order of appearance.

A. _____
_____ Deaths of Nadab and Abihu
_____ Holiday Laws
_____ Laws of Sacrifice
_____ Holiness Code

B. _____
_____ "The Blessings and the Curses"

_____ Moses' Death
_____ Shema
_____ Ten Commandments

C. _____
_____ Coat of Many Colors
_____ Binding of Isaac
_____ Jacob's Dream
_____ The Flood

D. _____
_____ Census
_____ Moses Hits Rock
_____ Balaam's Blessing
_____ Spies Report

E. _____
_____ Tabernacle Is Finished
_____ Moses Kills Egyptian
_____ Ten Plagues
_____ Ten Commandments

Score 8 points per correct book and 8 points per correct series (Total 80 points)

Total Score _____

Post-Test Text

Rabbi Ishmael, his son, says:
If one studies in order to teach,
it is granted to him to study
and to teach,
but if one studies in order to practice
it is granted to her to study
and to teach
and to observe
and to practice.

Pirke Avot 4.6

36

APPENDIX TO MODULE TWO

ANSWERS

Exercise 2.0

1. Genesis, Exodus, Leviticus, Numbers, Deuteronomy

2. Deuteronomy
   Genesis
   Leviticus
   Numbers
   Exodus
   Exodus
   Numbers
   Genesis
   Leviticus
   Deuteronomy
   Numbers
   Leviticus
   Genesis
   Exodus
   Exodus
   Deuteronomy
   Exodus
   Deuteronomy

3. Deuteronomy, chapter 5, verse 23
   Exodus, chapter 2, verse 4
   Leviticus, chapter 7, verse 23
   Genesis, chapter 48, verse 22
   Numbers, chapter 11, verse 15

4. A. 1, 3, 2
   B. 3, 1, 2
   C. 3, 1, 2
   D. 2, 1, 3
   E. 2, 1, 3
   F. 2, 1, 3
   G. 3, 1, 2
   H. 3, 2, 1
   I. 2, 1, 3
   J. 2, 1, 3
   K. 2, 1, 3

5. Beginning
   End
   Middle (also End)
   Beginning
   Beginning (end of Beginning)
   Beginning
   End
   Middle
   Middle
   Middle

Exercise 2.1

1. and said to him, 'Take thy son...'
2. Thou shalt not murder.
3. Thou shalt not murder.
4. ...the tenth day of this month is the day of atonement...
5. Now Israel loved Joseph more....
6. Thou shalt not take vengeance....
7. How goodly are your tents, O Jacob....
8. Hear, O Israel, the Lord Our God...
9. Now there arose a new king over Egypt...
10. The Lord bless thee, and keep thee...

The matches are: 8, 4, 7, 6, 2, 3, 2, 5, 10, 9

Exercise 2.2

1. 2	27. 49
2. 4	28. 50
3. 6	
4. 11	
5. 12	
6. 13	
7. 16	
8. 17	
9. 18	
10. 19	
11. 21	
12. 22	
13. 23	
14. 24	
15. 25	
16. 25	
17. 27	
18. 28	
19. 29	
20. 32	
21. 37	
22. 37	
23. 39	
24. 41	
25. 42	
26. 47	

Exercise 2.3

1. 1
2. 2
3. 2
4. 3
5. 7
6. 12
7. 14
8. 17
9. 18
10. 20
11. 21
12. 24
13. 25
14. 32
15. 34
16. 41

Exercise 2.4

1. The story seems to be out of order, and the building of the Tabernacle seems inserted into the drama, out of sequence. The tradition asserts that the Tabernacle was an addition to God's plan. Motivated by the Golden Calf, God recognized Israel's need for concrete symbols and not merely legal abstractions.

2. There are many possible answers, including yours. Among the two most popular are (1) that the Torah makes the appearance of the Golden Calf a jarring interruption into a calm narrative—we don't expect it. In that literary way, the actual shock of that moment is recreated. (2) Second, there is a talmudic principle which says that God creates cures before God creates illnesses. By introducing the Tabernacle before the Golden Calf, the Torah shows God has a solution to the people's need for a physical center for their spirituality.

Exercise 2.5

1. 1
2. 10
3. 11
4. 12
5. 19
6. 25
7. 26

1. daily offering, meal offering, peace offering, guilt offering, sin offering
2. They were killed in the Tabernacle after lighting a strange fire.
3. The Torah combines ritual and physical cleanliness. The priests were responsible for seeing that lepers were clean on both levels.
4. The laws in Leviticus 19 teach Jews how to be holy. It is a Code of Law which leads one to become holy.

Exercise 2.6

1. How goodly are your tents, O Jacob. 24.5
2. 74,600. 1.2 7
3. Caleb. 13.30
4. Rise up, O Lord. 10.35
5. A place where a person who kills by accident can hide from the angry family. 35.15

Exercise 2.7

1. 6. 4
2. 34.10
3. 11.26
4. 1.1
5. 5.16

Exercise 2.8—The Post-Test

1. Genesis, Exodus, Leviticus, Numbers, Deuteronomy
2. Leviticus, chapter 19, verse 1
   Numbers, chapter 8, verse 13
3. A. Leviticus, 2, 4, 1, 3
   B. Deuteronomy, 3, 4, 2, 1
   C. Genesis, 4, 2, 3, 1
   D. Numbers, 1, 3, 4, 2
   E. Exodus, 4, 1, 2, 3

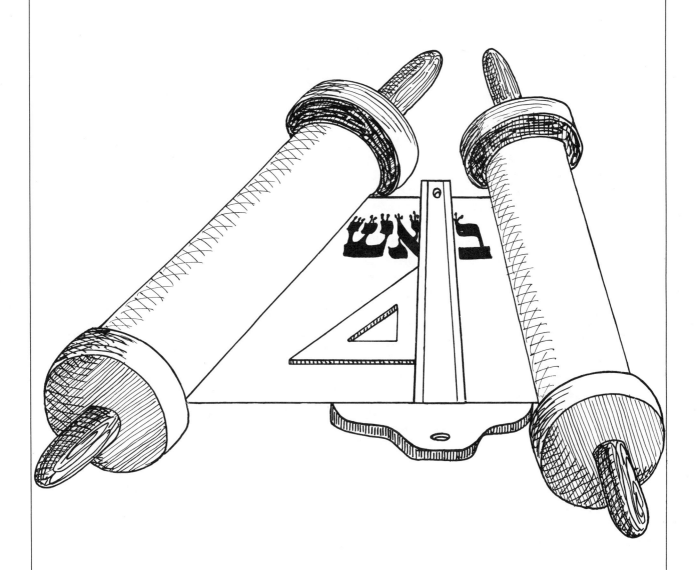

All creation is but these two things: Material and Form. Ibn Gabirol

When a human king builds a palace, he designs it with blueprints and doesn't work from memory, so he knows where to put rooms and entrances. In the same way, God consulted the Torah when designing the world.

Midrash Rabbah

PRESCRIPTION

All beginnings are hard. I can remember my mother murmuring those words while I lay in bed with fever. "Children are often sick, darling. That's the way it is with children. All beginnings are hard. You'll be all right soon."

I remember bursting into tears one evening because a passage of Bible commentary had proved too difficult for me to understand. I was about nine years old at the time. "You want to understand everything immediately," my father said, "just like that? You only began to study commentary last week. All beginnings are hard. You have to work at the job of studying. Go over it again and again."

The man who later guided me in my studies would welcome me warmly into his apartment and, when we sat at his desk, say to me in his gentle voice, "Be patient, David. The Midrash says, 'All beginnings are hard.' You cannot swallow all the world at one time."

I say it myself today when I stand before a new class at the beginning of a school year or am about to begin a new book or research paper: All beginnings are hard. Teaching the way I do is hard, for I touch the raw nerves of faith, the beginnings of things. Often students are shaken. I say to them what was said to me, "Be patient; you are learning a new way of understanding the Bible. All beginnings are hard." And sometimes I add what I have learned on my own: "Especially a beginning that you make by yourself. That is the hardest beginning of all."

Chaim Potok, **In the Beginning**

In Module Three we are going to learn a small piece of Torah. In doing so, we are beginning the process of learning the ways the Torah asks us to read it. For most of us, studying is usually a process of reading a passage quickly, identifying the major points, and then discussing them. The nature of Torah demands that we develop specific skills for reading and analyzing its text.

In this module, we will explore the first two chapters of Genesis in two different ways. By the time we are finished, the need to "**close-read**" the Bible will be clear.

We are going to:

1. Play a board game.
2. Draw some conclusions.
3. Compare two stories.
4. Draw some additional conclusions.

By the time you are done, you should be able to:

3.1 Describe the basic structure of the first story of creation.

3.2 Identify five exceptions to or emphases of that structure.

3.3 Find five contradictions between the two creation stories.

3.4 Describe three differences between these stories.

3.5 Create a list of things you need to look for when you study a biblical passage.

PLAYING BARA (Created)

On the following pages, you are going to find a board game called BARA. By playing it, you will learn something about the way the Torah is written.

STEP # 1

The entire first chapter of Genesis is written out within the squares of the game board. Before you can begin to play, you will need to color in the squares. Use the following color code:

BLUE — each of the six days of creation.
YELLOW — each time God saw that things were good or very good.
GREEN — each evening and morning.
RED — each time God calls something by name.
ORANGE — each time God creates something by "saying."
PURPLE — each time the thing which God creates comes into being.
PINK — each time God blesses.

Before you begin playing, see what patterns you can find.

STEP # 2

To play the game, you will need two to six players. All of you can play on one game board, but each player will need his/her own marker. (Use buttons, coins, pieces of paper, etc.)

You will also find in the following pages the question cards. They need to be cut out, shuffled, and stacked with the print facedown.

STEP # 3

The first player to finish the board (and to make it to Shabbat) wins.

To take a turn, a player draws a question card from the deck and tries to answer it. If the player answers the question correctly, she/he advances the indicated number of spaces.

It is **not** cheating to look at the game board. The idea of the game is for you to look *closely* at the board.

STEP # 4

Once you have finished playing, read the rest of the module and answer all the questions on the worksheets. These will help you to focus on the things that you've learned through playing the game.

Start

In the beginning God created the heaven and the earth.

Now the earth was unformed and void, and darkness was upon the face of the deep; and the spirit of God hovered over the face of the waters.

And God said: "Let there be light."

And there was light.

And God saw the light, that it was good.

And God divided the light from the darkness.

And God called the light Day, and the darkness He called Night.

And there was evening and there was morning,

ONE DAY

And God said: "Let there be a firmament in the midst of the waters, and let it divide the waters from the waters."

And God made the firmament, and divided the waters which were under the firmament from the waters which were above the firmament;

And the earth brought forth grass, herb yielding seed after its kind, and tree bearing fruit, wherein is the seed thereof, after its kind;

And it was so.

And God said: "Let the earth put forth grass, herb yielding seed, and fruit-tree bearing fruit after its kind, wherein is the seed thereof, upon the earth."

And God saw that it was good.

And God called the dry land Earth, and the gathering together of the waters called He Seas;

And it was so.

And God said: "Let the waters under the heaven be gathered together unto one place, and let the dry land appear."

A SECOND DAY

And there was evening and there was morning,

And God called the firmament Heaven.

And it was so.

And God saw that it was good.

And there was evening and there was morning,

A THIRD DAY

Bara

And God blessed them; and God said unto them: "Be fruitful, and multiply, and replenish the earth, and subdue it; and have dominion over the fish of the sea, and over the fowl of the air, and over every living thing that creepeth upon the earth."

And God created man in His own image, in the image of God created He him; male and female created He them.

And God said: "Let us make man in our image, after our likeness; and let them have dominion over the fish of the sea, and over the fowl of the air, and over the cattle, and over all the earth, and over every creeping thing that creepeth upon the earth."

And God saw that it was good.

And God made the beast of the earth after its kind, and the cattle after their kind, and everything that creepeth upon the ground after its kind;

And it was so.

42

And God said: "Let there be lights in the firmament [of] the heaven to divide the day from the night; and [let] them be for signs, and for seasons, and for days [and] years; and let them be for lights in the firma[m]ent of the heaven to give light upon the earth."

And it was so.

And God made the two great lights: the greater light to rule the day, and the lesser light to rule the night; and the stars.

A Creation Game

And God said: "Behold, I have given you every [he]rb yielding seed, which is upon the face of all [th]e earth, and every tree, in which is the fruit of a [tre]e yielding seed—to you it shall be for food; and [to] every beast of the earth, and to every fowl of [th]e air, and to every thing that creepeth upon the [ear]th, wherein there is a living soul, [I have given] [ev]ery green herb for food."

And it was so.

And God set them in the firmament of the heaven to give light upon the earth, and to rule over the day and over the night, and to divide the light from the darkness;

And God saw that it was good.

And there was evening and there was morning,

A FOURTH DAY

And God saw every thing that He had made, and, behold, it was very good.

And God said: "Let the waters swarm with swarms of living creatures, and let fowl fly above the earth in the open firmament of heaven."

These are the generations of the heaven and of the earth when they were created....

And God blessed the seventh day, and hallowed it; because that in it He rested from all His work which God in creating had made.

And on the SEVENTH DAY God finished His work which He had made; and He rested on the seventh day from all His work which He had made.

And there was evening and there was morning,

THE SIXTH DAY

And the heaven and the earth were finished, and all the host of them.

And God created the great sea-monsters, and every living creature that creepeth, wherewith the waters swarmed, after its kind, and every winged fowl after its kind;

[An]d God said: "Let the [ear]th bring forth the living [cr]eature after its kind, cat[tle], and creeping thing, [an]d the beast of the earth af[ter] its kind."

A FIFTH DAY

And there was evening and there was morning,

And God blessed them, saying: "Be fruitful, and multiply, and fill the waters in the seas, and let fowl multiply in the earth."

And God saw that it was good.

The translation used in this game is taken from the 1917 Jewish Publication Society (JPS) translation of the Bible, the Standard Jewish Version (SJV). While it presents us with some difficulties, including sexist language and a basic formality of language, it makes other things clear. This translation was the product of years of work by a committee of the best American Bible scholars. It is based on the style of the King James Edition—a Christian English translation of the Bible. Later in this volume we will contrast this style of translation to others.

Exercise 3.1— DEBRIEFING THE BARA GAME

The first chapter of Genesis is a highly structured text. It is a poem with patterns and exceptions. Both are ongoing and planned. The writer of this story carefully uses both the patterns and the breaks in those patterns to communicate the story's messages. This exercise will help us decode some of these patterns and exceptions.

PART # 1

Look at the way most of the days of creation are described:

	Color	Action/Concept	
BEGINNING			What two squares come at the beginning of each day?

ENDING			What two squares come at the end of each day?

1. What day doesn't fit the pattern?_____
2. Which days have two orange squares?_____
3. Which three days have the usual format naming (numbering) the day changed?

_____   _____   _____

MIDDLE
4. How many yellow squares are there? _____
5. Which days have two? _____
6. How many red squares are there? _____
7. How many pink squares are there? _____
8. Which days have red squares? _____
9. Which days have pink squares? _____
10. What other patterns do you see? _____

From the things you've found so far—what days seem like they might be paired?

_____

_____

PART # 2

Let's use what was created on each of the days (orange squares) to look at the pattern of this story.

What does God create on the first day?			What does God create on the fourth day?
What two things does God create the second day?			What two kinds of life does God create on the fifth day?
What two things does God make on the third day?			What two kinds of life are created on the sixth day?

	Is anything created on the seventh day?

11. What is the connection between what was created on the first three days and what was created on the next three days?

_____

_____

12. How does the distribution of pink and red squares (namings and blessings) relate to this?

_____

_____

_____

DRAWING SOME CONCLUSIONS

What do you think the author of this story was trying to say about creation?

_____

_____

_____

How does the style of this story differ from that of most other literature you have read?

_____

_____

_____

What kinds of "elements" do you have to look for?

_____

_____

_____

How does the style of this story help the writer to communicate the message about creation?

_____

_____

_____

COMPARISONS

In the first part of this module, we did some close-reading of the first chapter of the Torah. It taught us something of the careful use of patterns and exceptions which the biblical author uses to convey meaning. In the next part of this module, we are going to compare two chapters and see some of the other things that the TORAH asks us to discover.

The first chapter of Genesis tells the story of the creation of the world in seven days. The second chapter tells the story of creation from a different perspective—that of the Garden of Eden. Read and compare these two stories and then answer the questions at the end of the module.

בְּרֵאשִׁית בָּרָא אֱלֹהִים אֵת הַשָּׁמַיִם וְאֵת הָאָרֶץ: וְהָאָרֶץ הָיְתָה תֹהוּ וָבֹהוּ וְחֹשֶׁךְ עַל־פְּנֵי תְהוֹם וְרוּחַ אֱלֹהִים מְרַחֶפֶת עַל־פְּנֵי הַמָּיִם: וַיֹּאמֶר אֱלֹהִים יְהִי אוֹר וַיְהִי־אוֹר: וַיַּרְא אֱלֹהִים אֶת־הָאוֹר כִּי־טוֹב וַיַּבְדֵּל אֱלֹהִים בֵּין הָאוֹר וּבֵין הַחֹשֶׁךְ: וַיִּקְרָא אֱלֹהִים לָאוֹר יוֹם וְלַחֹשֶׁךְ קָרָא לָיְלָה וַיְהִי־עֶרֶב וַיְהִי־בֹקֶר יוֹם אֶחָד:

וַיֹּאמֶר אֱלֹהִים יְהִי רָקִיעַ בְּתוֹךְ הַמָּיִם וִיהִי מַבְדִּיל בֵּין מַיִם לָמָיִם: וַיַּעַשׂ אֱלֹהִים אֶת־הָרָקִיעַ וַיַּבְדֵּל בֵּין הַמַּיִם אֲשֶׁר מִתַּחַת לָרָקִיעַ וּבֵין הַמַּיִם אֲשֶׁר מֵעַל לָרָקִיעַ וַיְהִי־כֵן: וַיִּקְרָא אֱלֹהִים לָרָקִיעַ שָׁמָיִם וַיְהִי־עֶרֶב וַיְהִי־בֹקֶר יוֹם שֵׁנִי:

וַיֹּאמֶר אֱלֹהִים יִקָּווּ הַמַּיִם מִתַּחַת הַשָּׁמַיִם אֶל־מָקוֹם אֶחָד וְתֵרָאֶה הַיַּבָּשָׁה וַיְהִי־כֵן: וַיִּקְרָא אֱלֹהִים לַיַּבָּשָׁה אֶרֶץ וּלְמִקְוֵה הַמַּיִם קָרָא יַמִּים וַיַּרְא אֱלֹהִים כִּי־טוֹב: וַיֹּאמֶר אֱלֹהִים תַּדְשֵׁא הָאָרֶץ דֶּשֶׁא עֵשֶׂב מַזְרִיעַ זֶרַע עֵץ פְּרִי עֹשֶׂה פְּרִי לְמִינוֹ אֲשֶׁר זַרְעוֹ־בוֹ עַל־הָאָרֶץ וַיְהִי־כֵן: וַתּוֹצֵא הָאָרֶץ דֶּשֶׁא עֵשֶׂב מַזְרִיעַ זֶרַע לְמִינֵהוּ וְעֵץ עֹשֶׂה־פְּרִי אֲשֶׁר זַרְעוֹ־בוֹ לְמִינֵהוּ וַיַּרְא אֱלֹהִים כִּי־טוֹב: וַיְהִי־עֶרֶב וַיְהִי־בֹקֶר יוֹם שְׁלִישִׁי:

וַיֹּאמֶר אֱלֹהִים יְהִי מְאֹרֹת בִּרְקִיעַ הַשָּׁמַיִם לְהַבְדִּיל בֵּין הַיּוֹם וּבֵין הַלָּיְלָה וְהָיוּ לְאֹתֹת וּלְמוֹעֲדִים וּלְיָמִים וְשָׁנִים: וְהָיוּ לִמְאוֹרֹת בִּרְקִיעַ הַשָּׁמַיִם לְהָאִיר עַל־הָאָרֶץ וַיְהִי־כֵן: וַיַּעַשׂ אֱלֹהִים אֶת־שְׁנֵי הַמְּאֹרֹת הַגְּדֹלִים אֶת־הַמָּאוֹר הַגָּדֹל לְמֶמְשֶׁלֶת הַיּוֹם וְאֶת־הַמָּאוֹר הַקָּטֹן לְמֶמְשֶׁלֶת הַלַּיְלָה וְאֵת הַכּוֹכָבִים: וַיִּתֵּן אֹתָם אֱלֹהִים בִּרְקִיעַ הַשָּׁמַיִם לְהָאִיר עַל־הָאָרֶץ: וְלִמְשֹׁל בַּיּוֹם וּבַלַּיְלָה וּלְהַבְדִּיל בֵּין הָאוֹר וּבֵין הַחֹשֶׁךְ וַיַּרְא אֱלֹהִים כִּי־טוֹב: וַיְהִי־עֶרֶב וַיְהִי־בֹקֶר יוֹם רְבִיעִי:

When God began to create the heaven and the earth—the earth being unformed and void, with darkness over the surface of the deep and a wind from God sweeping over the water—God said, "Let there be light"; and there was light. God saw that the light was good, and God separated the light from the darkness. God called the light Day, and the darkness He called Night. And there was evening and there was morning, a first day.

God said, "Let there be an expanse in the midst of the water, that it may separate water from water." God made the expanse, and it separated the water which was below the expanse from the water which was above the expanse. And it was so. God called the expanse Sky. And there was evening and there was morning, a second day.

God said, "Let the water below the sky be gathered into one area, that the dry land may appear." And it was so. God called the dry land Earth, and the gathering of waters He called Seas. And God saw that this was good. And God said, "Let the earth sprout vegetation: seed-bearing plants, fruit trees of every kind on earth that bear fruit with the seed in it." And it was so. The earth brought forth vegetation: seed-bearing plants of every kind, and trees of every kind bearing fruit with the seed in it. And God saw that this was good. And there was evening and there was morning, a third day.

God said, "Let there be lights in the expanse of the sky to separate day from night; they shall serve as signs for the set times—the days and the years; and they shall serve as lights in the expanse of the sky to shine upon the earth." And it was so. God made the two great lights, the greater light to dominate the day and the lesser light to dominate the night, and the stars. And God set them in the expanse of the sky to shine upon the earth, to dominate the day and the night, and to separate light from darkness. And God saw that this was good. And there was evening and there was morning, a fourth day.

וַיֹּאמֶר אֱלֹהִים יִשְׁרְצוּ הַמַּיִם שֶׁרֶץ נֶפֶשׁ חַיָּה וְעוֹף יְעוֹפֵף עַל־הָאָרֶץ עַל־פְּנֵי רְקִיעַ הַשָּׁמָיִם: וַיִּבְרָא אֱלֹהִים אֶת־הַתַּנִּינִם הַגְּדֹלִים וְאֵת כָּל־נֶפֶשׁ הַחַיָּה הָרֹמֶשֶׂת אֲשֶׁר שָׁרְצוּ הַמַּיִם לְמִינֵהֶם וְאֵת כָּל־עוֹף כָּנָף לְמִינֵהוּ וַיַּרְא אֱלֹהִים כִּי־טוֹב: וַיְבָרֶךְ אֹתָם אֱלֹהִים לֵאמֹר פְּרוּ וּרְבוּ וּמִלְאוּ אֶת־הַמַּיִם בַּיַּמִּים וְהָעוֹף יִרֶב בָּאָרֶץ: וַיְהִי־עֶרֶב וַיְהִי־בֹקֶר יוֹם חֲמִישִׁי:

וַיֹּאמֶר אֱלֹהִים תּוֹצֵא הָאָרֶץ נֶפֶשׁ חַיָּה לְמִינָהּ בְּהֵמָה וָרֶמֶשׂ וְחַיְתוֹ־אֶרֶץ לְמִינָהּ וַיְהִי־כֵן: וַיַּעַשׂ אֱלֹהִים אֶת־חַיַּת הָאָרֶץ לְמִינָהּ וְאֶת־הַבְּהֵמָה לְמִינָהּ וְאֵת כָּל־רֶמֶשׂ הָאֲדָמָה לְמִינֵהוּ וַיַּרְא אֱלֹהִים כִּי־טוֹב: וַיֹּאמֶר אֱלֹהִים נַעֲשֶׂה אָדָם בְּצַלְמֵנוּ כִּדְמוּתֵנוּ וְיִרְדּוּ בִדְגַת הַיָּם וּבְעוֹף הַשָּׁמַיִם וּבַבְּהֵמָה וּבְכָל־הָאָרֶץ וּבְכָל־הָרֶמֶשׂ הָרֹמֵשׂ עַל־הָאָרֶץ: וַיִּבְרָא אֱלֹהִים אֶת־הָאָדָם בְּצַלְמוֹ בְּצֶלֶם אֱלֹהִים בָּרָא אֹתוֹ זָכָר וּנְקֵבָה בָּרָא אֹתָם: וַיְבָרֶךְ אֹתָם אֱלֹהִים וַיֹּאמֶר לָהֶם אֱלֹהִים פְּרוּ וּרְבוּ וּמִלְאוּ אֶת־הָאָרֶץ וְכִבְשֻׁהָ וּרְדוּ בִּדְגַת הַיָּם וּבְעוֹף הַשָּׁמַיִם וּבְכָל־חַיָּה הָרֹמֶשֶׂת עַל־הָאָרֶץ:

וַיֹּאמֶר אֱלֹהִים הִנֵּה נָתַתִּי לָכֶם אֶת־כָּל־עֵשֶׂב זֹרֵעַ זֶרַע אֲשֶׁר עַל־פְּנֵי כָל־הָאָרֶץ וְאֶת־כָּל־הָעֵץ אֲשֶׁר־בּוֹ פְרִי־עֵץ זֹרֵעַ זָרַע לָכֶם יִהְיֶה לְאָכְלָה: וּלְכָל־חַיַּת הָאָרֶץ וּלְכָל־עוֹף הַשָּׁמַיִם וּלְכֹל רוֹמֵשׂ עַל־הָאָרֶץ אֲשֶׁר־בּוֹ נֶפֶשׁ חַיָּה אֶת־כָּל־יֶרֶק עֵשֶׂב לְאָכְלָה וַיְהִי־כֵן: וַיַּרְא אֱלֹהִים אֶת־כָּל־אֲשֶׁר עָשָׂה וְהִנֵּה־טוֹב מְאֹד וַיְהִי־עֶרֶב וַיְהִי־בֹקֶר יוֹם הַשִּׁשִּׁי:

וַיְכֻלּוּ הַשָּׁמַיִם וְהָאָרֶץ וְכָל־צְבָאָם: וַיְכַל אֱלֹהִים בַּיּוֹם הַשְּׁבִיעִי מְלַאכְתּוֹ אֲשֶׁר עָשָׂה וַיִּשְׁבֹּת בַּיּוֹם הַשְּׁבִיעִי מִכָּל־מְלַאכְתּוֹ אֲשֶׁר עָשָׂה: וַיְבָרֶךְ אֱלֹהִים אֶת־יוֹם הַשְּׁבִיעִי וַיְקַדֵּשׁ אֹתוֹ כִּי בוֹ שָׁבַת מִכָּל־מְלַאכְתּוֹ אֲשֶׁר־בָּרָא אֱלֹהִים לַעֲשׂוֹת:

God said, "Let the waters bring forth swarms of living creatures, and birds that fly above the earth across the expanse of the sky." God created the great sea monsters, and all the living creatures of every kind that creep, which the waters brought forth in swarms; and all the winged birds of every kind. And God saw that this was good. God blessed them, saying, "Be fertile and increase, fill the waters in the seas, and let the birds increase on the earth." And there was evening and there was morning, a fifth day.

God said, "Let the earth bring forth every kind of living creature: cattle, creeping things, and wild beasts of every kind." And it was so. God made wild beasts of every kind and cattle of every kind, and all kinds of creeping things of the earth. And God saw that this was good. And God said, "Let us make man in our image, after our likeness. They shall rule the fish of the sea, the birds of the sky, the cattle, the whole earth, and all the creeping things that creep on earth." And God created man in His image, in the image of God He created him; male and female He created them. God blessed them and God said to them, "Be fertile and increase, fill the earth and master it; and rule the fish of the sea, the birds of the sky, and all the living things that creep on earth."

God said, "See, I give you every seed-bearing plant that is upon all the earth, and every tree that has seed-bearing fruit; they shall be yours for food. And to all the animals on land, to all the birds of the sky, and to everything that creeps on earth, in which there is the breath of life, [I give] all the green plants for food." And it was so. And God saw all that He had made, and found it very good. And there was evening and there was morning, the sixth day.

The heaven and the earth were finished, and all their array. On the seventh day God finished the work which He had been doing, and He ceased on the seventh day from all the work which He had done. And God blessed the seventh day and declared it holy, because on it God ceased from all the work of creation which He had done. Such is the story of heaven and earth when they were created.

אֵלֶּה תוֹלְדוֹת הַשָּׁמַיִם וְהָאָרֶץ בְּהִבָּרְאָם בְּיוֹם עֲשׂוֹת יהוה אֱלֹהִים אֶרֶץ וְשָׁמָיִם: וְכֹל שִׂיחַ הַשָּׂדֶה טֶרֶם יִהְיֶה בָאָרֶץ וְכָל־עֵשֶׂב הַשָּׂדֶה טֶרֶם יִצְמָח כִּי לֹא הִמְטִיר יהוה אֱלֹהִים עַל־הָאָרֶץ וְאָדָם אַיִן לַעֲבֹד אֶת־ הָאֲדָמָה: וְאֵד יַעֲלֶה מִן־הָאָרֶץ וְהִשְׁקָה אֶת־ כָּל־פְּנֵי הָאֲדָמָה: וַיִּיצֶר יהוה אֱלֹהִים אֶת־ הָאָדָם עָפָר מִן־הָאֲדָמָה וַיִּפַּח בְּאַפָּיו נִשְׁמַת חַיִּים וַיְהִי הָאָדָם לְנֶפֶשׁ חַיָּה:

וַיִּטַּע יהוה אֱלֹהִים גַּן־בְּעֵדֶן מִקֶּדֶם וַיָּשֶׂם שָׁם אֶת־הָאָדָם אֲשֶׁר יָצָר: וַיַּצְמַח יהוה אֱלֹהִים מִן־הָאֲדָמָה כָּל־עֵץ נֶחְמָד לְמַרְאֶה וְטוֹב לְמַאֲכָל וְעֵץ הַחַיִּים בְּתוֹךְ הַגָּן וְעֵץ הַדַּעַת טוֹב וָרָע:

וְנָהָר יֹצֵא מֵעֵדֶן לְהַשְׁקוֹת אֶת־הַגָּן וּמִשָּׁם יִפָּרֵד וְהָיָה לְאַרְבָּעָה רָאשִׁים: שֵׁם הָאֶחָד פִּישׁוֹן הוּא הַסֹּבֵב אֵת כָּל־אֶרֶץ הַחֲוִילָה אֲשֶׁר־שָׁם הַזָּהָב: וּזֲהַב הָאָרֶץ הַהִוא טוֹב שָׁם הַבְּדֹלַח וְאֶבֶן הַשֹּׁהַם: וְשֵׁם־הַנָּהָר הַשֵּׁנִי גִּיחוֹן הוּא הַסּוֹבֵב אֵת כָּל־אֶרֶץ כּוּשׁ: וְשֵׁם הַנָּהָר הַשְּׁלִישִׁי חִדֶּקֶל הוּא הַהֹלֵךְ קִדְמַת אַשּׁוּר וְהַנָּהָר הָרְבִיעִי הוּא פְרָת.

וַיִּקַּח יהוה אֱלֹהִים אֶת־הָאָדָם וַיַּנִּחֵהוּ בְגַן־ עֵדֶן לְעָבְדָהּ וּלְשָׁמְרָהּ: וַיְצַו יהוה אֱלֹהִים עַל־הָאָדָם לֵאמֹר מִכֹּל עֵץ־הַגָּן אָכֹל תֹּאכֵל: וּמֵעֵץ הַדַּעַת טוֹב וָרָע לֹא תֹאכַל מִמֶּנּוּ כִּי בְּיוֹם אֲכָלְךָ מִמֶּנּוּ מוֹת תָּמוּת:

וַיֹּאמֶר יהוה אֱלֹהִים לֹא־טוֹב הֱיוֹת הָאָדָם לְבַדּוֹ אֶעֱשֶׂה־לּוֹ עֵזֶר כְּנֶגְדּוֹ: וַיִּצֶר יהוה אֱלֹהִים מִן־הָאֲדָמָה כָּל־חַיַּת הַשָּׂדֶה וְאֵת כָּל־עוֹף הַשָּׁמַיִם וַיָּבֵא אֶל־הָאָדָם לִרְאוֹת מַה־יִּקְרָא־ לוֹ וְכֹל אֲשֶׁר יִקְרָא־לוֹ הָאָדָם נֶפֶשׁ חַיָּה הוּא שְׁמוֹ: וַיִּקְרָא הָאָדָם שֵׁמוֹת לְכָל־הַבְּהֵמָה וּלְעוֹף הַשָּׁמַיִם וּלְכֹל חַיַּת הַשָּׂדֶה וּלְאָדָם

When the LORD God made earth and heaven—when no shrub of the field was yet on earth and no grasses of the field had yet sprouted, because the LORD God had not sent rain upon the earth and there was no man to till the soil, but a flow would well up from the ground and water the whole surface of the earth—the LORD God formed man from the dust of the earth. He blew into his nostrils the breath of life, and man became a living being.

The LORD God planted a garden in Eden, in the east, and placed there the man whom He had formed. And from the ground the LORD God caused to grow every tree that was pleasing to the sight and good for food, with the tree of life in the middle of the garden, and the tree of knowledge of good and bad.

A river issues from Eden to water the garden, and it then divides and becomes four branches. The name of the first is Pishon, the one that winds through the whole land of Havilah, where the gold is. (The gold of that land is good; bdellium is there, and lapis lazuli.) The name of the second river is Gihon, the one that winds through the whole land of Cush. The name of the third river is Tigris, the one that flows east of Asshur. And the fourth river is the Euphrates.

The LORD God took the man and placed him in the garden of Eden, to till it and tend it. And the LORD God commanded the man, saying, "Of every tree of the garden you are free to eat; but as for the tree of knowledge of good and bad, you must not eat of it; for as soon as you eat of it, you shall die."

The LORD God said, "It is not good for man to be alone; I will make a fitting helper for him." And the LORD God formed out of the earth all the wild beasts and all the birds of the sky, and brought them to the man to see what he would call them; and whatever the man called each living creature, that would be its name. And the man gave names to all the cattle and to the birds of the sky and

לֹא־מָצָא עֵזֶר כְּנֶגְדּוֹ: וַיַּפֵּל יְהוָה אֱלֹהִים תַּרְדֵּמָה עַל־הָאָדָם וַיִּישָׁן וַיִּקַּח אַחַת מִצַּלְעֹתָיו וַיִּסְגֹּר בָּשָׂר תַּחְתֶּנָּה: וַיִּבֶן יְהוָה אֱלֹהִים אֶת־הַצֵּלָע אֲשֶׁר־לָקַח מִן־הָאָדָם לְאִשָּׁה וַיְבִאֶהָ אֶל־הָאָדָם: וַיֹּאמֶר הָאָדָם

זֹאת הַפַּעַם עֶצֶם מֵעֲצָמַי וּבָשָׂר מִבְּשָׂרִי לְזֹאת יִקָּרֵא אִשָּׁה כִּי מֵאִישׁ לֻקֳחָה־זֹּאת:

עַל־כֵּן יַעֲזָב־אִישׁ אֶת־אָבִיו וְאֶת־אִמּוֹ וְדָבַק בְּאִשְׁתּוֹ וְהָיוּ לְבָשָׂר אֶחָד:

וַיִּהְיוּ שְׁנֵיהֶם עֲרוּמִּים הָאָדָם וְאִשְׁתּוֹ וְלֹא יִתְבֹּשָׁשׁוּ: וְהַנָּחָשׁ הָיָה עָרוּם מִכֹּל חַיַּת הַשָּׂדֶה אֲשֶׁר עָשָׂה יְהוָה אֱלֹהִים וַיֹּאמֶר אֶל־הָאִשָּׁה אַף כִּי־אָמַר אֱלֹהִים לֹא תֹאכְלוּ מִכֹּל עֵץ הַגָּן: וַתֹּאמֶר הָאִשָּׁה אֶל־הַנָּחָשׁ מִפְּרִי עֵץ־הַגָּן נֹאכֵל: וּמִפְּרִי הָעֵץ אֲשֶׁר בְּתוֹךְ־הַגָּן אָמַר אֱלֹהִים לֹא תֹאכְלוּ מִמֶּנּוּ וְלֹא תִגְּעוּ בּוֹ פֶּן־תְּמֻתוּן: וַיֹּאמֶר הַנָּחָשׁ אֶל־הָאִשָּׁה לֹא־מוֹת תְּמֻתוּן: כִּי יֹדֵעַ אֱלֹהִים כִּי בְּיוֹם אֲכָלְכֶם מִמֶּנּוּ וְנִפְקְחוּ עֵינֵיכֶם וִהְיִיתֶם כֵּאלֹהִים יֹדְעֵי טוֹב וָרָע: וַתֵּרֶא הָאִשָּׁה כִּי טוֹב הָעֵץ לְמַאֲכָל וְכִי תַאֲוָה־הוּא לָעֵינַיִם וְנֶחְמָד הָעֵץ לְהַשְׂכִּיל וַתִּקַּח מִפִּרְיוֹ וַתֹּאכַל וַתִּתֵּן גַּם־לְאִישָׁהּ עִמָּהּ וַיֹּאכַל: וַתִּפָּקַחְנָה עֵינֵי שְׁנֵיהֶם וַיֵּדְעוּ כִּי עֵירֻמִּם הֵם וַיִּתְפְּרוּ עֲלֵה תְאֵנָה וַיַּעֲשׂוּ לָהֶם חֲגֹרֹת:

וַיִּשְׁמְעוּ אֶת־קוֹל יְהוָה אֱלֹהִים מִתְהַלֵּךְ בַּגָּן לְרוּחַ הַיּוֹם וַיִּתְחַבֵּא הָאָדָם וְאִשְׁתּוֹ מִפְּנֵי יְהוָה אֱלֹהִים בְּתוֹךְ עֵץ הַגָּן: וַיִּקְרָא יְהוָה אֱלֹהִים אֶל־הָאָדָם וַיֹּאמֶר לוֹ אַיֶּכָּה: וַיֹּאמֶר אֶת־קֹלְךָ שָׁמַעְתִּי בַּגָּן וָאִירָא כִּי־עֵירֹם אָנֹכִי וָאֵחָבֵא: וַיֹּאמֶר מִי הִגִּיד לְךָ כִּי עֵירֹם אָתָּה הֲמִן־הָעֵץ אֲשֶׁר צִוִּיתִיךָ לְבִלְתִּי אֲכָל־מִמֶּנּוּ אָכָלְתָּ:

to all the wild beasts; but for Adam no fitting helper was found. So the LORD God cast a deep sleep upon the man; and, while he slept, He took one of his ribs and closed up the flesh at that spot. And the LORD God fashioned the rib that He had taken from the man into a woman; and He brought her to the man. Then the man said,

> "This one at last
> Is bone of my bones
> And flesh of my flesh.
> This one shall be called Woman,
> For from man was she taken."

Hence a man leaves his father and mother and clings to his wife, so that they become one flesh.

The two of them were naked, the man and his wife, yet they felt no shame. Now the serpent was the shrewdest of all the wild beasts that the LORD God had made. He said to the woman, "Did God really say: You shall not eat of any tree of the garden?" The woman replied to the serpent, "We may eat of the fruit of the other trees of the garden. It is only about fruit of tree in the middle of the garden that God said: You shall not eat of it or touch it, lest you die." And the serpent said to the woman, "You are not going to die, but God knows that as soon as you eat of it your eyes will be opened and you will be like divine beings who know good and bad." When the woman saw that the tree was good for eating and a delight to the eyes, and that the tree was desirable as a source of wisdom, she took of its fruit and ate. She also gave some to her husband, and he ate. Then the eyes of both of them were opened and they perceived that they were naked; and they sewed together fig leaves and made themselves loincloths.

They heard the sound of the LORD God moving about in the garden at the breezy time of day; and the man and his wife hid from the LORD God among the trees of the garden. The LORD God called out to the man and said to him, "Where are you?" He replied, "I heard the sound of You in the garden, and I was afraid because I was naked, so I hid." Then He said, "Who told you that you were naked? Did you eat of the tree from which I had forbidden you to eat?" The

וַיֹּאמֶר הָאָדָם הָאִשָּׁה אֲשֶׁר נָתַתָּה
עִמָּדִי הִוא נָתְנָה־לִּי מִן־הָעֵץ וָאֹכֵל: וַיֹּאמֶר
יְהוָה אֱלֹהִים לָאִשָּׁה מַה־זֹּאת עָשִׂית
וַתֹּאמֶר הָאִשָּׁה הַנָּחָשׁ הִשִּׁיאַנִי וָאֹכֵל: וַיֹּאמֶר
יְהוָה אֱלֹהִים אֶל־הַנָּחָשׁ

כִּי עָשִׂיתָ זֹּאת אָרוּר אַתָּה מִכָּל־הַבְּהֵמָה
וּמִכֹּל חַיַּת הַשָּׂדֶה עַל־גְּחֹנְךָ תֵלֵךְ וְעָפָר
תֹּאכַל כָּל־יְמֵי חַיֶּיךָ: וְאֵיבָה אָשִׁית בֵּינְךָ וּבֵין
הָאִשָּׁה וּבֵין זַרְעֲךָ וּבֵין זַרְעָהּ הוּא יְשׁוּפְךָ
רֹאשׁ וְאַתָּה תְּשׁוּפֶנּוּ עָקֵב:

אֶל־הָאִשָּׁה אָמַר הַרְבָּה אַרְבֶּה עִצְּבוֹנֵךְ
וְהֵרֹנֵךְ בְּעֶצֶב תֵּלְדִי בָנִים וְאֶל־אִישֵׁךְ
תְּשׁוּקָתֵךְ וְהוּא יִמְשָׁל־בָּךְ:

וּלְאָדָם אָמַר כִּי שָׁמַעְתָּ לְקוֹל אִשְׁתֶּךָ
וַתֹּאכַל מִן־הָעֵץ אֲשֶׁר צִוִּיתִיךָ לֵאמֹר לֹא
תֹאכַל מִמֶּנּוּ

אֲרוּרָה הָאֲדָמָה
בַּעֲבוּרֶךָ בְּעִצָּבוֹן תֹּאכֲלֶנָּה כֹּל יְמֵי חַיֶּיךָ:
וְקוֹץ וְדַרְדַּר תַּצְמִיחַ לָךְ וְאָכַלְתָּ אֶת־עֵשֶׂב
הַשָּׂדֶה: בְּזֵעַת אַפֶּיךָ תֹּאכַל לֶחֶם עַד שׁוּבְךָ
אֶל־הָאֲדָמָה כִּי מִמֶּנָּה לֻקָּחְתָּ כִּי־עָפָר אַתָּה
וְאֶל־עָפָר תָּשׁוּב:

וַיִּקְרָא הָאָדָם שֵׁם אִשְׁתּוֹ חַוָּה כִּי הִוא הָיְתָה
אֵם כָּל־חָי: וַיַּעַשׂ יְהוָה אֱלֹהִים לְאָדָם
וּלְאִשְׁתּוֹ כָּתְנוֹת עוֹר וַיַּלְבִּשֵׁם:

וַיֹּאמֶר יְהוָה אֱלֹהִים הֵן הָאָדָם הָיָה כְּאַחַד
מִמֶּנּוּ לָדַעַת טוֹב וָרָע וְעַתָּה פֶּן־יִשְׁלַח יָדוֹ
וְלָקַח גַּם מֵעֵץ הַחַיִּים וְאָכַל וָחַי לְעֹלָם:
וַיְשַׁלְּחֵהוּ יְהוָה אֱלֹהִים מִגַּן־עֵדֶן לַעֲבֹד אֶת־
הָאֲדָמָה אֲשֶׁר לֻקַּח מִשָּׁם: וַיְגָרֶשׁ אֶת־
הָאָדָם וַיַּשְׁכֵּן מִקֶּדֶם לְגַן־עֵדֶן אֶת־הַכְּרֻבִים
וְאֵת לַהַט הַחֶרֶב הַמִּתְהַפֶּכֶת לִשְׁמֹר אֶת־
דֶּרֶךְ עֵץ הַחַיִּים:

man said, "The woman You put at my side—she gave me of the tree, and I ate." And the LORD God said to the woman, "What is this you have done!" The woman replied "The serpent duped me, and I ate." Then the LORD God said to the serpent,

> "Because you did this,
> More cursed shall you be than all cattle
> And all the wild beasts:
> On your belly shall you crawl
> And dirt shall you eat
> All the days of your life.
> I will put enmity
> Between you and the woman,
> And between your offspring and hers;
> They shall strike at your head,
> And you shall strike at their heel."

And to the woman He said,

> "I will make most severe
> Your pangs in childbearing;
> In pain shall you bear children.
> Yet your urge shall be for your husband,
> And he shall rule over you."

To Adam He said, "Because you did as your wife said and ate of the tree about which I commanded you, 'You shall not eat of it,'

> Cursed be the ground because of you;
> By toil shall you eat of it
> All the days of your life:
> Thorns and thistles
> Shall it sprout for you.
> But your food shall be the grasses of the field;
> By the sweat of your brow
> Shall you get bread to eat,
> Until you return to the ground—
> For from it you were taken.
> For dust you are,
> And to dust you shall return."

The man named his wife Eve, because she was the mother of all the living. And the LORD God made garments of skins for Adam and his wife, and clothed them.

And the LORD God said, "Now that the man has become like one of us, knowing good and bad, what if he should stretch out his hand and take also from the tree of life and eat, and live forever!" So the LORD God banished him from the garden of Eden, to till the soil from which he was taken. He drove the man out, and stationed east of the garden of Eden the cherubim and the fiery ever-turning sword, to guard the way to the tree of life.

Answer each of these questions about each story.	STORY # 1	STORY # 2
1. What is God called in each story?	G-d	lord G-d
2. What things exist before creation begins?		
3. How does God create in each story?		
4. List the order in which things are created.		
5. When and how are man and woman created?		
6. In what style is the story written? (poem, folk-story, narrative, history, etc.)		
7. How does God relate to people?		
8. How much water is present in the world?		
9. Do the stories have different messages? What does each story say about creation? About people's role in the world? About the world?		

conCLUEsions

1. Now that you have compared these two sections of the biblical text, what problems/ questions/difficulties did you find?

_____

_____

_____

_____

2. How do you feel about discovering these "problems"? (Excited? Confused? Frustrated? Nothing?) Why?

_____

_____

_____

_____

3. Do you have some way of solving/resolving these problems? How? What conclusions have you drawn?

_____

_____

_____

_____

_____

In reading the first chapter of Genesis by itself and then in comparing the first two chapters, what have you learned about the way the Torah should be studied? What makes it different from reading short stories?

_____

_____

_____

_____

_____

The **Rx** for this module suggests that you should now be able to do five things. Check off those you think you can now accomplish:

_____ Describe the basic structure of the first story of creation.
_____ Identify five exceptions to or emphases of that structure.
_____ Find five contradictions between the two creation stories.
_____ Describe three differences between these stories.
_____ Create a list of things you need to look for when you study a biblical passage.

FOOTNOTE
In this exercise and throughout most of the book, biblical excerpts will follow the 1962 JPS translation, the New Jewish Version (NJV). Unlike the SJV used in the first exercise, this translation breaks free of the style of the King James Edition. In Module Five, we'll look at the kinds of things we can learn from differing translations.

AN INTERLUDE

(A personal reflection)

I really find learning the Bible is like exploring a haunted house. It always seems that something is lurking behind the words, phrases, and metaphors. Perhaps, what I sense is God's true voice, or maybe the ghosts of rabbinic sages past. It may be the secret identities of the "real authors," or merely the echoes of ancient footsteps. I am never sure, but the text seems to draw me in and demand that I listen carefully to it. It demands that I question it and regularly calls upon me to explain it.

I often see myself, candle in hand, brushing aside the cobwebs and dust of the ancient "thee"s and "thou"s, listening to the creaks and echoes, and to the things which go bump in the syntax. On some explorations I am skeptical. Other journeys bring concern or disappointment. However, every encounter is a quest for the forces which haunt and give continual renewed life to these ancient phrase-clauses.

We need to know how to prod the text and to listen to its answers. Often, as we have already seen, we need to go past the story to the way the story is told. The text itself seems to demand this kind of exploration. It is indeed like a marvelous haunted mansion—one which has been carefully and artistically crafted.

APPENDIX TO MODULE THREE

ANSWERS

Exercise 3.1

Part #1

The first chapter in the Torah is a story of creation. It is a story of order with variation. While creation has a clear pattern, moving from simple to complex, and while there are regular rhythms, nothing is mechanical and totally fixed.

Orange squares begin most days of creation; they involve God creating by speaking. These are almost always followed directly by **purple squares**. These squares show that the act of God speaking resulted in the act of creation occurring. God says it, and it comes to be.

Days end with **green squares** followed by **blue squares**. **Green squares** are "evening and morning"; they represent the regularity in creation.

1. The seventh day does not fit the pattern. Nothing active is created.

2. The third and sixth days both have two acts of creation.

3. The third, fourth, and fifth days have a **yellow square** (God saw that it was good), a **green square** (evening and morning), and a **blue square** with the formula A ___rd/th Day. All other days have variations on one of these three elements.

4. There are seven **yellow squares**. God sees that it is good seven times.

5. The second and sixth days both have two **yellow squares**.

6. There are three **red squares**. God names things on the first three days.

7. There are three **pink squares**. God blesses things on the last three days.

8. See the answer to 6.

9. See the answer to 7.

10. This is an open-ended question.

   Based on this data, there is a clear connection between the third and the sixth days. There is also a connection between the first three days and the last three days.

Part #2

When we look at the pattern of creation, we see that "raw products" are created on the first three days while the things which "complete" them are created on the next three days.

On the first day God creates **light**, and perhaps "heaven and earth," depending on your reading of the first sentence. On the fourth day God creates the things which give **light**.

On the second day God divides between **sky** and **waters**. On the fifth day God creates **fish** and **birds**.

On the third day God creates **dry land** and **plants**. On the sixth day God creates **animals** and **people**.

On the seventh day God creates **rest**.

11. The first three days are "raw products." The next three days are those things which "actualize" those raw products.

12. For the first three days, God names things. This is one level of personal involvement. On the last three days (excluding the fourth, but now including the seventh) God insures their fate by blessing the things which are created. A blessing from God is a commitment to a positive future.

   The author of this story is clearly telling us that creation is good. The story also makes it clear that creation has an order and a pattern, but not necessarily a predictable or perfectly symmetric pattern. There is a subtlety to creation, where new perceptions of the order are always becoming clear.

   This story is a kind of prose poetry where form and content interweave. In looking for patterns in the story, we are also taught about looking for patterns in creation. It is a work of art where the process of communicating the nature of creation echoes the story's message about creation.

Exercise 3.2

A comparison of the first three chapters of Genesis reveals two different stories of creation, each of which reveals a different view of the process and nature of people and creation.

1. God	Lord God
2. Maybe chaos	All earth except garden
3. By speaking	More "hands-on" creation
4. Plants, animals, people	Plants, man, animals, woman
5. Man and woman equal	Woman created out of man
6. Epic poem	Folktale (Just-so story)
7. God doesn't	God talks directly
8. World based on water	Very little water

9. People are the culmination of creation. All of creation leads up to people; they end the process.

   People are the reason for creation. Most creation was to provide an environment for people.

   Not only do these two stories of creation contradict each other, but they also seem to provide very different answers to some of life's most basic questions.

The ancient Hebrew writers purposefully nurtured and developed prose narration to take the place of the epic genre which by its content was intimately bound up with the world of paganism, and appears to have had a special standing in the polytheistic cults. The recitation of the epics was tantamount to an enactment of cosmic events in the manner of sympathetic magic. In the process of total rejection of the polytheistic religions and their ritual expressions in the cult, epic songs and also the epic genre were purged from the repertoire of the Hebrew authors.

Shemaryahu Talmon, **The "Comparative Method" in Biblical Interpretation—Principles and Methods**

The biblical tale, through the most rigorous economy of means, leads us again and again to ponder complexities of motive and ambiguities of character because these are essential aspects of its vision of man, created by God, enjoying or suffering all the consequences of human freedom.

Robert Alter, **The Art of Biblical Narrative**

PRESCRIPTION

In Module Three: "Close-Reading, " we saw the use of repetition, patterns, and exceptions in the text. We saw the differences between two tellings of the same story. From these examples we learned that the Torah demands "close-reading." In this module, we will learn to recognize five literary patterns used in the text and add them to our investigative skills. They are: Repetition, Twice-Told Tales, Finding the Motivation, Leading Words, and Word-Echoes.

In the course of this module, each of these patterns will be explained and a working example will be provided. Then, a second series of examples will allow you to apply these patterns—to see if you really understand them.

By the end of this module, you should be able to:

4.1 Compare "repeated" portions of the biblical text and identify changes in the pattern of repetition.
4.2 Compare versions of stories and laws which are presented more than once in the text and identify differences in these versions.
4.3 Explain the concepts of "back-story" and "sub-text" and (a) describe how some midrashim fill this in, and (b) explain why that midrash was demanded by the text.
4.4 Identify **leading word**(s) in a passage and describe their impact.
4.5 Trace a "word-echo" between several passages and draw the connection the text seems to be making.
4.6 Describe and give an example of how the biblical author uses each of these five patterns to editorialize the story.

Exercise 4.1—REPETITION

ABRAM   SARAI   LOT   POSSESSIONS

When we read the Bible, it often seems to repeat itself constantly. We find that often God tells somebody to do something, that person does the thing, and then someone else is told about it—all in more or less the same language. The key is in the "*more or less.*" As we saw in Genesis, chapter I, pattern and variation are important tools of the biblical author. Look at this example.

When Abram left Ur and then Haran, he was accompanied by Lot, his brother's son. He travels with him from chapter 12 of Genesis through most of 13; then the text tells us:

> **The land could not support them staying together; for their possessions were so great that they could not remain together. And there was quarreling between the herdsmen of Abram's cattle and those of Lot's cattle.** (13:6-7)

But this may not be the whole story. If we look closely at two other passages (and notice the subtle change in the pattern of repetition), we see that the biblical narrator is giving us more information.

When Abram leaves Haran we are given the following description of his family:

> **(1) Abram took (2) Sarai his wife, and (3) Lot, his brother's son, and (4) all their possessions...** (12:5)

But just before the quarrel Abram and family return from Egypt and the description is *more or less* repeated:

> **(1) Abram went up into the Negev. He, and (2) his wife and (3) all that he possessed, and (4) Lot with him...** (13:1)

Here, in what seems like just a repetition of the cast, is a clue from the biblical narrator as to what is about to happen.

I. The order of people is the same in both passages, but how is the ownership of property changed?

_____

2. Does this insight into the change in Abram's and Lot's relationship make anything clearer about the fighting between their shepherds?

_____

3. Can you draw a lesson from this?

_____

As you can see, repetition in the Bible requires close examination.

EXERCISE 4.2—TWICE-TOLD TALES

We have already seen that sometimes a biblical story is told more than once and that sometimes the details seem to change.

Compare the following two versions of the story about the spies who scouted *Eretz Yisrael.*

The Lord spoke to Moses, saying: "Send men to scout the land of Canaan, which I am giving to the Israelite people: send one man from each of their ancestral tribes, each one a chief among them." So Moses, by the Lord's command, sent them out from the wilderness of Paran, all the men being leaders of Israel. (Num.13:1-3)	Then all of you came back to me [Moses] and said: "Let us send men ahead to reconnoiter the land for us and bring back word on the route we shall follow and the cities we shall come to." I approved of the plan, and so I selected twelve of your men, one from each tribe. (Deut. 1:22-23)
When they returned, they reported: "We came to the land you sent us to; it does indeed flow with milk and honey, and this is its fruit. However, the people who inhabit the country are powerful, and the cities are fortified and very large...." Caleb hushed the people before Moses and said, "Let us by all means go up, and we shall gain possession of it, for we shall surely overcome it." But the men who had gone up with him said, "We cannot attack that people, for it is stronger than we." Thus they spread calumnies among the Israelites about the land they had scouted, saying, "The land that we traversed and scouted is one that devours its settlers...." (Num. 13:27-28; 30-32)	...And they gave us this report, "It is a good land that the Lord our God is giving to us." Yet you refused to go up, and flouted the command of the Lord your God. You sulked in your tents and said, "It is because the Lord hates us that He brought us out of the land of Egypt.... What kind of place are we going to? Our kinsmen have taken the heart out of us, saying, "We saw there a people stronger and taller than we, large cities with walls sky-high...."(Deut. 1:25-28)

I. Who decides that the spies should be sent?

2. Who were the spies? What were their qualifications?

3. Compare Moses' responsibility. (Clue: What is God's role?)

4. Who is responsible for the people refusing to go up?

5. What new "theological" idea (about God) is added in the Deuteronomy passage?

As in the two stories of creation, we have found here that there are some details which differ. Let's spend a moment looking at what various scholars have done with these two versions (to give them meaning).

Give some evidence (or answer the specific questions) for each interpretation.

1 The "documentary hypothesis" is an approach to the text which suggests that the Bible was assembled by collecting various documents/texts which had been written by different groups, under different influences, in different time periods. What evidence is there that these two passages might indeed be two different accounts (from different sources) about the same event?

_____

_____

_____

2 Several traditional commentators say that there is no "real" contradiction between the two accounts. They are simply (like two news reporters) choosing to focus on different details. Can you explain how both excerpts are "factual"?

_____

_____

3 A traditional commentator, the Ramban (Nachmanides), suggests that the two versions of the story were designed to fit the needs of two audiences. The first was written about and for the generation which left Egypt—the generation which died in the desert. The second was written for the generation which was about to enter the Land of Israel—the generation which was born and raised in the desert. What evidence can support this point of view?

_____

_____

_____

_____

4 A modern commentator, David Hoffman, suggests that the two accounts have two different purposes. The version in Numbers was written to give us the historical details, while the version in Deuteronomy was created to teach us a "moral lesson." Give evidence supporting this point of view.

_____

_____

_____

5 One of my students, Danny Kaufman, suggested that the two versions simply reflect aging. Moses is forty years older when he presents the second account. Do you have a comment?

_____

_____

_____

6 Why do you think the Torah includes two separate accounts of this incident? What are we supposed to learn from them?

_____

_____

_____

Exercise 4.3—FINDING THE MOTIVATION

"Back-Stories"

Imagine that you are an actor and someone has just handed you a script, asking you to play the part of a lawyer. Before you can begin playing the part (and have a sense of how to approach your lines), you need to know something about this lawyer. You want to know if she/he is bright or stupid, rich or poor, idealistic or crooked, if she/he is related to Oliver Wendell Holmes or was self-taught while in prison, etc. This background on the character helps the actor understand the motivation for the lines—in the theater it's called the character's "**back-story.**" Often, an actor has to figure out what a character's back-story is because the playwright hasn't filled in the details. She/he has to read the script and then fill in the missing details with imagination (extrapolated from the given data). The Bible often leaves us in the same position.

Here is an example from Genesis:

> Now this is the line of Terah: Terah begot Abram, Nahor, and Haran; and Haran begot Lot. Haran died in the lifetime of his father Terah, in his native land, Ur of the Chaldeans....
> (11:27-28)

> Terah took his son Abram, his grandson Lot, the son of Haran, and his daughter-in-law Sarai, the wife of his son Abram, and they set out together from Ur of the Chaldeans for the land of Canaan; but when they had come as far as Haran, they settled there. (11:31)

The Bible introduces the cast—Terah, Abram, Lot, and Sarai—but we are told nothing about them. We know what they do, but not why. We know their names and family relationships, but nothing about their *motivations.*

Write your own back-story for Abram which explains:

1. Why the family left Ur.
2. Why the family left Haran.
3. Why the Lord chose to talk to Abram.
4. Why Abram listened and went.

EXERCISE 4.4

Consider the following midrashim which serve as back-stories.

A wicked king wanted to kill all newborn babies. Abram's parents hid him in a cave. This is what the midrash says happened there.

He left the cave and walked along the edge of the valley. When the sun sank and the stars came forth, he said, "These are gods!" But when the dawn came, and the stars could be seen no longer, then he said, "I will not pay worship to these, for they are no gods." Thereupon the sun came forth, and he spoke, "This is my god, him will I extol." But again the sun set, and he said, "He is no god," and beholding the moon he called her his god to whom he would pay divine homage. Then the moon was obscured, and he cried out, "This, too, is no god! There is only One who sets them all in motion." Ginzberg, *Legends of the Jews*, *p. 189*

Rabbi Chiyya taught: Terah was an idol-maker. Once, he went away and left Abram to sell the idols in his place. A man came and wished to buy one. Abram asked him, "How old are you?" "Fifty years," the man answered. Abraham said, "You are fifty years old and you would worship a thing made yesterday?" The man became ashamed and left.

Another time, a woman came with a plateful of flour. She said to Abram, "Take this and offer this to them." He took a stick, broke them, and put the stick in the hand of the largest. When his father returned, he asked, "What have you done to them?" Abram said, "I cannot tell a lie. A woman came with a plateful of fine meal and requested me to offer it to them. One idol said, 'I must eat first.' Another said, 'I must eat first.' At that moment, the largest idol took a stick and broke them."

"Do you take me for a fool?" his father asked. "They have no intelligence." Abram said, "Listen to your words."

Genesis Rabbah 38:12

How did the tradition which created these back-stories/midrashim solve these questions?

1. What was Abram's childhood like? What was he like as a child?

_____

2. Why did God choose Abram?

_____

3. How did Abram meet and come to relate to God?

_____

4. What else do these midrashim teach? What details do they fill in which weren't directly "demanded" by the biblical text?

_____

EXERCISE 4.5—FINDING THE MOTIVATION

"Sub-text"

Actors have a concept called "**sub-text**." The sub-text of a line is the message which is being communicated by the ways words are spoken, not just by what the words mean. Think of it this way: Imagine two people sitting at the breakfast table: one asks the other, "PASS THE MILK, PLEASE." Usually we think that person A is just asking person B for the milk. But, if they had just had a fight, person A could ask for the milk in a tone which really said: "*I am mad at you.*" Or, "*I am really hurt.*" Or, "*Do you want to make up?*" Or even, "*You know, I really love you.*" The message behind the words is called the sub-text.

The Bible is written in such a manner that we often have to figure out the sub-text for ourselves. Most biblical stories are written in a format which scholars call **biblical narrative**, which is made up of two parts: dialogue and narration. The narration describes action and almost never discusses the feelings or motivation. We have to guess at what characters are feeling or thinking by what they say. This means we are often trying to discover the **sub-text**.

In the following passage, Jacob is trying to fool his father, Isaac, into giving him the blessing which was intended for his brother, Esau. Underline all the dialogue.

Rebekah said to her son Jacob, "I overheard your father speaking to your brother Esau, saying, 'Bring me some game and prepare a dish for me to eat, that I may bless you, with the LORD's approval, before I die.' Now, my son, listen carefully as I instruct you. Go to the flock and fetch me two choice kids, and I will make of them a dish for your father, such as he likes. Then take it to your father to eat, in order that he may bless you before he dies." Jacob answered his mother Rebekah, "But my brother Esau is a hairy man and I am smooth-skinned. If my father touches me, I shall appear to him as a trickster and bring upon myself a curse, not a blessing." But his mother said to him, "Your curse, my son, be upon me! Just do as I say and go fetch them for me."

He got them and brought them to his mother, and his mother prepared a dish such as his father liked. Rebekah took the best clothes of her older son Esau, which were there in the house, and had her younger son Jacob put them on; and she covered his hands and the hairless part of his neck with the skins of the kids. Then she put in the hands of her son Jacob the dish and the bread that she had prepared.

He went to his father and said, "Father." And he said, "Yes, which of my sons are you?" Jacob said to his father, "I am Esau, your first-born; I have done as you told me. Pray sit up and eat of my game, that you may give me your innermost blessing." Isaac said to his son, "How did you succeed so quickly, my son?" And he said, "Because the LORD your God granted me good fortune." Isaac said to Jacob, "Come closer that I may feel you, my son—whether you are really my son Esau or not." So Jacob drew close to his father Isaac, who felt him and wondered, "The voice is the voice of Jacob, yet the hands are the hands of Esau." He did not recognize him, because his hands were hairy like those of his brother Esau; and so he blessed him.

He asked, "Are you really my son Esau?" And when he said, "I am," he said, "Serve me and let me eat of my son's game that I may give you my innermost blessing." So he served him and he ate, and he brought him wine and he drank. Then his father Isaac said to him, "Come close and kiss me, my son" ... (Gen. 27:6-26)

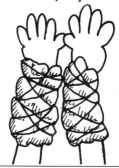

If you were an actor playing the part of Isaac, would you be fooled by Jacob or not? It is clear that you have some doubts, but, by the end of the dialogue, do you believe that it is Esau you're blessing, or do you know that it is Jacob?

(In other words, what is the sub-text of the line "The voice is the voice of Jacob, yet the hands are the hands of Esau"?)

Explain how and why you would make your choice.

_____

_____

_____

_____

_____

_____

The Bible often leaves us with the problem of understanding the tone of the dialogue.

Exercise 4.6—LEADING WORDS

The biblical text uses **leading words** in telling a story, a technique not often found in English stories. Read this passage and follow the directions. See if you can figure out the definition of a "leading word."

HIS word was to Yona, son of Amittai, saying:
Arise,
go to Nineveh, the great city,
and call out concerning it
that their evil-doing has come before my face.
Yona arose
to flee to Tarshish, away from HIS face.
He went down to Yafo, found a ship traveling to Tarshish, gave (them) the fare,
and went down aboard it, to travel to Tarshish, away from HIS face.
But HE hurled a great wind upon the sea,
so that the ship was on the brink of breaking up.
The sailors were afraid, they cried out, each man to his god,
and hurled the implements which were in the ship into the sea,
to be lightened from them.
Now Yona had gone down into the hindmost deck, had lain down
and had gone to sleep.
The captain approached him and said to him:
How can you sleep?
Arise, call upon your god!

Jonah 1:1-6
Translated by Everett Fox, **Response**, *Summer 1974*

1 Give a quick summary of the plot of this passage.

_____

_____

_____

_____

_____

_____

2 Does the text tell us anything about what Jonah was thinking or feeling? (Why does he run from God's order?)

_____

3 Go back to the text and mark the use of the verbs "arise" and "went down." Does seeing this usage of these verbs give you a clue to Jonah's psychology?

_____

_____

_____

continued*

4 If the use of "arise" and "went down" is a good example of a "leading word," can you define the concept?

_____

_____

_____

(If you can't define the concept, look at the way Martin Buber defined it below.)

The Original Statement (in translation)

By "leading word" we mean a word or word-stem which is ingeniously repeated within a text, a series of texts, a group of related texts: to one who pays attention to these repetitions is disclosed or made clear an interpretation of the text....It need not be the same word but merely the same word-stem which recurs in this manner; through the momentary variations, the dynamic effect of the whole is often magnified. I call it *dynamic* because a kind of movement takes place between the articulations of sound which are interrelated: one for whom the whole is present feels the waves beating back and forth.

Leitwortstil in der Erzaehlung des Pentateuchs
Translated by E. Fox, Response, *Summer 1972*

A translation in "regular" English

*Hebrew is based on three-letter roots. Grammarians call these three-letter roots "word-stems." Often, the biblical narrator weaves a word or word-stems into a passage. That word seems to be used far more frequently than is necessary, and both its sound and its meaning add something to a passage. Sometimes, even the exact number of times it is used may be a clue to its importance. Like a poet, the biblical narrator can hide the interpretation of the text in the words used to tell the tale. **Leading words** is one of these devices.*

EXERCISE 4.7—WORD-ECHOES

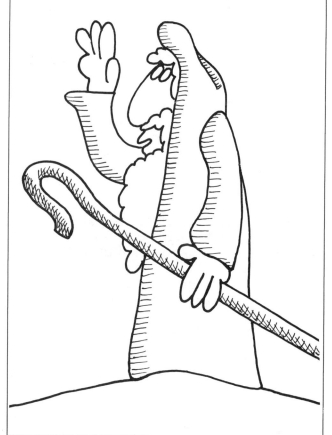

Three related incidents.

Incident # 1—The Binding of Isaac

Some time afterward, God put Abraham to the test. He said to him, "Abraham," and he answered, "הִנֵּנִי /*Hineni* (I am here)." And He said, "Take your son, your favored one, Isaac, whom you love, and go to the land of Moriah, and offer him there as a burnt offering upon one of the heights which I will point out to you." (Gen. 22:1-2)

Then, Isaac said to his father Abraham, "Father!" And he answered, "הִנֶּנִּי / *Hineni* (I am here), my son." And he said, "הִנֵּה / *Hineh* (Here) are the firestone and the wood; but where is the sheep for the burnt offering?" And Abraham said: "God will see to the sheep for His burnt offering, my son...." (Gen. 22:7-8)
Then an angel of the LORD called to him from heaven: "Abraham! Abraham!" And he answered, "הִנֵּנִי / *Hineni* (I am here)." (Gen. 22:11)

The word-stem ה־נ־ה /H-N-H, which means "here is," is a leading word in this passage.

Incident # 2—The Burning Bush

An angel of the Lord appeared to him in a blazing fire out of a bush. He gazed, and הִנֵּה /hineh (here) was a bush all aflame, yet the bush was not consumed.... When the LORD saw that he had turned aside to look, God called to him out of the bush: "Moses! Moses!" He answered: " הִנֵּנִי /Hineni (I am here)." (Exod. 3:2-4)

Incident # 3—God calls Samuel

...Samuel was sleeping in the temple of the LORD where the ark of God was. The LORD called out to Samuel, and he answered, " הִנֵּנִי /Hineni (I am here)." He ran to Eli and said, " הִנֵּנִי /Hineni (I am here); you called for me." But he replied, "I did not call you; go back to sleep." He went back and lay down. Again the LORD called "Samuel!" Samuel rose and went to Eli and said, " הִנֵּנִי /Hineni (I am here); you called for me." But he replied, "I didn't call, my son; go back to sleep." —Now Samuel had not yet experienced the LORD; the word of the LORD had not yet been revealed to him.—The LORD called Samuel again, a third time, and he rose and went to Eli and said, " הִנֵּנִי /Hineni (I am here); you called me." Then Eli understood that the LORD was calling the boy. And Eli said to Samuel, "Go, lie down; if you are called again, say, 'Speak, LORD, for Your servant is listening.'" So Samuel went to his place and lay down. The LORD came, and stood and He called as before: "Samuel! Samuel!..." (1 Sam. 3:3-10)

1 Abraham, Moses, and Samuel were all great Jewish leaders. With each one, Jewish life began a new phase. What did each one start?

Abraham _____

Moses _____

Samuel _____

2 How does the word הִנֵּנִי / hineni with its variety of forms link these stories? How does it teach us that these three leaders have something in common?

_____

_____

3 There is a second word-echo which connects these stories. God calls all three of these leaders in the same way. Explain that form.

_____

_____

4 What do we learn by bringing these three incidents together?

_____

_____

A SHORT REVIEW

So far, you have been exposed to five patterns of exploring a biblical text. In your own words, describe the kind of things you are looking for when you use one of these patterns.

REPETITION _____

TWICE-TOLD TALES _____

THE MOTIVATION:
"BACK-STORIES" _____

"SUB-TEXT" _____

LEADING WORDS _____

WORD-ECHOES _____

In the exercise which follows, you will find six sets of texts. Apply what you have already learned to each by "decoding" some of their hidden meanings.

REPETITION

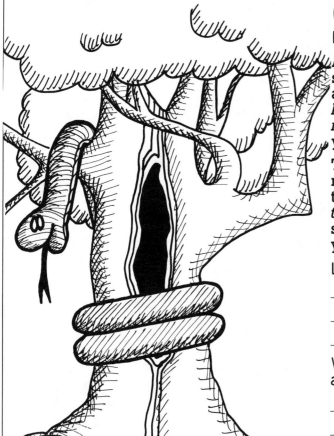

Compare the actual instructions God gives Adam and Eve with the way Eve repeats them to the serpent.

And the LORD God commanded the man, saying, "Of every tree in the garden you are free to eat, but as for *the tree of knowledge of good and bad, you must not eat of it*; for as soon as you eat of it, you shall die." (Gen. 2:16-17)

The woman replied to the serpent, "We may eat of the fruit of the other trees of the garden. It is only of the fruit of *the tree in the middle of the garden* that God said: *You shall not eat it or touch it*, lest you die." (Gen. 3:2-3)

List the differences you find.

_____

_____

_____

What do these differences teach you about Eve?

_____

_____

TWICE-TOLD TALES

Here are two versions of the fourth commandment. What can you learn from comparing them?

Remember the sabbath day and keep it holy. Six days you shall labor and do all your work, but the seventh day is a sabbath of the LORD your God: you shall not do any work—you, your son or daughter, your male or female slave, or your cattle, or the stranger who is within your settlements. For in six days the LORD made heaven and earth and sea, and all that is in them, and He rested on the seventh day; therefore the LORD blessed the sabbath day and hallowed it. (Exod. 20:8-11)

Observe the sabbath day and keep it holy, as the LORD your God has commanded you. Six days you shall labor and do all your work, but the seventh day is a sabbath of the LORD your God: you shall not do any work—you, your son or your daughter, your male or female slave, your ox or ass, or any of your cattle, or the stranger in your settlements, so that your male and female slaves may rest as you do. Remember that you were a slave in the land of Egypt and the LORD your God freed you from there with a mighty hand and an outstretched arm; therefore the LORD your God has commanded you to observe the sabbath day. (Deut. 5:12-15)

1 Underline the portions of the text that are the same in both versions.

2 Circle the portions of the text which are parallel (more or less the same words in the same place).

3 What should be left are the portions of the two versions which are different. List the differences.

4 What can be learned from comparing these two versions of the laws? (Look at the clues which follow.)

_____

_____

_____

_____

Clue # 1— לְכָה דוֹדִי /Lechah Dodi

Beloved, come to meet the bride;
(Come) greet the face of Shabbat.

"*Observe*" and "*Remember*": a single command,
the one God caused us to hear;
the LORD is one and His name is one.
His are honor and glory and praise.

לְכָה דוֹדִי לִקְרַאת כַּלָּה
פְּנֵי שַׁבָּת נְקַבְּלָה
"שָׁמוֹר וְזָכוֹר" בְּדִבּוּר אֶחָד
הִשְׁמִיעָנוּ אֵל הַמְיֻחָד
יְיָ אֶחָד וּשְׁמוֹ אֶחָד
לְשֵׁם וּלְתִפְאֶרֶת וְלִתְהִלָּה.

Clue # 2— קִדּוּשׁ לְשַׁבָּת /The Shabbat Kiddush

Praised are You, LORD our God
Ruler of the universe
Creator of the fruit of the vine.

בָּרוּךְ אַתָּה יְיָ אֱלֹהֵינוּ
מֶלֶךְ הָעוֹלָם
בּוֹרֵא פְּרִי הַגָּפֶן.

Praised are You, LORD our God
Ruler of the universe
who hallows us with His mitzvot
and takes delight in us.
His holy Shabbat
in love and favor
He has made our heritage
as a reminder of the work of creation.
It is a day of celebration
a holy gathering
a reminder of the Exodus from Egypt.
It is us You have chosen
and us from among all people whom You made holy
and Your holy Shabbat
in love and favor
You gave us as an inheritance.
Praised are You, LORD our God
who makes Shabbat holy.

בָּרוּךְ אַתָּה יְיָ אֱלֹהֵינוּ
מֶלֶךְ הָעוֹלָם
אֲשֶׁר קִדְּשָׁנוּ בְּמִצְוֹתָיו
וְרָצָה בָנוּ.
וְשַׁבַּת קָדְשׁוֹ
בְּאַהֲבָה וּבְרָצוֹן
הִנְחִילָנוּ
זִכָּרוֹן לְמַעֲשֵׂה בְרֵאשִׁית.
כִּי הוּא יוֹם תְּחִלָּה
לְמִקְרָאֵי קֹדֶשׁ
זֵכֶר לִיצִיאַת מִצְרָיִם.
כִּי־בָנוּ בָחַרְתָּ
וְאוֹתָנוּ קִדַּשְׁתָּ מִכָּל־הָעַמִּים
וְשַׁבַּת קָדְשְׁךָ
בְּאַהֲבָה וּבְרָצוֹן
הִנְחַלְתָּנוּ.
בָּרוּךְ אַתָּה יְיָ
מְקַדֵּשׁ הַשַּׁבָּת.

I. When *Lechah Dodi* says that God makes "Observe" and "Remember" a single commandment, what does it mean?

_____

_____

2. How does the Shabbat Kiddush draw its two "remembrance" themes from the two sets of the Ten Commandments? What has the Kiddush learned from the two sets?

_____

_____

Here are some midrashim about Joshua. The Torah tells us very little about Joshua. We are given no story of his birth, no details about his family. He just appears after the Exodus as Moses' assistant. He comes with no background other than being "the son of Nun." The purpose of these midrashim was to fill in some of the gaps in his background. As you read them, try to list the questions they are answering.

First you may want to research the biblical sources of these midrashim. The following references will be helpful: Exod. 17:8-14; 24:12-14; 32:15-17; 33:9-11. Num. 11:26-29; 13-14; 27:15-23.

Baby Joshua was swallowed by a whale but did not die. The sea monster spit him out at a point way down the seacoast. He was found by a kind stranger and was adopted. He grew up without knowing any of his real family.

When he had grown up, he was appointed to the office of local hangman. As luck would have it, his own father was sentenced to death. By the law of the land, the wife of the executed man was given to the executioner. Just as Joshua was about to execute his own father, a miracle happened...milk began to flow from his mother's breasts. He was suspicious, began inquiries, and learned the truth. (Rabbah Pe'alim 12a)

Later Joshua, who was so ignorant that he was called a fool by most people, became Moses' attendant. God rewarded his faithful service by making him Moses' successor. (Yalkut)

When Moses was about to die, he sent for Joshua and invited him to ask him any questions about the Torah and the Oral Law. Joshua answered: "I have no need to ask questions, because I have listened attentively to all the lessons of Moses my teacher. Right after Moses' death, Joshua forgot 300 *halachot* (laws) and had doubts about 700 others. The people were angry. (Talmud, Temurah 16a)

Directly after Moses' death, God commanded Joshua to go to war, so that the people might forget their grievances against him.

It is false to think that Joshua was only a military hero. When God appeared to him, to give him instructions concerning the war, God found Joshua studying the Book of Deuteronomy. In response, God told him, "Be strong and be of good courage; the book of the law shall never leave your mouth." (Bereshit Rabbah 6:9)

List a couple of the questions you think these midrashim are answering.

_____

_____

_____

_____

_____

_____

_____

_____

_____

_____

FINDING THE MOTIVATION—Sub-Text

One of the most frightening and powerful stories in the Torah is the "Binding of Isaac," where Abraham almost sacrifices his son. Look at this small piece of the action, and see if you can answer the following questions about the motivations of Abraham and Isaac. These are questions of sub-text.

1 Does Isaac (a) know or (b) suspect what is happening, or (c) is his question honestly naive?

2 Does Abraham (a) know or (b) suspect that Isaac knows or suspects, or (c) is his answer an attempt to keep things hidden, or (d) does he let his son understand that he understands (if either of them indeed understands)?

> Abraham took the wood for the burnt offering and put it on his son Isaac. He himself took the firestone and the knife; and the two walked off together. Then Isaac said to his father Abraham, "Father!" And he answered, "Yes, my son." And he said, "Here are the firestone and the wood; but where is the sheep for the burnt offering?" And Abraham said, "God will see to the sheep for His burnt offering, my son."
> (Gen. 22:6-8)

3 Using your best guess at the "sub-texts," what is happening in this conversation? What do Abraham and Isaac believe is going on?

_____

_____

_____

4 What "outside" information did you use to reach your conclusion?

_____

_____

_____

_____

Exercise 4.8e
LEADING WORDS

Most of the passages we have examined have been stories. Here is a legal text in which we can also learn from the use of a leading word.

When your brother sinks down
and his hand falters
beside you
hold him fast
sojourner and settler
let him live
beside you
You may not take from him interest or
    multiplication
Stand in fear before your God
your brother shall live beside you
Do not give him your money on interest
for multiplication do not give your food
I am your God
who brought you out of the land of Egypt
to give you the land of Canaan
to be God to you.
When your brother sinks down beside you
and sells himself to you
you shall not make him serve the service
    of a serf
As a hired-hand
as a settler
shall he be beside you
Until the year of Recall he is to serve
beside you
then he is to go out from beside you
he and his children beside him
and return to his clan
to the plot of his fathers he shall return
For they are My servants
whom I brought out of the land of Egypt
they shall not be sold in servant-selling.

Lev. 25:35-42

Translated by Everett Fox, Response,
Winter 1971-1972

1 Can you identify the *leading words* in this passage? What phrase seems to echo over and over again?

_____

2 What two laws does this passage teach?

_____

_____

_____

3 What theological rationale is given for both commandments?

_____

_____

_____

4 Underline the *leading word*. What does this repeated word add to your understanding of the reason for these commandments?

_____

_____

_____

_____

Exercise 4.8f
WORD-ECHOES

Look at the following passages:

1. Identify the words which connect them.
2. Draw a "message" from the connection.

And He said to Abram, "Know well that your offspring shall be strangers in a land not theirs...." (Gen. 15:13)

Then Abraham rose...saying, "I am a resident stranger among you...." (Gen. 23:3-4)

She bore a son whom he [Moses] named Gershom (meaning the stranger), for he said, "I have been a stranger in a foreign land." (Exod. 2:22)

There shall be one law for the citizen and for the stranger who dwells among you. (Exod. 12:49)

When a stranger resides with you in your land, you shall not wrong him. The stranger who resides with you shall be to you as one of your citizens; you shall love him as yourself, for you were strangers in the land of Egypt.... (Lev. 19:33-34)

1 The word which connects these passages is: _____

2 The lesson which is learned by connecting these passages is:

_____

_____

_____

POST-TEST PEP TALK

If the last two modules have been effective, learning Torah should now seem both more difficult and more exciting. Things have been made more complicated, but we've also opened up new things to find. Most importantly, you've begun to master new tools which you can use to look for meaning.

At the beginning of the midrash to Song of Songs, the rabbis had a dialogue on what it felt like to learn Torah. They talked both about the difficulty and confusion experienced in trying to unlock a text and about the excitement and joy in finding meaning. Here is part of their conversation.

NARRATOR: Besides being wise, Solomon also taught knowledge to the people. He was the first biblical commentator. He measured and searched out meaning, set many things in order, and taught parables and explanations. Before Solomon, Torah learning was difficult. After him, all could enter into the text.

VOICE ONE: Learning Torah is like trying to explore a palace with many doors and hallways. Everyone who went into this palace used to get lost. Finally, one wise person (Solomon) tied a string at the entrance and found his way by unrolling it as he entered, and rerolling it as he left. Since then, everyone can use his method.

VOICE TWO: No, it is more like this thick forest of thorns through which no one could pass. Finally, one person (Solomon) took out a sickle and cut a trail. After that, all could pass through using his trail.

VOICE THREE: Think of it this way. There was a big pot of boiling water which no one could lift. Then, along came someone (Solomon) who invented handles. Now there was a way for anyone to carry that pot.

VOICE FOUR: I think it was like the time when once there was a basket of ripe fruit which no one could pick up until someone (Solomon) came and attached handles. After that, everyone could get the fruit home.

VOICE FIVE: Picture a deep well. Its water was clear and sweet, yet none could reach down to drink from it. One wise person (Solomon) took pieces of rope and tied them together, and then attached a bucket. Now all could drink from the Torah's deep, sweet water.

Song of Songs **Rabbah 1**

For the rabbis, learning Torah was like
finding their way through a maze
cutting a path through a thorn forest
lifting a pot of boiling water
carrying an overfull basket
reaching down into a deep well

To reach the meaning of a passage, the rabbis said that people need to
trace their route through the many paths in the maze
cut their own path through the obstacles
invent their own handles
attach other handles
tie one thing to another

When they succeed, they get their reward
the joy of finding the center of the maze
the ease of a direct path
the use of the boiling water to cook and clean
the reward of the "fruits" of knowledge
the sweet, pure water of Torah

So far, we have only begun to experience these rewards. At this point, rather than providing a post-test for this module, we're going to provide you with a different experience. Here are two passages from Genesis.

They will provide you with a chance to find repetitions, questions of motivation, leading words, and word-echoes. After finding all of these, you'll then have a chance to draw your own "meaning" from these patterns.

וַיֹּאמֶר יהוה אֶל־אַבְרָם
לֶךְ־לְךָ
מֵאַרְצְךָ
וּמִמּוֹלַדְתְּךָ
וּמִבֵּית אָבִיךָ
אֶל־הָאָרֶץ
אֲשֶׁר אַרְאֶךָּ

The LORD said to Abram
Take yourself
from your *land*
from your birthplace
from your father's house
to the land:
there I will let you *see*

וְאֶעֶשְׂךָ לְגוֹי גָּדוֹל
וַאֲבָרֶכְךָ
וַאֲגַדְּלָה שְׁמֶךָ
וֶהְיֵה בְּרָכָה:
וַאֲבָרְכָה מְבָרְכֶיךָ
וּמְקַלֶּלְךָ אָאֹר

(1) And I will make you a great nation
(2) And I will BLESS you
(3) And I will make your name great.
(4) And you will be a BLESSING
(5) And I will BLESS those who BLESS you.
(6) (And I will curse anyone who curses you)—

וְנִבְרְכוּ בְךָ כֹּל מִשְׁפְּחֹת הָאֲדָמָה:

(7) All the families of the earth will be BLESSED through you.

וַיֵּלֶךְ אַבְרָם כַּאֲשֶׁר דִּבֶּר אֵלָיו יהוה
וַיֵּלֶךְ אִתּוֹ לוֹט
וְאַבְרָם בֶּן־חָמֵשׁ שָׁנִים וְשִׁבְעִים שָׁנָה בְּצֵאתוֹ מֵחָרָן:

ABRAM went as the LORD had told him,
and LOT went with him.
ABRAM was seventy-five years old when he left Haran.

וַיִּקַּח אַבְרָם אֶת־שָׂרַי אִשְׁתּוֹ
וְאֶת־לוֹט בֶּן־אָחִיו
וְאֶת־כָּל־רְכוּשָׁם אֲשֶׁר רָכָשׁוּ
וְאֶת־הַנֶּפֶשׁ אֲשֶׁר־עָשׂוּ בְחָרָן
וַיֵּצְאוּ לָלֶכֶת אַרְצָה כְּנַעַן:

ABRAM took SARAI his wife,
and LOT his nephew
and all they owned
and the people acquired in Haran
and they left for the *land* of Canaan.
They came to the *land* of Canaan.

וַיָּבֹאוּ אַרְצָה כְּנָעַן:
וַיַּעֲבֹר אַבְרָם בָּאָרֶץ עַד מְקוֹם
שְׁכֶם עַד אֵלוֹן מוֹרֶה
וְהַכְּנַעֲנִי אָז בָּאָרֶץ:
וַיֵּרָא יהוה אֶל־אַבְרָם
וַיֹּאמֶר
לְזַרְעֲךָ אֶתֵּן אֶת־הָאָרֶץ הַזֹּאת
וַיִּבֶן שָׁם מִזְבֵּחַ
לַיהוה הַנִּרְאֶה אֵלָיו:

ABRAM crossed the *land* as far as Shechem, to the Oak of Moreh
(The Canaanites then lived in the *land*.)
The LORD was *seen* by ABRAM.
The LORD said:
"To your future family I will give this *land*."
ABRAM built an altar
to the LORD who is *seen* by him.

Genesis 12:1-7,
Translated by Joel Lurie Grishaver, from **Being Torah**

LEADING WORDS:

_____

_____

WORD-ECHO:
(Look at the word *seen*.)

_____

_____

_____

וַיַּעַל אַבְרָם מִמִּצְרַיִם
הוּא וְאִשְׁתּוֹ וְכָל־אֲשֶׁר־לוֹ
וְלוֹט עִמּוֹ הַנֶּגְבָּה:
וְאַבְרָם כָּבֵד מְאֹד בַּמִּקְנֶה בַּכֶּסֶף וּבַזָּהָב....
וְגַם־לְלוֹט הַהֹלֵךְ אֶת־אַבְרָם
הָיָה צֹאן־וּבָקָר וְאֹהָלִים:

ABRAM went up from Egypt into the Negev.
He and his wife, and all that was his.
And LOT went with him.
ABRAM was very rich in herds, in silver
and in gold....
And LOT (who went with ABRAM)
also owned sheep, oxen, and tents.

וְלֹא־נָשָׂא אֹתָם הָאָרֶץ
לָשֶׁבֶת יַחְדָּו
כִּי־הָיָה רְכוּשָׁם רָב

לֹא־יָכְלוּ לָשֶׁבֶת יַחְדָּו:
וַיְהִי־רִיב בֵּין
רֹעֵי מִקְנֵה־אַבְרָם וּבֵין רֹעֵי מִקְנֵה־לוֹט
וְהַכְּנַעֲנִי
וְהַפְּרִזִּי אָז יֹשֵׁב בָּאָרֶץ:

The *land* would not support
both of them SETTLING together
They had so many belongings that they
were not able to SETTLE together.
There was feuding between
ABRAM's herdsmen and LOT's herdsmen.
(At the same time, the Canaanites and the
Perizzites were SETTLED in the *land.*)

וַיֹּאמֶר אַבְרָם אֶל־לוֹט
אַל־נָא תְהִי מְרִיבָה בֵּינִי וּבֵינֶךָ
וּבֵין רֹעַי וּבֵין רֹעֶיךָ
כִּי־אֲנָשִׁים אַחִים אֲנָחְנוּ:
הֲלֹא כָל־הָאָרֶץ לְפָנֶיךָ הִפָּרֶד נָא מֵעָלָי
אִם־הַשְּׂמֹאל וְאֵימִנָה
וְאִם־הַיָּמִין וְאַשְׂמְאִילָה:

ABRAM said to LOT:
"Let there be no feud between me and you,
between my herdsmen and between your
herdsmen,
because we are *men* who are like *brothers.*
The whole *land* is before you—
please leave me.
If you go to the left, I will go to the right.
If you go to the right, I will go to the left."

וַיִּשָּׂא־לוֹט אֶת־עֵינָיו
וַיַּרְא אֶת־כָּל־כִּכַּר הַיַּרְדֵּן
כִּי כֻלָּהּ מַשְׁקֶה....
וַיִּבְחַר־לוֹ לוֹט אֵת כָּל־כִּכַּר הַיַּרְדֵּן
וַיִּסַּע לוֹט מִקֶּדֶם

LOT lifted up his eyes
and saw the plain of the Jordan
It had much water....
LOT chose the Jordan plain
and journeyed eastward.

וַיִּפָּרְדוּ
אִישׁ מֵעַל אָחִיו:
אַבְרָם יָשַׁב בְּאֶרֶץ־כְּנַעַן
וְלוֹט יָשַׁב בְּעָרֵי הַכִּכָּר
וַיֶּאֱהַל עַד־סְדֹם:
וְאַנְשֵׁי סְדֹם רָעִים
וְחַטָּאִים לַיהוה מְאֹד:

So they were divided—
each *man* from his *brother.*
ABRAM SETTLED in the *land* of Canaan.
LOT SETTLED in the cities of the plain
and pitched his tents near Sodom.
The men of Sodom were evil
and sinned on purpose.

וַיהוה אָמַר אֶל־אַבְרָם...
שָׂא נָא עֵינֶיךָ וּרְאֵה מִן־הַמָּקוֹם אֲשֶׁר־אַתָּה שָׁם
צָפֹנָה וָנֶגְבָּה וָקֵדְמָה וָיָמָּה:
כִּי אֶת־כָּל־הָאָרֶץ אֲשֶׁר־אַתָּה רֹאֶה לְךָ אֶתְּנֶנָּה

וּלְזַרְעֲךָ עַד־עוֹלָם:

The LORD said to ABRAM...
"Lift up your eyes and look around.
North, South, East, and West.
All the *land* which you see, I give it to you
and to your future family forever.
Your future family will be like dust covering
the *land.*
Like the dust of the *land*—
Your future family will be impossible to
count.
Get up and walk the *land,*
from end to end
and from side to side.
because I give it to you."

וְשַׂמְתִּי אֶת־זַרְעֲךָ כַּעֲפַר הָאָרֶץ
אֲשֶׁר אִם־יוּכַל אִישׁ לִמְנוֹת אֶת־עֲפַר הָאָרֶץ
גַּם־זַרְעֲךָ יִמָּנֶה:
קוּם הִתְהַלֵּךְ בָּאָרֶץ
לְאָרְכָּהּ
וּלְרָחְבָּהּ
כִּי לְךָ אֶתְּנֶנָּה:

וַיֶּאֱהַל אַבְרָם וַיָּבֹא
וַיֵּשֶׁב בְּאֵלֹנֵי מַמְרֵא אֲשֶׁר בְּחֶבְרוֹן
וַיִּבֶן־שָׁם מִזְבֵּחַ לַיהוה:

ABRAM moved his tents
and **SETTLED** at the Oaks of Mamre near
Hebron.
There he built an altar to the LORD.

Genesis 13:1-18
Translated by Joel Lurie Grishaver, from **Being Torah**

LEADING WORDS:

_____

_____

_____

WORD-ECHOES:
(Look at *men* and *brothers*.)

_____

_____

_____

REPETITIONS:

I. What did we learn in Exercise 4.1 about the order of march?

_____

_____

2. Compare the blessing given to Abram here in Genesis 13:1-18 to that in Genesis 12:1-7.

_____

_____

_____

MOTIVATION:

Rabbi Berekiah said that Rabbi Judah had taught him this:
Abraham used to muzzle his cattle (to keep them from grazing off fields owned by others) while Lot did not muzzle his cattle. Abraham's herdsmen said: "Why do you allow your cattle to steal?" Lot's herdsmen answered, "God already told Abraham: 'To your future family I will give this land.' Abraham is like a barren mule who cannot father children—therefore Lot will be his heir; if our cattle are eating, they are eating what they will own."

God said, "To your future family I *will* give this land." However, right now "the Canaanites and the Perizzites are SETTLED in the land." So far they still have the right to the land. (Genesis Rabbah 41:5)

_____

_____

_____

_____

EVALUATION

Check off those skills which you believe you have now mastered.

_____ 4.1 Compare "repeated" portions of the biblical text and identify changes in the pattern of repetition.

_____ 4.2 Compare versions of stories and laws which are presented more than once in the text and identify differences in these versions.

_____ 4.3 Explain the concepts of "back-story" and "sub-text" and (a) describe how some midrashim fill this in, and (b) explain why that midrash was demanded by the text.

_____ 4.4 Identify "leading word"(s) in a passage and describe their impact.

_____ 4.5 Trace a "word-echo" between several passages and draw the connection the text seems to be making.

_____ 4.6 Describe and give an example of how the biblical author uses each of these five patterns to editorialize the story.

Which of the following metaphors fits your image of the biblical text?

_____ Haunted house
_____ Maze-like palace
_____ Thorn forest
_____ Basket of ripe fruit
_____ Pot of boiling water
_____ Deep well of sweet water.

Based on your experience of learning Torah, when has it felt like you were:

winding and unwinding a ball of string through a maze? _____

_____

cutting through the underbrush? _____

_____

inventing handles? _____

_____

tying string to string? _____

_____

Based on your experience of learning Torah, complete the following:

I think the Torah is like _____

_____

_____

_____

In order to study Torah I need to_____

_____

_____

APPENDIX TO MODULE FOUR

ANSWERS

Exercise 4.1—Repetition

1. At first, the property was held collectively, "all their possessions." Later Abram had his own possessions and Lot, too, had his own.
2. It seems that the fighting between the herdsmen is an echo of a division within the family.
3. Yes. (Draw one of your own!)

Exercise 4.2—Twice–Told Tales

page 60

1. The Lord	The people
2. Tribal chiefs	"Men"
3. Moses follows God's orders	Moses acts as the leader
4. Some of the spies	All of the spies

5. Entering the land = Following God's commandments. The idea of following or not following commandments (and getting rewards or punishments as a result) is the center of Deuteronomic theology.

page 61

1. Different facts are the result of different sources.
2. The first account focuses on the specific facts: it includes the differing reports of various spies, and the fact that Moses checked with God. The second account is more general; it just gives the end results: the impact of the spies' report and Moses' final decision.
3. The first text is immediate: it points out the good and the bad (allowing people to learn from their mistakes). The second text is a retrospective, teaching a moral principle (follow commandments) for the entry into the land.
4. See the answer to number 3.
5. Do you?
6. What is your opinion?

Exercise 4.3—Finding the Motivation

Your original back-story cannot be evaluated.

Exercise 4.4

1. Abram grew up in a place where idolatry was the norm. As a child he wondered a lot about God and other such questions.
2. God chose Abram because Abram figured out that there was only one god to worship. Abram really chose God.
3. It is the end result of Abram's inquiry into the true God of the universe. Abram seeks God and when he arrives at the truth, God reveals God's self.
4. Abram made fun of people who worshiped idols.

Exercise 4.5—Finding the Motivation

This exercise calls for original conclusions.

Exercise 4.6—Leading Words

1. God orders Jonah to go to Nineveh. Jonah decides to run. God uses a storm to stop the ship on which he is fleeing.
2. We are given no direct clues as to Jonah's feelings or motivations.
3. The text takes Jonah down further and further. It seems to suggest that he is getting depressed.
4. Repeated words buried in the narration often clue us as to the text's meaning or theme.

Exercise 4.7—Word-Echoes

1. All three answer their God's call: *"Hineni."*
2. All three of them respond to their call in the same way. They all share the same openness and willingness to serve.
3. All three of them are called twice: "Abraham, Abraham," "Moses, Moses," and "Samuel, Samuel."
4. A prototype of how to serve God (and how to be a Jewish leader).

Exercise 4.8a—Repetition

God calls the tree "The tree of the knowledge of good and bad," while Eve calls it, "the tree in the middle of the garden." God warns people, "As soon as you eat of it, you shall die." Eve restates this as "You shall not eat it or touch it."

At best, Eve fails to remember the real lessons that God is teaching; at worst, she completely misunderstands God.

Exercise 4.8b—Twice-Told Tales

3. One command is "Remember"; the other is "Observe." One is rooted in the creation and the other is rooted in the Exodus.
4. The Shabbat is an echo of two different historical experiences.

Exercise 4.8c—Back-Stories

Among the questions which these midrashim answer are:

What does Joshua "Bin Nun" mean? (One meaning of "Nun" is fish.)
Why was Joshua chosen to follow Moses?
Why does Joshua fail to be a great teacher?
Why doesn't Joshua succeed completely?
Why does Joshua spend so much time fighting?

Exercise 4.8d—Sub-Text

This exercise calls for original conclusions.

Exercise 4.8e—Leading Words

1. "Beside you."
2. Don't take interest, and carefully follow the rules for keeping a Hebrew slave.
3. Your "brother" is like you; he is "beside you."
4. Yes. Explain it yourself.

Exercise 4.8f—Word-Echoes

1. "Strangers."
2. God made the Jewish people "strangers" in Egypt on purpose, because the experience taught us how to be ethical and treat all other "strangers" in the world.

Exercise 4.9a

Leading Words: The word **Abram** and the word **land** are both used seven times. These are also matched with seven verses of **blessing.** The word **bless** is used five times. Cassuto teaches that God gave Abraham a total of five blessings.

Word-Echo: Martin Buber teaches that "see" is Abraham's theme word, which is involved in virtually every Abraham story. In this case, God promises to let Abram "see" the land where they are going. When they reach that land, Abram does "see" God.

Exercise 4.9b

Leading Words: The word **land** is used seven times. The word **settle** is only used six times, but also seems to be an important part of the theme. This is a story about settling in the land.

Word-Echoes: The repetition of **men** and **brothers** shows the importance of the idea that all men should treat one another as brothers — something which doesn't fully happen in the story. It is reminiscent of Cain and Abel ("Am I my **brother's** keeper?"). Here, at least, the conflict ends peacefully.

Repetitions: (1) The change in family attitudes is echoed by their shepherds' behavior. (2) In both, God gives a two-part promise of making Abram's family great and giving them the Land of Israel.

Motivation: In answering the question of why Abram and Lot divided their possessions and eventually divided up, the midrash extrapolates the view that they had different values.

MODULE FIVE: TRANSLATION

The good translator must be a good artist. Bialik

One who translates a passage the way it looks translates lies. Talmud, Kiddushin

Once a translation is made, the original vanishes. Shi Levin

Sometimes one must not translate the lines themselves, but what is between them. Bialik

Even the best translation cannot fully provide the exact meaning of a text. Mendelssohn

A people's entry into universal history is marked by the moment at which it makes the Bible its own in a translation. Franz Rosenzweig

The translator is a commentator and every commentator adds something of himself...to the deepening of the matter...its explanation and its emphasis. Bialik

One who knows Judaism in translation is like one who kisses his mother through a veil. Bialik

RX

5.1 Be able to describe some of the elements which make translating the Bible difficult.

5.2 Be able to describe the different approaches to translation used in differing renditions of the biblical text.

5.3 When comparing renditions, be able to distinguish differences which are ornamental or stylistic from those which present a different understanding of the passage.

5.4 Be able to use multiple English renditions to closer approach the meaning of the Hebrew text.

TRANSLATION

This book is written in English. It talks about learning Torah in English. We study the Bible in translation.

Every translation is a rewriting. No two languages are "equal." Translation is not just mechanically substituting one set of words for another. The translator must take the entire experience of one culture and transplant it into terms developed through the experiences of another culture. Words are tools that the translator must use. Any choice of words always seems inadequate.

When a translation is made, two things happen:

1. The translator works like a bulldozer. When she/he is finished—the Torah text is leveled and even. Many of the problems, the ambivalences, the echoes, and the clues are missing. It is not that the translation is poor; it is just the limitations of pushing one language into the words of another.

2. The translator is also a trailblazer who marks a path through the text for us—sharing insights and connections. The translator points out places of interest along the way. The translator becomes our guide, not only making the text understandable, but aiding our exploration.

No translation of the Torah captures its true meaning:

• There are many places in the Torah which no one really understands. If it is unclear in Hebrew, then translation into another language is a problem.

• Through its long history of handwritten transmission, the Torah has places where we don't understand the grammar or spelling. In addition, there are places where scribal tricks (large or small letters, upside down letters, etc.) have become part of the text. Such mistakes in the Torah are difficult (if at all possible) to reproduce in another language.

• It is Jewish to read multiple meanings into a single line of the Torah (no vowels and no punctuation make this easy)—ambivalence is difficult to translate.

• Much of the Bible is written in a kind of combined prose-poetry. It uses the echoing of sounds, the reuse of word-stems, and other kinds of devices which are all but impossible to translate.

Yet translations are made.

The Bible Needs to Be Read Aloud
From an article by Everett Fox in *Response* magazine.

I have been asked by the editors to describe "what goes on in your soul when you face the text," a question to which I can only respond with an ironic smile. Anyone who has grappled with translating knows that the soul is not the only part of oneself involved in the process. A good deal of the time it must recede into the background, in favor of the brain.

Translating, especially the translating of the Hebrew Bible, is after all the most pedantic of artistic pursuits. It is often downright unromantic. There one sits, surrounded by texts, lexicons, dictionaries, thesauruses, scholarly articles, and commentaries—hardly the stuff of which artistic dreams are made. The work is time-consuming and often frustrating: one can spend hours and even days on a single word, only to be forced in the end to admit defeat....In short, it is the devil's work, a kind of dangerous flirtation with foreign gods. Not for nothing does one rabbinic tradition hold that the day on which the Bible was translated into Greek was as disastrous as the one on which the Golden Calf was made.

But of the making of golden calves there is no end, and so those of us who undertake these translations should explain ourselves publicly. We have an obligation to divulge something of why and how we work—especially in an era which has seen numerous English versions of the Bible.

...It has become my task to...demonstrate the extent to which the Hebrew Bible needs to be read out loud. I proceed in a way similar to Buber's own, learning to read the text in a slow, intense manner, paying attention to its inner rhythm. This means working phrase by phrase, becoming aware of the structure of the text by means of sound. It means ... keeping my ears open for allusions, cross-references, and echoes.

There is really no "final"translation of a biblical text, but only one's current understanding, which must inevitably change. It might therefore be useful to think of my renditions as performances, rather than as fixed, petrified works.

Everett Fox is a modern Bible scholar, whose rendition, **Genesis and Exodus,** is published by Schocken Books.

NIGHTMARES

Imagine being a translator and trying to deal with the following kinds of passages.

1 In the Joseph story, there is a point where, after he has interpreted Pharaoh's dreams, Joseph is made the number-two person in Egypt. He is dressed in special clothing, put in a chariot, and the people shout "ABREK!"

No one knows what the word אַבְרֵךְ / AVRECH means.

There are some guesses:

- "Kneel" from a Hebrew root
- "Attention" from context
- "Grand Vizier"— his title

Many translators don't translate it—they just leave it: **And they cried "ABREK" before him.** (Gen. 41:43)

2 At the end of the first story of creation, there is a wrap-up line: **"Such is the story of heaven and earth when they were created...."** In the Hebrew text, the word "created" has one letter that is smaller than the others. (Gen. 2:4)

In Hebrew the word בְּהִבָּרְאָם / behibaram is written with a half-sized letter ה (hei). It is believed that the ה was added by a later scribe to correct a mistake (a missing letter). Because it was a correction to an older text, the scribe added a smaller letter.

All of the translations ignore this graphic detail, but the commentators explain: "After people were created, their stature was made smaller because of their sin." (Small ה/Small people)

3 Isaac is old and blind. His son Jacob fools him by putting goatskins on his hands, so that Isaac will think that he is Esau. When Isaac asks him who he is, he answers: **"I am Esau, your first-born."** (Gen. 27:19)

In the Torah there is no punctuation. In English the passage is usually translated:

> **"It is I, Esau, your first-born."**

The rabbis found another way to read the passage—a way which would keep Jacob from lying to his father.

> **"It is I [Jacob]; Esau *is* your first-born."**

A translation can't reflect both possibilities.

4 Later on, Jacob has a wrestling match at the ford of the Jabbok River. The angel touches him in a place called the גִּיד הַנָּשֶׁה / *gid hanasheh*. It is a funny term which only appears in one verse in the Bible. (Gen. 32:33)

Gid hanasheh is usually translated as the "sinew of the thigh vein" (though some scholars suggest that it may mean penis).

Regardless of its meaning, there is an echo in this word.

The Jabbok River is the border between the land which later belonged to the two tribes— Gad and Manasseh. Look at this.

גִּיד הַנָּשֶׁה   Gid Hanasheh
גַּד מְנַשֶּׁה   Gad Menasheh

EXERCISE 5.1— A LOOK AT TRANSLATION

Take a look at the three translations of Genesis 8:20-22 and compare these elements:
1. The literary style/language
2. The graphic format
3. The use/lack of "and "
4. What is going on in the underlined sections
5. What you think are the basic rules/principles behind each translation

Indicate which of the "principles" of translation listed below are utilized in the three renderings of Gen. 8:20-22 we have examined.

	SJV	NJV	FOX
1. Translating the Hebrew into "modern" English.			
2. Using English to express the "ancient Hebrew" exactly.			
3. Expressing the "ancient Hebrew" in English syntax.			
4. Translating the Hebrew *vav* (which means *and*) every time it is used.			
5. Translating the *vav* as *and* only when needed in English syntax (or when it really connects two things).			
6. Rendering the whole text as prose (in paragraphs).			
7. Rendering the narrative parts of the text as prose and the poetic sections as poetry.			
8. Rendering the whole text as poetry.			
9. Using "formal" English styles (as in the King James Edition).			
10. Using ordinary English.			
11. Being most concerned with making the text's ideas understandable to ordinary people.			
12. Being most concerned with letting the Hebrew text speak in English.			

THE MASORETIC TEXT

The Bible was originally written down without vowels or punctuation. During the late rabbinic period, a group of scholars called the Masoretes punctuated the text, adding vowels, notes for cantillation, and marking the end of sentences. (Chapter and verse numbers were added in the Middle Ages.) Today, we still use the Masoretic text as the basic Hebrew version. (Module Eight will detail more of their work.)

Here is the Hebrew text of Gen. 8:20-22.

SJV

THE STANDARD JEWISH VERSION

As indicated earlier, the Jewish Publication Society of America released a translation of the Bible in 1917. It was the product of long years of work by a committee of the best American Bible scholars. This translation was based on the style of the King James Edition, which was the first English (though Christian) translation of the Bible. This translation has become the standard Jewish translation.

וַיִּבֶן נֹחַ מִזְבֵּחַ לַיהוה וַיִּקַּח מִכֹּל הַבְּהֵמָה הַטְּהֹרָה וּמִכֹּל הָעוֹף הַטָּהוֹר וַיַּעַל עֹלֹת בַּמִּזְבֵּחַ: וַיָּרַח יהוה אֶת־רֵיחַ הַנִּיחֹחַ וַיֹּאמֶר יהוה אֶל־לִבּוֹ לֹא אֹסִף לְקַלֵּל עוֹד אֶת־הָאֲדָמָה בַּעֲבוּר הָאָדָם כִּי יֵצֶר לֵב הָאָדָם רַע מִנְּעֻרָיו וְלֹא־ אֹסִף עוֹד לְהַכּוֹת אֶת־כָּל־חַי כַּאֲשֶׁר עָשִׂיתִי: עֹד כָּל־יְמֵי הָאָרֶץ זֶרַע וְקָצִיר וְקֹר וָחֹם וְקַיִץ וָחֹרֶף וְיוֹם וָלַיְלָה לֹא יִשְׁבֹּתוּ:

And Noah built an altar unto the LORD; and took of every clean beast and every clean fowl, and offered burnt-offerings on the altar. And the Lord smelled the sweet savour; *And the LORD said in His heart*: "I will not again curse the ground any more for man's sake; for the imagination of man's heart is evil from his youth; neither will I again smite any more every thing living, as I have done. While the earth remaineth, seedtime and harvest, and cold and heat, and summer and winter, and day and night shall not cease."

NJV

THE NEW JEWISH VERSION

In 1962, the Jewish Publication Society of America published a new translation of the Torah. (Since then the rest of the Bible has also been retranslated.) This translation, too, was the work of a committee of scholars—but this time they had a new philosophy of translation. (It used very different rules from those in the King James Edition.) Dr. Harry Orlinsky, a professor at the Hebrew Union College, headed this committee.

Then Noah built an altar to the LORD and, taking of every clean animal and of every clean bird, he offered burnt offerings on the altar. The LORD smelled the pleasing odor, *and the LORD said to HIMSELF:* "Never again will I doom the earth because of man, since the devisings of man's mind are evil from his youth; nor will I ever again destroy every living being, as I have done.

So long as the earth endures,
seedtime and harvest,
cold and heat,
summer and winter,
day and night
shall not cease."

EVERETT FOX

In 1972, *Response* magazine published an edition of the Book of Genesis prepared by Everett Fox. It has since appeared in a book from the Schocken Press. His work is based on a translation of the Bible which was done by two German Jewish scholars, Martin Buber and Franz Rosenzweig.

Noah built a slaughter-site to HIM.
He took from all clean animals and from all clean fowl
And offered up offerings upon the slaughter-site.
Then HE smelled the soothing smell
And HE said to his heart.
I will not henceforth curse the ground again on man's account, since the fashioning of man's heart from his youth onward is evil,
I will not henceforth strike down all living things as I have done,
henceforth, all the days of the earth,
seed and harvest
cold and heat,
summer and winter
day and night
will never rest.

When we learn Torah in English translation, our problem is to get back to the real meanings and feel of the Hebrew. No matter how good a translation is, it can't give you everything. Using two (or more) translations helps.

וַיֹּאמֶר יהוה אֶל־לִבּוֹ

VAYOMER ADONAI EL LIBO

AND THE LORD SAID IN HIS HEART (SJV)

The SJV is a literal word translation. It translates every word exactly as the English will allow.

AND THE LORD SAID TO HIMSELF (NJV)

The NJV is an idiomatic translation. It takes each Hebrew phrase and translates it into an equivalent English expression.

IN HIS HEART
Gives us a feel for the Hebrew tone (it is more emotional).

TO HIMSELF
Gives us the basic meaning of the text (in our terms).

When we use both, we are closer to the full meaning of the text.

When we compare translations, we find three kinds of differences between them.

1. ORNAMENTAL DIFFERENCES—use of *You* rather than *Thou, fowl* vs. *bird*. These are just the particular words the translator chose; their meaning is the same.

2. STYLISTIC DIFFERENCES—different translations differ in their "philosophy of translation." Some want to produce the clearest possible English; others want to stay as close as possible to the patterns of the Hebrew. That is the difference between *To Himself* and *In His Heart*.

3. DIFFERENT UNDERSTANDINGS—Sometimes two different renditions will reflect two different understandings of what the words actually mean.

Exercise 5.2

Compare these pairs of translations and decide whether the differences are:

1. ornamental
2. stylistic
3. different in meaning

1. (Gen. 12:1)

Now the Lord said unto Abram: "Get thee out of **thy country, and from thy kindred, and from thy father's house**, unto the land that I will show thee...."(SJV)

The Lord said to Abram, "Go forth from **your native land and from your father's house** to the land that I will show you...."(NJV)

A. *Now the Lord* _____
B. **Thy country** _____

2. (Gen. 1:1-3)

In the beginning God created the heaven and the earth. Now the earth was unformed and void, and darkness was upon **the face of the deep**: and **the spirit of God hovered** over the face of the waters. And God said: "Let there be light."...(SJV)

When God began to create the heaven and the earth—the earth being unformed and void, with darkness over **the surface of the deep** and **a wind from God sweeping** over the water—God said: "Let there be light."...(NJV)

A. *In the beginning...* _____
B. **The face...** _____
C. The spirit of God... _____

3. (Gen. 15:9)

And He said unto him, "Take Me a heifer of three years old, and a she-goat of three years old, and a ram of three years old...."(SJV)

And He said unto Him, 'Take Me three heifers, three she-goats and three rams....(Rashi)

Three _____

4. (Exod. 36:8)

And every **wise-hearted man** among them that wrought the work made the tabernacle with ten curtains: of fine twisted **linen,** and blue, and purple, and scarlet, *with cherubim the work of the skillful workman made he them.* (SJV)

Then all **the skilled** among those engaged in the work made the tabernacle of ten strips of cloth, which they made of fine twisted linen, blue, purple, and crimson yarns; *into these they worked a design of cherubim.* (NJV)

A. *And every* _____
B. **Wise-hearted man** _____
C. And blue, and... _____
D. *With cherubim...* _____

5. (Gen. 1:14)

And God said: "Let there be lights in the *firmament of the heaven* to divide the day from the night; and let them be for **signs, and for seasons, and for days and for years**...."(SJV)

God said, "Let there be lights in the *expanse of the sky* to separate day from night; they shall serve as **signs for the set times—the days and the years**...."
(NJV)

A. *Firmament...* _____
B. **Signs...** _____

6. (Deut. 1:7)

Turn you, and take your journey, and go to the hill-country of the Amorites and unto all the places nigh thereunto, in the Arabah, in the hill-country, and in **the lowland, and in the south, and by** the sea-shore, the land of the Canaanites, and Lebanon....(SJV)

Start out and make your way to the hill country of the Amorites and to all their neighbors in the Arabah, the hill country, **the Shephelah, the Negeb,** *the seacoast,* the land of the Canaanites, and the Lebanon....(NJV)

A. *Turn...* _____
B. **The lowland...** _____
C. The sea-shore... _____

89

EXERCISE 5.3

Here is another set of renditions for you to compare.

1. (Exod. 1:10)

"...come, let us deal *wisely* with them, lest they multiply, and it come to pass, that, **when there befalleth** us any war, they also join themselves unto our enemies, and fight against us, and get them up out of the land."(SJV)

"...Let us deal *shrewdly* with them, so that they may not increase; otherwise **in the event of war** they may join our enemies in fighting against us and rise from the ground."(NJV)

A. *Wisely...* _____
B. **When there befalleth...** _____
C. Get them up out of the land... _____

2. (Lev. 19:15-16)

Ye shall do no unrighteousness in judgment; thou shalt not *respect the person of the poor*, nor favor the person of the mighty; but in righteousness shalt thou judge thy neighbor. Thou shalt not **go up and down as a talebearer among thy people**; neither shalt thou stand idly by the blood of thy neighbor. (SJV)

You shall not render an unfair decision: *do not favor the poor* or show deference to the rich; judge your neighbor fairly. **Do not deal basely with your fellows.** Do not profit by the blood of your neighbor. (NJV)

A. *Respect the person...* _____
B. **Go up and down...** _____
C. Stand idly... _____

3. (Deut. 30:6)

And the Lord thy God *will circumcise thy heart*, and the heart of thy **seed**, to love the Lord thy God with all thy heart and with all thy soul, that thou mayest live. (SJV)

Then the Lord your God will *open up your heart* and the hearts of your **offspring** to love the Lord your God with all your heart and soul, in order that you may live. (NJV)

A. *Will circumcise...* _____
B. **Seed...** _____

4. (Deut. 34:10-12)

And there hath not arisen a prophet since in Israel like unto Moses, **whom the LORD knew face to face**; in all the signs and the wonders, which the LORD sent him to do in the land of Egypt, to Pharaoh, and to all his servants, and to all his land; and in *all the mighty hand, and in all the great terror,* which Moses **wrought in the sight** of all Israel. (SJV)

Never again did there arise in Israel a prophet like Moses—**whom the Lord singled out, face to face,** for the various signs and portents that the Lord sent him to display in the land of Egypt, against Pharaoh and all his courtiers and his whole country, and for all the *great might and awesome power* that Moses **displayed before** all Israel. (NJV)

A. *And there hath not...* _____
B. **Whom the Lord knew...** _____
C. Servants... _____
D. *All the mighty hand...* _____
E. **Wrought...** _____

5. (Num. 10:35-36)

And it came to pass, *when the ark set forward*, that Moses said: "**Rise up**, O Lord, and let Thine enemies be scattered; and let them that hate Thee flee before Thee." And when it rested, he said: "Return, O Lord, unto the ten **thousands** of the families of Israel."(SJV)

When the ark was to set out, Moses would say: **Advance**, O Lord! May Your enemies be scattered and may Your foes flee before You! And when it halted, he would say: Return, O Lord, You who are Israel's myriads of thousands! (NJV)

A. *When the ark set...* _____
B. **Rise up...** _____
C. Of the families... _____

6. (Exod. 21:20)

And if a man *smite his bondman*, or his bondwoman, with a rod, and he die **under his hand**, he shall surely be punished. (SJV)

When a man *strikes his slave*, male or female, with a rod, and he dies **there and then**, he must be avenged. (NJV)

A. *Smite...* _____
B. **Under his hand...** _____
C. Surely be punished... _____

7. (Num. 14:4)

And they said one to another: "*Let us make a captain*, and let us return into Egypt."(SJV)

And they said to one another, "Let us head back for Egypt."(NJV)

Let us make a captain... _____

8. (Deut. 10:14)

Behold, unto the Lord thy God belongeth the heaven, *and the heaven of heavens*, the earth and all that therein is. (SJV)

Mark, the heavens *to their uttermost reaches* belong to the Lord your God, the earth and all that is on it! (NJV)

And the heaven of heavens... _____

REVIEW

When we can't read the Bible in Hebrew, we are always left with a limited impression of the text. It's like only being able to view one side of a three-dimensional sculpture. Torah isn't only a literature which was written down in Hebrew; it is a communications form whose mindset and world view is rooted in Hebrew syntax. We've already seen (back in Module Four) that the Torah communicates on many levels. It uses repeated echoes and patterns, makes subtle changes in forms, and often teaches through what it leaves out. Torah evolves its own rhythm of expression, and that rhythm comes in Hebrew. Robert Alter, a modern American scholar, has said:

The monotheistic writer works not only with very different theological assumptions but also with a radically different sense of literary form.

The Art of Biblical Narrative

For us, this means that much of the Torah's message is woven into the way its story is told, and those stories are in Hebrew. There is a gap we must struggle to cross, and that crossing begins with a recognition of the limitations of translations we use.

T he time has now come for you to apply your insight into differing translations to a whole passage. Here are three renditions (SJV, NJV, and Fox) of a single story, chapter 22 of Genesis, the Binding of Isaac. Compare all three translations, and mark the places where, because of significant differences, you should focus your study.

MASORETIC TEXT (Gen. 22:1-14)

וַיְהִי אַחַר הַדְּבָרִים הָאֵלֶּה וְהָאֱלֹהִים נִסָּה אֶת־אַבְרָהָם וַיֹּאמֶר אֵלָיו אַבְרָהָם וַיֹּאמֶר הִנֵּנִי:

וַיֹּאמֶר קַח־נָא אֶת־בִּנְךָ אֶת־יְחִידְךָ אֲשֶׁר־אָהַבְתָּ אֶת־יִצְחָק וְלֶךְ־לְךָ אֶל־אֶרֶץ הַמֹּרִיָּה וְהַעֲלֵהוּ שָׁם לְעֹלָה עַל אַחַד הֶהָרִים אֲשֶׁר אֹמַר אֵלֶיךָ:

וַיַּשְׁכֵּם אַבְרָהָם בַּבֹּקֶר וַיַּחֲבֹשׁ אֶת־חֲמֹרוֹ וַיִּקַּח אֶת־שְׁנֵי נְעָרָיו אִתּוֹ וְאֵת יִצְחָק בְּנוֹ וַיְבַקַּע עֲצֵי עֹלָה וַיָּקָם וַיֵּלֶךְ אֶל־הַמָּקוֹם אֲשֶׁר־אָמַר־לוֹ הָאֱלֹהִים:

בַּיּוֹם הַשְּׁלִישִׁי וַיִּשָּׂא אַבְרָהָם אֶת־עֵינָיו וַיַּרְא אֶת־הַמָּקוֹם מֵרָחֹק:

וַיֹּאמֶר אַבְרָהָם אֶל־נְעָרָיו שְׁבוּ־לָכֶם פֹּה עִם־הַחֲמוֹר וַאֲנִי וְהַנַּעַר נֵלְכָה עַד־כֹּה וְנִשְׁתַּחֲוֶה וְנָשׁוּבָה אֲלֵיכֶם:

וַיִּקַּח אַבְרָהָם אֶת־עֲצֵי הָעֹלָה וַיָּשֶׂם עַל־יִצְחָק בְּנוֹ וַיִּקַּח בְּיָדוֹ אֶת־הָאֵשׁ וְאֶת־הַמַּאֲכֶלֶת וַיֵּלְכוּ שְׁנֵיהֶם יַחְדָּו:

וַיֹּאמֶר יִצְחָק אֶל־אַבְרָהָם אָבִיו וַיֹּאמֶר אָבִי וַיֹּאמֶר הִנֶּנִּי בְנִי וַיֹּאמֶר הִנֵּה הָאֵשׁ וְהָעֵצִים וְאַיֵּה הַשֶּׂה לְעֹלָה:

וַיֹּאמֶר אַבְרָהָם אֱלֹהִים יִרְאֶה־לּוֹ הַשֶּׂה לְעֹלָה בְּנִי וַיֵּלְכוּ שְׁנֵיהֶם יַחְדָּו:

וַיָּבֹאוּ אֶל־הַמָּקוֹם אֲשֶׁר אָמַר־לוֹ הָאֱלֹהִים וַיִּבֶן שָׁם אַבְרָהָם אֶת־הַמִּזְבֵּחַ וַיַּעֲרֹךְ אֶת־הָעֵצִים וַיַּעֲקֹד אֶת־יִצְחָק בְּנוֹ וַיָּשֶׂם אֹתוֹ עַל־הַמִּזְבֵּחַ מִמַּעַל לָעֵצִים:

SJV

And it came to pass after these things, that God did prove Abraham, and said unto him: "Abraham"; and he said: "Here I am."

And He said: "Take now thy son, thine only son, whom thou lovest, even Isaac, and get thee into the land of Moriah; and offer him there for a burnt-offering upon one of the mountains which I will tell thee of."

And Abraham rose early in the morning, and saddled his ass, and took two of his young men with him, and Isaac his son; and he cleaved the wood for the burnt-offering, and rose up, and went unto the place of which God had told him.

On the third day Abraham lifted up his eyes, and saw the place afar off.

And Abraham said unto his young men: "Abide ye here with the ass, and I and the lad will go yonder; and we will worship, and come back to you."

And Abraham took the wood of the burnt-offering, and laid it upon Isaac his son; and he took in his hand the fire and the knife; and they went both of them together.

And Isaac spoke unto Abraham his father, and said: "My father." And he said: "Here am I, my son." And he said: "Behold the fire and the wood; but where is the lamb for a burnt-offering?"

And Abraham said: "God will provide Himself the lamb for a burnt-offering, my son." So they went both of them together.

And they came to the place which God had told him of; and Abraham built the altar there, and laid the wood in order, and bound Isaac his son, and laid him on the altar, upon the wood.

NJV

Some time afterward, God put Abraham to the test. He said to him, "Abraham," and he answered, "Here I am."

And He said, "Take your son, your favored one, Isaac, whom you love, and go to the land of Moriah, and offer him there as a burnt offering on one of the heights which I will point out to you."

So early next morning, Abraham saddled his ass and took with him two of his servants and his son Isaac. He split the wood for the burnt offering, and he set out for the place of which God had told him.

On the third day Abraham looked up and saw the place from afar.

Then Abraham said to his servants, "You stay here with the ass. The boy and I will go up there; we will worship and we will return to you."

Abraham took the wood for the burnt offering and put it on his son Isaac.

He himself took the firestone and the knife; and the two walked off together.

Then Isaac said to his father Abraham, "Father!" And he answered, "Yes, my son." And he said, "Here are the firestone and the wood; but where is the sheep for the burnt offering?"

And Abraham said, "God will see to the sheep for His burnt offering, my son." And the two of them walked on together.

They arrived at the place of which God had told him. Abraham built an altar there; he laid out the wood; he bound his son Isaac; he laid him on the altar, on top of the wood.

FOX

Now after these events it was
that God tested Avraham
and said to him:
Avraham!
He said:
Here I am.
He said:
Pray take your son,
your only-one,
whom you love,
Yitzhak,
and go-you-forth to the land of Moriyya/
    Seeing,
and offer him up there as an offering-up
upon one of the mountains
that I will tell you of.
Avraham (arose) early in the morning,
he saddled his ass,
he took his two serving-lads with him
    and Yitzhak his son,
he split wood for the offering-up
and arose and went to the place that God
    had told him.
On the third day Avraham lifted up his
    eyes
and saw the place from afar.
Avraham spoke to his lads:
You stay here with the ass,
and I and the lad will go yonder;
we will bow down and then return to you.
Avraham took the wood for the
    offering-up,
he placed them upon Yitzhak his son,
in his hand he took the fire and the knife.
Thus the two of them went together.
Yitzhak said to Avraham his father, he said:
Father!
He said:
Here I am, my son.
He said:
Here are the fire and the wood,
but where is the lamb for the offering-up?
Avraham said:
God will select for himself the lamb
    for the offering-up,
my son.
Thus the two of them went together.
They came to the place that God had told
    him of;
there Avraham built the slaughter-site
and arranged the wood
and bound Yitzhak his son
and placed him on the slaughter-site atop
    the wood.

וַיִּשְׁלַח אַבְרָהָם אֶת־יָדוֹ וַיִּקַּח אֶת־
הַמַּאֲכֶלֶת לִשְׁחֹט אֶת־בְּנוֹ:

וַיִּקְרָא אֵלָיו מַלְאַךְ יהוה מִן־הַשָּׁמַיִם
וַיֹּאמֶר אַבְרָהָם אַבְרָהָם וַיֹּאמֶר הִנֵּנִי:

וַיֹּאמֶר אַל־תִּשְׁלַח יָדְךָ אֶל־הַנַּעַר וְאַל־
תַּעַשׂ לוֹ מְאוּמָה כִּי עַתָּה יָדַעְתִּי כִּי־
יְרֵא אֱלֹהִים אַתָּה וְלֹא חָשַׂכְתָּ אֶת־
בִּנְךָ אֶת־יְחִידְךָ מִמֶּנִּי:

וַיִּשָּׂא אַבְרָהָם אֶת־עֵינָיו וַיַּרְא וְהִנֵּה־
אַיִל אַחַר נֶאֱחַז בַּסְּבַךְ בְּקַרְנָיו וַיֵּלֶךְ
אַבְרָהָם וַיִּקַּח אֶת־הָאַיִל וַיַּעֲלֵהוּ לְעֹלָה
תַּחַת בְּנוֹ: וַיִּקְרָא אַבְרָהָם שֵׁם־הַמָּקוֹם
הַהוּא יהוה יִרְאֶה אֲשֶׁר יֵאָמֵר הַיּוֹם
בְּהַר יהוה יֵרָאֶה:

And Abraham stretched forth his hand, and took the knife to slay his son.

And the angel of the LORD called unto him out of heaven, and said: "Abraham, Abraham." And he said: "Here am I."

And he said: "Lay not thy hand upon the lad, neither do thou any thing unto him; for now I know that thou art a God-fearing man, seeing thou hast not withheld thy son, thine only son, from Me."

And Abraham lifted up his eyes, and looked, and behold behind him a ram caught in the thicket by his horns. And Abraham went and took the ram, and offered him up for a burnt-offering in the stead of his son. And Abraham called the name of that place Adonai-jireh; as it is said to this day: "In the mount where the LORD is seen."

_____
_____
_____
_____
_____
_____
_____
_____
_____
_____
_____
_____
_____
_____
_____
_____

And Abraham picked up the knife to slay his son.

Then an angel of the LORD called to him from heaven. "Abraham, Abraham!" And he answered, "Here I am."

And he said, "Do not raise your hand against the boy, or do anything to him. For now I know that you fear God, since you have not withheld your son, your favored one, from Me."

When Abraham looked up, his eye fell upon a ram, caught in the thicket by its horns. So Abraham went and took the ram and offered it up as a burnt offering in place of his son.

And Abraham named that site Adonai-yireh, whence the present saying, "On the mount of the LORD there is vision."

Avraham stretched out his hand,
he took the knife to slay his son.
But YHWH's messenger called to him
    from heaven
and said:
Avraham, Avraham!
He said:
Here I am.
He said:
Do not stretch out your hand against the
    lad,
do not do anything to him!
For now I know
that you are God-fearing—
you have not withheld your son, your
    only-one, from me.
Avraham lifted up his eyes and saw:
there, a ram caught behind in the thicket
    by its horns!
Avraham went,
he took the ram
and offered it up as an offering-up in
    place of his son.
Avraham called the name of that place:
    YHWH sees.
As it is still said today: On YHWH's
    mountain (it) is seen.

ANSWERS

Exercise 5.1

These three different translations use different methods to reveal the meaning of the text.

The SJV: The SJV uses classical English to reproduce the syntax of the Hebrew in English. It reproduces every *vav* and treats the text as prose. Its central concern is to accurately express the Hebrew (word and clause by word in clause) into classical (formal) English.

The NJV: The NJV is a modern English translation which tries to express the Hebrew of the biblical text as contemporary English. Rather than translating word by word, it reproduces phrase for phrase and idiom for idiom. It reproduces prose as prose and poetry as poetry. Its prime concern is creating a translation which reads as contemporary English and is completely understandable.

Fox: Everett Fox works differently: his English is a mixture of classical and modern, but his use of English follows the Hebrew text very precisely. Rather than bend the meaning to fit English, he adjusts the English to express the nuances of the Hebrew. He uses poetry to keep the syntax and flow of the Hebrew as close to the original as possible (without reducing it to pure English).

Exercise 5.2

1. A. 2 (The meaning of "vav")
   B. I

2. A. 3
   B. 2
   C. 3

3. A. 3

4. A. I
   B. 2
   C. 2
   D. I

5. A. I
   B. I

6. A. I
   B. 2
   C. I

Exercise 5.3

1. A. I
   B. I
   C. 2

2. A. I
   B. 2
   C. 3

3. A. 2
   B. 2

4. A. I
   B. 3
   C. I
   D. 2
   E. I

5. A. 2
   B. 2
   C. 3

6. A. I
   B. 3
   C. 2

MODULE SIX: "WHO DONE IT?"

The early Hebrews have created the Bible out of their lives and their descendants created their lives out of the Bible.

Abram Leon Sachar

Words of Torah are like golden vessels:

The pages of the Bible are God's love letters.

Julius Mark

The more you scour and polish them, the more they glisten and reflect the face of him who looks at them.

Talmud

The Torah is the Jews' portable holy land.

Heinrich Heine

HOLY LAND

The Torah is a coat of many colors.

Abraham Neuman

The Bible is and at all times was a world full of fresh life, not a dead book. Hence, every period, every school, every individuality introduced into the Bible its own way of regarding the contents of the Bible.

Abraham Geiger

The Bible is a seed, God is the sun, but we are the soil. Every generation is expected to bring forth new understandings, new realization.

Aberman

Rx

In Module Six we are going to look at three possible understandings of how the Torah was written and how we should relate to it. By the time you are finished, you should be able to:

6.1 Describe the "chain of the tradition" and put in the right order the links in that chain.

6.2 Describe the "documentary hypothesis" and somewhat identify the source/document of given passages.

6.3 Describe two different systems which weave divine and human authorship of the Bible.

6.4 Describe how the three understandings of how the Torah was written solve each of the problems in the Genesis texts (indicated below).

6.5 State your own beliefs about the authorship and authority of the Torah.

THREE PROBLEMS

In Module Three, "Close-Reading," we looked at the first two chapters of Genesis and uncovered many questions/problems/contradictions/etc. In this module, we are going to use three of these problems to understand different ways of learning. We'll see how the various ways we believe the Torah was written lead us to find different answers.

PROBLEM 1 In the two creation stories, God is called by two different names. Each name has a distinct personality and style.

PROBLEM 2 The two stories contradict each other, presenting the order of creation differently and sometimes repeating certain creative acts.

PROBLEM 3 The two stories of creation present different explanations of when, how, and why people were created.

GOD WROTE IT

There are many ways of looking at the Torah:

As literature
As history
As God's words
As a collection of ethics and values
As a law code
All of the above
Some of the above

The way we learn Torah is totally dependent upon our beliefs about how the Torah was written. Each set of assumptions creates another disciplined way of learning Torah. Each disciplined way asks its own questions.

We're going to use three of these problems to understand different ways of learning. We'll see how the various ways we believe the Torah was written lead us to find different answers.

GOD WROTE IT

We can believe that God designed the Torah and one way or another transmitted it to the world via the Jewish people.

If we believe that the Torah is God's words, we have to believe that it is perfect. Every word and even every letter has meaning. It is our job to discover what each of these is trying to teach us.

There can be no mistakes in the Torah. Every difficulty, everything which looks confusing, every place which feels like a contradiction is only a clue. It is our job to figure out what God is trying to teach us in each of these passages.

THIS IS THE BASIS OF TRADITIONAL TORAH STUDY.

PEOPLE WROTE IT

We can believe that the Torah was written by people over a period of years. The Torah was created, passed on by word of mouth, edited, and then written down.

If we see the Torah as a collection of humanity's writing, every flaw, every contradiction is a clue. By studying these, along with archeological and historical data, we try to come to understand the people who created the Torah.

We can begin to understand the Torah as a mixture of periods, beliefs, and influences. Each generation adds and transforms that which it received from its predecessors.

THIS IS THE BASIS OF CRITICAL TORAH STUDY.

GOD AND PEOPLE WROTE IT

Or we can believe that God inspired the people who wrote the Torah. We can see in it both revelation (God's messages) and the historical process.

This means that we have to find a way to fuse critical Torah study with traditional Torah study. We have to be able to see and understand the same thing in many different ways.

Both traditional Torah study and biblical criticism work with the same difficulties, problems, and questions in the text. For each, they are clues to different kinds of answers.

As modern Jews, we have to be able to balance these two disciplines of Torah study.

PASS IT ON—THE CHAIN OF THE TRADITION

For the Jewish tradition, the Torah was written by God and dictated to Moses. The "chain of the tradition," שַׁלְשֶׁלֶת הַקַּבָּלָה / shalshelet hakabalah, is very carefully traced from Moses to us.

At Mt. Sinai, God revealed to Moses not only the Ten Commandments and not only the *Chumash* (his five books) and not only the whole Written Torah (the Bible) but the whole Oral Torah.

Moses wrote down his five books (except for the last eight lines of Deuteronomy) and told the rest to Joshua and the elders. Joshua wrote the last eight lines of the Torah (about Moses' death) and the Book of Joshua. Samuel studied with the elders of his day and wrote down Judges, Ruth, and Samuel. David was anointed by Samuel. David wrote the Psalms. Solomon, his son, wrote Proverbs, Song of Songs, and Ecclesiastes. Along came the prophets who wrote their own books. The prophet Jeremiah wrote his book and Lamentations. Ezra, a scribe and the first leader of the Great Assembly, wrote Ezra and Chronicles. The men of the Great Assembly wrote down the rest of the Bible.

Talmud, Baba Batra 14b

Moses received the Torah at Sinai, and passed it on to Joshua. And Joshua passed it on to the elders, and the elders passed it on to the prophets, and the prophets passed it on to the men of the Great Assembly. Pirke Avot 1:1

This is the Torah that Moses set before the Children of Israel, from the mouth of God and the hand of Moses. Siddur

... I will give you the tablets of stone, and the Torah and the Mitzvah, which I have written, that you may teach them.

Exod. 24:12

Rabbi Levi Bar Chama said that Rabbi Shimon Ben Lakish said:
tablets of stone = the Ten Commandments,
Torah = the *Chumash*,
Mitzvah = the Mishnah,
which I have written = the Prophets and Writings,
that you may teach them = the Talmud.

Thus we learn that the whole Torah was given to Moses at Mt. Sinai.

Talmud, Berachot 5a

THE ORAL LAW

Meanwhile, the Great Assembly kept on meeting, though it became known as the Sanhedrin. Later, the same meetings took place at the great academies. Studying and trying to apply the Torah, Prophets, and Writings to their own times, they evolved the Oral Law. A member of the Great Assembly had the title "rabbi." The rabbis wrote three great works: the Mishnah, the Gemara, and the Midrash.

Mishnah + Gemara = Talmud. The Talmud is the organization and application of the laws of the Torah. Reading the Talmud, you get the whole conversation surrounding the law. There are two Talmuds, the Jerusalem Talmud, (תַּלְמוּד יְרוּשַׁלְמִי /Talmud Yerushalmi), and the Babylonian Talmud, (תַּלְמוּד בַּבְלִי /Talmud Bavli), which is the most important legal source book.

Midrash is a collection of stories and explanations (some of which also teach about laws).

When the Oral Law was being written, people still had to figure out how it applied to them. A group of men—the commentators— began collecting and writing down explanations. But, with all these laws and commentaries being recorded, people began to need a simple way to find answers (without getting fifty opinions), so they began collecting the Oral Law in books of codes.

Even with the codes of law, there were still questions. People wrote to the great scholars and elders of their time. These questions and the scholars' answers became books of **responsa.**

THE TELEPHONE SYNDROME

Quite often we compare the oral "chain of the tradition" to a game of telephone. We figure that things will get lost and confused as they go from mouth to ear. Actually our ancestors were better at remembering and retelling things than we are. They did a good job of keeping things unchanged...but—

When Moses died...Joshua forgot three hundred laws and had seven hundred doubts about the law....During the mourning period for Moses, three thousand laws were forgotten. The people said to Joshua, "Ask." But he answered..."It is not possible to tell you." And he told the people..."It is not in heaven." The people asked Samuel to "ask." But he answered them, "These are the commandments" (meaning that this is all we have—no one can add to them).... All the scholars who were from the days of Moses until Rabbi Yose Ben Yoezer were free from blemish, but after him all scholars have some blemish.

Talmud, Temurah 16a

AUTHORITY

In spite of some "missing pieces," the traditional attitude is... "Well, this is all we have" — "These are the commandments." Because of the problem of "lost laws," they worked out a principle—the older the source, the closer to Moses getting the word at Sinai, the more authority it has. The older the quote, the more authority. Torah is more important than the rest of the Bible. The decision of a rabbi from the Mishnah will always take precedence over that of a rabbi from the Gemara.

TRADITIONAL TORAH STUDY

Traditional Torah study is predicated on the belief that God wrote the Torah and gave it to Moses on Mt. Sinai. Moses received not only the Written Law but also the Oral Law. So when you learn Torah traditionally, you never do it without commentaries, codes, and the other explanations. You need the Oral Law to understand the real meaning of the Written Torah.

Traditional Torah study is based on the assumption that each generation understands less about Torah than the preceding generations. The closer you are to Sinai (in time), the more you understand.

Traditional Torah study is based on the belief that the Torah is God's word and that God's word must be perfect. In spite of the long "telephone game" involved in the "chain of the tradition," traditional Torah study states: "These are the commandments." If we don't understand something, it is our fault and not the Torah's fault. We simply no longer have the level of scholarship necessary. In generations before ours, these things were understood.

Traditional Torah study requires our finding "problems" in the text and then showing that rather than being mistakes (God doesn't make mistakes) these "problems" are clues left for us—forcing us to understand the Torah on deeper levels.

Traditional Torah study considers the Torah to be not just a book of laws and stories but a bottomless source of understanding.

Ben Bag Bag said—Turn it and turn it— for all is in it.

Pirke Avot 5:25

ASSUMPTIONS

In this section we've been looking at traditional Jewish beliefs about the Torah's origins. Whether or not we accept the divine authorship of the Torah, it is important for us to be able to work with these traditional assumptions which formed the basis of all Jewish scholarship up to the 1800s. To study Talmud, Midrash, codes, and commentaries, we'll have to learn to think (not believe) that God revealed everything to Moses. In other words:

1. God wrote the whole Torah (oral and written).

2. If God wrote it, it must be flawless and perfect (no mistakes, contradictions, etc.).

3. Everything that seems like a "mistake" or that feels like it might be a "problem" is really a clue to a deeper meaning.

4. If we can't understand something, it is the result of our lack of understanding, not a flaw in the text.

5. The Torah has many levels of meaning.

6. The older the source—the closer in time to God's revelation to Moses—the more authority it has.

Exercise 6.1

According to the assumptions of the "chain of the tradition," place the following in the right chronological order:

_____ Prophets
_____ Joshua
_____ Moses
_____ The rabbis (The people of the Great Assembly)
_____ God
_____ The elders
_____ Us

PEOPLE WROTE IT

BIBLICAL CRITICISM

Biblical criticism starts with the assumption that people (not one person and not God) wrote the Torah. Given that assumption, our job is to try to figure out who wrote it, when, and why.

In the seventeenth century, people began to seriously question the idea that God had single-handedly written the Torah. Out of these doubts came new schools of biblical learning: biblical criticism and scientific criticism. The most prominent and influential advocates of this kind of study were two German (non-Jewish) scholars—Karl Heinrich Graf and Julius Wellhausen.

The Hexateuch (the Pentateuch plus the Book of Joshua) does not present a history of Israel: rather, it provides the source material through which that history can be reconstructed.

(Paraphrased from the introduction to the *Prolegomena to the History of Ancient Israel*)

For them, Bible study was a kind of archeology, digging into the Torah; using the text as clues to piece together and reconstruct a picture of the periods and cultures which produced the Torah.

Biblical criticism uses such clues as literary style, the kind of language utilized, the names God is called, and the images individual texts present. With these, the modern biblical scholar tries to isolate layers or periods in the text.

Biblical criticism doesn't mean pointing out what is wrong with the Bible; rather, it is a technical term for the exacting use of the scientific method.

THE DOCUMENTARY HYPOTHESIS

Graf and Wellhausen defined four major sources/periods/authors/layers in the "biblical material." For them, the major clue was something we've already noticed—the contradictions between different versions of the same story, especially where different names of God are used. These four major sources or documents are called J, E, P, and D.

J = Jehovah/ *Yahweh/Adonai*

THE LORD יהוה

J is a storyteller; his people are real people, and his God talks directly to people. His God can be talked to (and even argued with). His God is described in human terms.

J tells stories about pain and pleasure, ambition and promise, love and hate. All his characters have real strengths and weaknesses.

J is people- and earth-centered.

J tells the story of a people. For him, people have free will.

E = *Elohim*

GOD אֱלֹהִים

E is writing history. His stories all show the importance of the Jewish people and how their one God has helped them. His people are perfect, his God is in total control, and people talk to God via angels and messengers.

E is God- and heaven-centered.

E's history is a story of events, and God predetermined and ordered everything.

D = Deuteronomy

D is concerned with the covenant. D talks about blessings for those who follow God's laws and curses for those who break them.

D is believed to be the author of Deuteronomy, which was found by King Josiah (621 B.C.E.). It was a time when many of the people worshiped idols and other gods. D summons the people to enter into a covenant with God and to pledge themselves to abide loyally by God's rules.

P stands for the priests.

P is a lawyer more than anything else. The priests were teachers and their style is legal.

P lists births, deaths, measurements, and statistics. P also lists every law over and over in every combination (so that no one can mistake them).

P describes in great detail sacrifices, the Tabernacle, and other priestly duties.

PROOF-TEXT: And Hilkiah the high priest said unto Shaphan the scribe: "I have found the book of the Law in the House of the LORD....At the king's summons, all the elders of Judah and Jerusalem assembled before him. The king went up to the House of the LORD, together with all the men of Judah and all the inhabitants of Jerusalem, and the priests and prophets—all the people, young and old. And he read to them the entire text of the covenant scroll (Deuteronomy) which had been found in the House of the Lord. The king stood by the pillar and solemnized the covenant before the LORD: that they would follow the LORD and observe His commandments, His injunctions, and His laws with all their heart and soul; that they would fulfill all the terms of the covenant as inscribed upon the scroll. And all the people entered into the covenant. II Kings 22:8, 23:1-3

ASSUMPTIONS

Biblical criticism is a scientific way of approaching the biblical text. When it is done at its best, it starts with no assumptions. For the critical biblical scholar, everything must be proved through the use of evidence taken from either internal (the Bible itself) or external (e.g., archeological findings) sources. It is a slow, careful process of reconstructing the history and social fabric which produced and compiled the Bible.

Biblical criticism works from the same basic phenomena as does traditional Torah learning. For biblical criticism, the "mistakes" in the text aren't secret messages from God, but rather clues to authorship.

RECONSTRUCTION

In the same way that an archeologist can reconstruct the shape of a piece of pottery from a small shard, a modern biblical scholar working creatively from the biblical text and archeological evidence can reconstruct the history and culture of the biblical period.

EXERCISE 6.2

1 Look up the following selections and try to identify the source documents (J, E, P, D).

DEUT. 27:15-26	___
GEN. 36:1-6	___
GEN. 18:20-32	___
EXOD. 2:23-25	___
EXOD. 25:1-9	___
GEN. 22:1-14	___
GEN. 22:15-18	___
LEV. 23:23-25	___
GEN. 46:8-27	___
GEN. 6:9-22	___
GEN. 7:1-5	___
DEUT. 6:1-9	___
NUM. 1:1-54	___

2 As a biblical critic—what can you learn from this quotation?

God spoke to Moses, and said to him, "I am the Lord. I appeared to Abraham, to Isaac, and to Jacob, as God Almighty, but by My name יהוה I made Me not known to them." Exod. 6:2-3

_____

_____

_____

_____

Hints: Look at the names of God that are used and you should be able to tell what sources cannot be the root of this quote. How about a combination?

R IS REDACTOR

R stands for the redactor. The redactor is the name given to the editor(s) who pieced together the J,E,D, and P materials. Some see R as being P, reworking the J,E, and D materials. Others see R as an independent party, weaving together the J,E,D sources and the P source.

In either case, whoever R was, the result was the Torah—where the threads of all these sources are woven together—and the teaching tradition of Israel.

(Note: This may help you answer Question 2 on Exodus 6:2-3)

EXERCISE 6.3

I.D. CHECK

Without peeking, identify and describe the following:

R_____

J_____

E_____

D_____

P_____

GRAF-WELLHAUSEN_____

RECONSTRUCTION_____

DOCUMENTARY HYPOTHESIS_____

GOD AND PEOPLE WROTE IT

Basically, there are two methodologies for learning the Bible. You can study Torah using traditional commentaries and assume that "GOD WROTE IT," that the Torah was revealed to Moses at Sinai. Or, you can study the Bible critically (using the scientific method and archeological findings) and assume that "PEOPLE WROTE IT" over a series of years and influences.

Even though there are only two basic methods of Bible study (each reflecting a theology), today many Jewish thinkers are looking for some middle ground...for a way to understand the Torah as a product of both people and God. This section will present a series of different models of how BOTH OF THEM might HAVE DONE IT. At the end of the section we'll take a look at ways to combine traditional and scientific Bible study.

METAPHORS AND MODELS

Revelation is the fancy name for the process of God talking to people. Traditionally, the Torah was considered to be a revealed document. God told it to Moses (etc.). If we believe that both God and people were involved, then we have to come up with new metaphors and models which help us imagine the process. Here are a few.

1. Order in the universe
God created an orderly universe, with a set of rules (both natural laws and moral laws). When people looked at the world, they began to understand something of the divine order, and from that the laws by which all should live. Their understanding of this order formed the basis of the Torah.

2. The single zap
In some way, which only God knows, God can communicate with people. We don't know if God whispers in ears, uses mental telepathy, or just "zaps" what He wants people to know into their ears. Some people, like Moses, received "revelations" from God, which they wrote down in their own words. The Torah, then, is the human expression of God's revelation.

3. The "domino theory"
God communicates with one person (A) who then retells his/her experience to (B), who uses his/her own words to tell it to (C), and so on....

TORAH = GOD + A + B + C + D.

4. The multiple zap
The multiple zap is a complex version of the single zap. In God's mysterious way, God reveals "truth" to a number of people. All of these people use their own words to tell others about their experiences. When all this "truth" is collected and written down as the Torah, we have multiple versions of what people have learned from God.

5. "Divine inspiration"
In the "God zaps" model, God is the active party. "Divine inspiration" suggests that people, either mystically or rationally, are able to understand "God's will." Here, people do the searching, and their understandings become the Torah.

6. The course of history
Working from a master plan, God could also shape both individual and national historical events in such a way that the sum total of all these events, and the individual responses to these events, is a Torah written totally by people as per God's design.

7. Mix and match
It is easy to imagine one or more of these models working at once.

Not at all   A Little   Some   A lot

8. Your model:

_____

_____

_____

_____

_____

EXERCISE 6.4

Look at these quotations from famous Jewish scholars. Decide to which of the above models (if any) these correspond.

1 To the question of the "truth" of Genesis the sensitive response can only be: It is, indeed, true; not in the sense in which a statement of a physical law is true, but few things that really matter to the poet ever are. It is true in the way that great poetry is always true: to the imagination of the human heart and the orderliness of the human mind. The God-and-Israel centered account discriminates, as every good historical narrative must, in its choice of events and presents us with history not, perhaps, as it was but as it ought to have been.

Stanley Gevirtz (quoted from *The Torah: A Modern Commentary*, edited by W. Gunther Plaut)

2 Alone atop the mountain, above the clouds, I experienced cold and hunger and loneliness and anxiety about my purpose. I prayed to Him from time to time, and He answered my prayers. I wrote and scratched out what I wrote. Then, when still not finished, I became weary of writing; I found a huge flat rock, and on it I chiseled the Ten Words He had spoken; it was a double rock, as if two tablets of stone had been miraculously joined together.

The laws of property, of crime, of judicial procedures all come easy to me. More difficult was the need to fashion laws for worship, to limit sacrifices....But so determined was I that I should not be thought of as a ruler, or king, that I wanted there to be an important office which I would never hold. My laws must never be mine, must never come from the imposition by a tyrant of his will on a cowered and subdued people. Rather, my people had to be the unique people I needed them to be. In the interest of my role as the framer of their laws, I felt the need for a priest, while I would always remain Moses without a title.

I wrote the laws on the sheets of parchment, trying to find different ways to express them. One way was to be very brief, for example: "Whoever kills a man is to be put to death." I wrote and re-wrote, I thought and rethought, and again wrote and rewrote. I imagined that I was a Hebrew, a hundred years later, in prosperous Canaan, and I wrote laws and regulations for worship which seemed to me could be suitable for that future time.

In every single item which I wrote there was my conviction that there must be a special people, a kingdom of priests and a holy nation, a moral people, an elevated people. Surely without this conviction I would not have had the impulse to write, not the persistence to rethink and rewrite and to press on and on. The laws, as you know, have been copied with some minor confusions. There comes in the midst of them now what I wrote as their very beginning:

"Justice, truest justice, must be our pursuit." I had the sheets of parchment before me. Should I bring down with me those sheets on which I had written the beginning of thoughts, the first efforts to

express in words what needed to be recorded?...I separated the sheets into the preparatory and the acceptable. I arranged the sheets of the acceptable in their right order and smiled at myself for having forgotten to bring along needle and thread to sew the sheets together before rolling them up. I wrapped them in the cloth that I used to cover myself against the cold winds....I dared not leave two tablets. Heavy as they were, and weakened as I was, I picked them up, and, burdened with them and the sheets of parchment, I began to go down the mountainside.

I heard the noise of the camp before I was able to see it. I heard shouting and singing and was reminded of the dancing around Jethro's altar. They were dancing, and my brother Aaron was dancing, and it was not around an altar that they danced, but a golden calf! As the men danced they repeatedly pointed their fingers at the calf, singing. "Here is your god, O Israel."... I spoke only these words, which all of them heard. "You shall have no other gods beside Me. You shall make no graven images."... Then my fury welled up in me, and I threw down the two tablets, and I saw them fall onto a huge boulder and shatter. I unwrapped my garment and let the parchment sheets float down, pushed by the winds, and I did not care what happened to them.

I sent for Caleb. "Did you read the parchment sheets?" He nodded his head.

"Did you understand them? I mean, are they clear?"

"Some sheets would be clear except that other sheets say somewhat different things."

I know that he meant the first sheets and the final ones. "Forgetting these differences, what did the parchments say to you?"

"They are laws to govern us."

He looked at me. "Except for the disorder in them." Samuel Sandmel (from his novel, *Alone Atop the Mountain*)

---

3 I may not accept the account the Bible gives of our origin and descent...and yet look upon God as the creator of all that is or was or shall be. I may not believe that the moral laws of the Bible had been written by the hand of God, and yet follow them more scrupulously than he that does subscribe to that belief. Joseph Krauskopf

---

4 We recognize in the Mosaic legislation a system of training the Jewish people for its mission during its national life in Palestine, and today we accept as binding only such ceremonies as elevate and sanctify our lives, but reject all such as are not adapted to the views and habits of modern civilizations.

The Pittsburgh Platform

---

5 The unique character of the Bible consists in furnishing us both the revelation of God to man as given in the Pentateuch and in the Prophets, and the revelation of man to God, as contained in the Psalms and in other portions of the Scriptures of a liturgical nature. Solomon Schechter

ANSWERS TO OUR THREE PROBLEMS

Module Three raised some questions about the first two chapters of the Book of Genesis. Previously, we defined three specific "problems" in the text. To understand how theology can make a difference in what we learn from the text, we'll compare the way both traditional Torah study and biblical criticism make use of these three "problems."

ANSWERS—Traditional Torah Study

PROBLEM 1   In the two creation stories, God is called by two different names. Each name has a distinct personality and style.

For the tradition, God has many names, and each name reflects aspects of God's personality. It was assumed that the Torah chose the particular name by which God was called to reflect the divine attribute which was being demonstrated.

אֱלֹהִים /Elohim (God)...stands for מִדַּת הַדִּין / midat hadin (God's attribute of justice).

יהוה /Adonai (the Lord)...stands for מִדַּת הָרַחֲמִים / midat harachamim (God's attribute of mercy).

But does God's name change during the stories of creation? A midrash uses this insight into names to teach that the world was originally created by God (Elohim) as a place of justice. But later the Divinity is called the Lord-God (Adonai-Elohim) because God realized that the world could not survive without the added quality of mercy.

> **To what can this be compared? To a king who owned expensive goblets of cut crystal. If he filled them with hot water, they would crack; and, if he filled them with cold water, they would shatter. So the king took two containers and filled the goblets with both hot and cold water. So it was when God created the world with both justice and mercy.** *Genesis Rabbah*

PROBLEM 2　The two stories contradict each other, presenting the order of creation differently and sometimes repeating certain creative acts.

The tradition has two ways of resolving the contradictions:

First, there is the rabbinic principle:
En mukdam ume'uchar batorah—There is no before or after in the Torah.

Written order doesn't always mean chronological order.

Second, the rabbis found ways to explain individual contradictions. To our eyes, the creation of plants on the third day of creation (chapter I), and then the statement at the beginning of chapter 2— "and every plant of the field was not yet on the earth"— presents a problem. For the rabbis, there was a simple explanation. In chapter I, God sets up the plants, and in chapter 2 they begin to grow.

> At the time when creation of the world was completed on the sixth day before people were created, no plant was "yet on the earth" because even though it says "The earth brought forth sprouts, etc.," on the third day...this doesn't mean that they came above ground—but they remained just at the surface till the sixth day. Adapted from Rashi

The tradition always finds ways of resolving each apparent contradiction.

PROBLEM 3　The two stories of creation present different explanations of when, how, and why people were created.

Story #I teaches us:

> People were created last to show us that, if a person gets arrogant or haughty, we can tell him/her: "The gnat, the fly, and the mosquito are older than you." Genesis Rabbah

Story #2 teaches us:

> God formed Adam out of dust from all over the earth: yellow clay, white sand, black loam, and red soil, so that no one can claim that a person does not belong somewhere. All soil is people's homes. Genesis Rabbah

For the tradition, both stories complement each other and each gives a different lesson.

ANSWERS—Critical Torah Study

PROBLEM 1 In the two creation stories, God is called by two different names. Each name has a distinct personality and style.

Biblical criticism uses the documentary hypothesis to explain the differences in the two stories.

Story #2 uses יהוה /Adonai (The Lord) and it can be considered a J text. It is a good story that has God and people talking to each other. Its characters are real (God has to improve the world, which was just created).

Even though it uses אֱלֹהִים /Elohim (God), story #I is a P document. Its major concern is order and it very carefully sets up the structure of life and defines people's roles.

PROBLEM 2 The two stories contradict each other, presenting the order of creation differently and sometimes repeating certain creative acts.

The documentary hypothesis has already taught us that these two stories come from two different sources. It is to be assumed that different people writing in different environments would have differing views of the genesis of creation. Critical text study has us look into the origins of these stories.

The Babylonians have a creation story found in an epic called the *Enuma Elish*. In it there are two gods, Apsu and Tiamat. Marduk, one of their offspring, eventually kills Tiamat and creates the world. This happens in seven steps.

1. Water chaos of Apsu and Tiamat (unformed and void).
2. Birth of Marduk, "Sun of Heaven" (creation of light).
3. Sky is made from half of Tiamat's body (creation of heaven).
4. Earth is made from the other half of Tiamat (gathering of waters forms earth).
5. Setting up the constellations (creation of lights in the firmament).
6. Making people to serve gods (people created to rule over creation).
7. Divine banquet (God rested—Shabbat).

Scholars have suggested that the biblical author reworked this pagan seven-step version of creation into a seven-step monotheistic creation epic in Genesis.

Other biblical stories also have their parallels in the literature of the ancient Near East. Some of these include: the Garden of Eden story and the story of the Tree of Knowledge of Good and Evil.

PROBLEM 3 The two stories of creation present different explanations of when, how, and why people were created.

Critical Bible study leads us to accept the views of God's relationship to people as the result of two authors and two traditions which were woven together by R during his/her time. Judaism needed both stories and both images.

The first story sees people distant from their Creator—but as a culmination of the creation process. They are created in God's image—and it was "very good." The second story sees people as part of a working, changing notion of creation—in dialogue with the Deity.

The exciting part of this kind of study is that we can watch the Jewish tradition take root in ancient Near Eastern myths—while adding its own unique value system.

(We will see this more clearly in Module Eight.)

ANSWERS—Making a Synthesis

In both traditional Torah study and scientific criticism our beliefs about who wrote the Torah automatically suggest a way of learning. But, when we try to work with the assumption that both God and people wrote the Torah, we need to find a way to fuse the traditional insights into the text (Midrash, commentaries, etc.) with the analytic tools of scientific criticism (archeology, historical documents and events, form criticism, etc.).

We need to synthesize the traditional and critical answers to our problems.

PROBLEM 1 In the two creation stories, God is called by two different names. Each name has a distinct personality and style.

The tradition explains that each of the names used for God communicates a different attribute or understanding of God. Here we fuse a name which manifests justice with a name which manifests mercy; the conclusions: IT TAKES BOTH JUSTICE AND MERCY TO CREATE AND SUSTAIN THE WORLD.

Biblical criticism suggests that the two names were rooted in two differing source documents. Story #1 uses אֱלֹהִים / ELOHIM and it is a P document (priests were formal and orderly) while story #2 (יהוה /ADONAI) is a J document and was probably the product of an author who lived in the Southern Kingdom. We know that R decided that both were important.

The TRADITIONAL scholar looks at these stories and teaches us that there are various ways of describing the relationship between God and people. We can relate to God in many ways. Similarly, the CRITICAL scholar sees the two stories and says that they reflect two different views of God that were important to the Jewish people. We learn similar lessons.

PROBLEM 2 The two stories contradict each other, presenting the order of creation differently and sometimes repeating certain creative acts.

The tradition, bothered by the contradictions in the two stories, goes to great effort to "cover up" the "contradictions" and show the consistency of the text. For the rabbis, each of these problems provided an opportunity for study and for expanding their belief that the whole Torah flows together.

Biblical criticism is secure in the knowledge that each story is constructed from ancient myths and finds no difficulty with the fact that the stories appear inconsistent. Yet, in the end, the central learning comes from R. Because the redactor chose to include both versions, weaving them together, both must be important. In the end, what emerges is an evolving but confluent Jewish tradition.

Both approaches suggest that, in spite of the "contradictions," we have something to learn from the totality formed by the "two versions."

PROBLEM 3 The two stories of creation present different explanations of when, how, and why people were created.

Through the Midrash we learn different messages about "people's nature" from the two creation stories. From one we learn that people were created last to teach them humility, while from the other we learn that people are made from dust to show the common origins of all humankind.

Critical study showed us that these two world views—people as the culmination of an ordered creation, and people as partners of God in an evolving creation—are both part of the Jewish tradition.

Fill in your own synthesis of this third problem. _____

POST-TEST

1 Quickly describe the steps in the "chain of the tradition."

_____

_____

_____

_____

_____

_____

2 According to the "documentary hypothesis," what is the source (J,E,D, or P) for each of the following:

A. _____ An angel of the Lord appeared to him in a flaming fire out of the midst of the bush. (Exod. 3:2)

B. _____ God said to Noah, "I have decided to put an end to all flesh, for the earth is filled with lawlessness because of them; I am about to destroy them with the earth...." (Gen. 6:13)

C. _____ The Lord spoke to Moses, saying: Command Aaron and his sons thus: This is the ritual of the burnt offering: The burnt offering itself shall remain where it is burned upon the altar all night until the morning.... (Lev. 6:1-2)

D. _____ We set out from Horeb and traveled the great terrible wilderness that you saw, along the road to the hill country of the Amorites, as the Lord our God had commanded us.... (Deut. 1:19)

3 Describe two ways in which both God and people could have been involved in the creation of Torah.

_____

_____

_____

_____

_____

_____

4 Fill in the following chart:

	How does the tradition solve this? What does it teach us from these problems?	How does biblical criticism teach us that we can learn from these problems?	What could we learn by comparing both models?
PROBLEM 1 In the two creation stories, God is called by two different names. Each name has a distinct personality and style.			
PROBLEM 2 The two stories contradict each other, presenting creation in differing orders and sometimes repeating certain creative acts.			
PROBLEM 3 The two stories present two different explanations of when, how, and why people were created.			

5 HOW DO YOU THINK THE TORAH WAS WRITTEN?

_____

_____

_____

_____

_____

_____

_____

_____

_____

_____

_____

_____

_____

EVALUATION

Now that you've completed Module Six, you should be able to:

____ 6.1 Describe the "chain of the tradition" and, when given links in the chain, order them correctly.

____ 6.2 Describe the "documentary hypothesis" and correctly identify the source document of given passages.

____ 6.3 Describe two systems which weave divine and human authorship of the Bible.

____ 6.4 Describe how the three understandings of Torah solve each of the problems in the Genesis texts (included in this module).

____ 6.5 State your own beliefs about the authorship and authority of the Torah.

The Lord does not object even if a person misunderstands what she/he learns, providing she/he tries to understand it all out of his/her love of learning. It is like a parent whose beloved child is asking a question in stumbling words—the parent still delights at the child's words.

The Baal Shem Tov

APPENDIX TO MODULE SIX

Answers

Exercise 6.1

The correct order in the "chain of the tradition" is: God to Moses to Joshua to the elders to the prophets to the rabbis to us.

Exercise 6.2

1. Deut. 27:15-26—Presence of "curses" makes classic D text.

Gen. 36:1-6—The genealogy clues this as a P document.

Gen. 18:20-32—The use of "the Lord" (*Adonai*) indicates this is a J document.

Exod. 2:23-25—While at first this looks like an E document, it is assumed to be a P document, tying together two other pieces of the narration. The "remembering" and the "covenant" are the clues. But there is no reason you should have recognized that at this point in your studies.

Exod. 25:1-9—This literal description of the Tabernacle ritual is an obvious P (priest) passage.

Gen. 22:1-14—The story begins by talking about "God." It is a telling of the E part of the story.

Gen. 22:15-18—At this point in the narration the God name switches to "the Lord," making this a J passage. There are some suggestions that R is also at work here.

Lev. 23:23-25—This passage (which we saw in the last module too) is a typical legal P passage.

Gen. 46:8-27—The use of the name Jacob rather than Israel suggests that this is a J document. In the next verse, 28, the name switches to Israel and E probably takes over the narration.

Gen. 6:9-22—The story here uses the name "God," making it look like an E document. However, the genealogy and the focus on right and wrong (and punishment) suggest that this is really P speaking.

Gen. 7:1-5—At this point in the narrative the God name switches to "the Lord." Here it seems that J continues the narrative.

Deut. 6:1-9—While it is safe to assume that most Deuteronomy is D, the emphasis on "rewards" (e.g., lengthened days) suggests that this is pure D.

Num.1:1-54—The Book of Numbers begins with this very precise listing of the tribes. Exact attention to numbers and details is pure P.

2. This passage reveals that God's name changes. Some names are indeed older than others.

Exercise 6.3

R = Redactor

J = "Jehovah" (*Adonai*) a.k.a. the Lord

E = "*Elohim*" a.k.a. God

D = Deuteronomy

P = Priests

Graf and Wellhausen are the two scholars who evolved the documentary hypothesis.

Reconstruction is the process of trying to discover true history by assembling pieces of the information which has been preserved.

Documentary Hypothesis is the theory that the Torah is made up of a series of older documents which have been woven together.

Exercise 6.4

1. This seems to be connected to the "order in the universe" theory.

2. The single zap.

3. Order in the universe.

4. The domino theory (though you may need more than this quote to understand this).

5. Divine inspiration.

Post-Test

1. God to Moses to Joshua to the elders to the prophets to the rabbis to us.

2. A. J
   B. E
   C. P
   D. D

3. See page 106.

4. **Problem 1:** The tradition suggests that the two names represent two different attributes of God: justice and mercy. Biblical criticism suggests that these two stories evolve from different traditions. When we put them together, we learn (possibly) that by joining traditions together, Judaism evolves a diverse and dynamic vision of God.

Problem 2: The tradition suggests that the differing facts aren't really contradictions, but the retelling of the story from differing viewpoints. They teach differing views of God and people. Biblical criticism suggests that each of the two stories is rooted in folktales borrowed from other cultures and then reworked into an Israelite, monotheistic form. Joining the two, we learn that Judaism was able to absorb the insights apparent in many local pagan forms and elevate them to ultimately paint a diverse picture of the one true God.

Problem 3: The same basic conclusion. Two stories evolved to teach us a diverse perspective. Truth (God and people) has many facets.

MODULE SEVEN: READING THE TORAH WITH RABBINIC EYES
(Part One)—MIDRASH

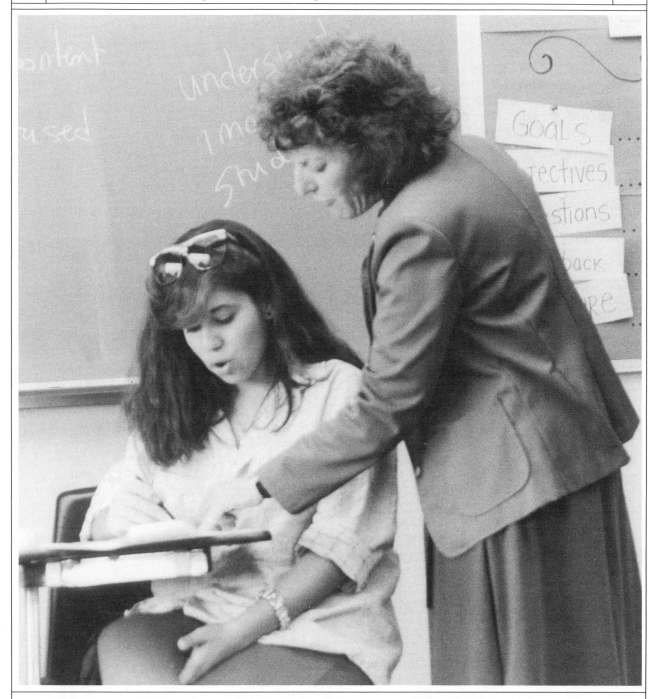

One should learn from his teacher until he becomes fluent in the text and its plain meaning. After that he should consider what he has learned, comparing things to one another, asking questions and answering them. But at first he must not do that because he will waste time and the teacher might not always be available again; after he has learned much, he will get a clearer idea of his work and be able to smooth over difficulties by himself. Talmud, Avodah Zarah 19a

Rx

In Module Six: "Who Done It?" we examined three ways the Torah might have been written. In this module we are going to follow through the first of those theologies—the "GOD WROTE IT" assumptions—and we are going to look at traditional text study and learn how to read Torah with rabbinic eyes. We are going to follow the "chain of the tradition" through the Midrash (in Module Seven) into the commentaries (in Module Eight) and understand how to use these tools.

In Module Four: "Five Patterns" and in Module Five: "Translation" we learned about some of the patterns and forms the biblical A/author(s) used. In this module we are going to see how the rabbinic tradition related to these "phenomena" and used them as questions that contributed to an understanding of the Torah.

By the end of this module you should be able to:

7.1 Trace the "chain of the tradition" through the works which expound on the Torah's meaning.

7.2 Describe the evolution of midrashic literature.

7.3 Examine a piece of midrash and identify (I) the parts of that midrash which are taken from the Torah, (2) the answer given to the biblical problem, and (3) the message or moral of that midrash.

7.4 Identify the technique a given midrash uses to solve a biblical problem.

Last module we learned that the heart of the "GOD WROTE IT" theology of Torah was the belief that God taught the entire Torah to Moses on Mt. Sinai. At that time, God taught Moses two Torahs—Written Torah (The Five Books) and the Oral Torah (rabbinic literature). The Oral Law comprised the explanations, commentaries, interpretations, and applications which were the key to understanding the Written Law.

The Oral Tradition was then passed on from generation to generation. This was called the שַׁלְשֶׁלֶת הַקַּבָּלָה / *shalshelet hakabalah* (the chain of the tradition). Last module we saw a short version of this from the Mishnah.

Moses received the Torah at Sinai and passed it on to Joshua. And Joshua passed it on to the elders, and the elders passed it on to the prophets, and the prophets passed it on to the men of the Great Assembly. Pirke Avot 1:1

To begin this module, here is an expanded version of this chain as described in the introduction to Maimonides' *Mishneh Torah*. (Rambam will introduce himself at the end of the passage, and we'll give you a fuller biography later on.)

THE "CHAIN OF THE TRADITION"

MOSES wrote the entire Torah before he died and presented a copy to each tribe. He placed one copy in the ark as a witness but did not write down the mitzvah (commandment), which is the interpretation of the Torah. This he left to the ELDERS, and to JOSHUA, and to all the people. For this reason, it is called the Oral Law. Although the Oral Law was not committed to writing, MOSES taught the whole of it to the seventy ELDERS who were included in his court. He handed it to JOSHUA and charged him concerning it. Many ELDERS received the Oral Tradition from JOSHUA. ELI received it from the ELDERS, SAMUEL received it from ELI and his court, and DAVID received it from SAMUEL and his court....

RABBI JUDAH compiled the Mishnah. From the time of MOSES to the time of RABBI JUDAH, the Oral Law was taught publicly but not written. In each generation, however, some prophet or the head of the *Bet Din* (the court) would make private notes in order to teach publicly the traditions which he had received from his teachers. Everyone could note down for his/her own use the traditional interpretations of the Torah and all the basic rules of conduct based upon it. RABBI JUDAH compiled all the traditions, laws, comments, and interpretations of the Bible which had been taught by our teacher MOSES, by the prophets, and by the courts of preceding generations. Then he taught it to his students, who made copies of it and taught it everywhere so that the Oral Law might not be forgotten among the Jewish people.

RABBI YOCHANAN BEN NAPPAHA compiled the Jerusalem Talmud in *Eretz Yisrael* about three centuries after the destruction of the Temple. RAVINA and RAV ASHI were the last sages of the Talmud. RAV ASHI compiled the Babylonian Talmud in Babylon about one century after RABBI YOCHANAN's compilation of the Jerusalem Talmud.

The scholars who arose shortly after the compilation of the Talmud and studied it deeply became famous for their wisdom. They are called the GEONIM. They arose in *Eretz Yisrael*, Babylon, Spain, and France, studied the method of the Talmud, explaining its obscure passages and teaching its subject matter. For, indeed, the ways of the Talmud are exceedingly deep.

The GEONIM of successive generations wrote commentaries on the Talmud. Some interpreted specific laws, while others explained chapters which were found to be difficult in their time. They also made compilations of well established rules (codes of law) concerning what is permissible or forbidden, so as to make them intelligible to anyone who cannot penetrate the depths of the Talmud.

The inhabitants of every town addressed many questions to each contemporary

AND SO IT GOES UNTIL ISRAEL AND JUDAH ARE CONQUERED BY BABYLON AND GO INTO EXILE.

EZRA THE SCRIBE

RABBI JUDAH

RABBI YOCHANAN

RAVINA AND RAV ASHI

THE GEONIM

Gaon and asked for explanations of difficult passages in the Talmud. The GEONIM would answer the questions to the best of their knowledge. Those who posed the questions compiled the responsa into books for the purpose of study.

In the year 1177 C.E. Maimonides decided to write down the Oral Law. He explains why:

At the present time (1177 C.E.), when severe disasters keep following one another and the needs of the moment brush all things aside, our wise men lose their wits, and the understanding of our clever people is hidden.

Hence, the commentaries, the codes of law, and the responsa, which were written by the GEONIM, who regarded them as easily intelligible, have presented difficulties in our day, so that a mere few are capable of understanding the subject matter properly.

I, MOSES BEN MAIMON (Rambam), the Sefardi, made a thorough study of all these books and decided to put down in writing, in plain language and concisely, the entire Oral Law in order that no one should have need of any other work dealing with the laws of Israel, so that all the laws can be open to old and young alike. I have named it *Mishneh Torah* (The Repetition of the Torah), because anyone who reads first the Written Torah and then this work will know the entire Oral Law.

Exercise 7.1

1 What do you know about Moses Ben Maimon?

_____

_____

2 Compare Rambam's time with our own. (How are needs the same/ different?)

_____

_____

3 IDENTIFY THE FOLLOWING:

Moses _____

Mishnah_____

Prophets _____

Eli _____

Rabbi Judah _____

Oral Law _____

Geonim _____

Ezra _____

Talmud_____

Responsa _____

Commentaries_____

Midrash _____

*Mishneh Torah*_____

4 Without looking back, arrange the following according to the "chain of the tradition":

____ David
____ Ezra
____ The prophets
____ Moses
____ The geonim
____ All of us
____ God
____ Joshua
____ Samuel
____ Rabbi Judah
____ Eli
____ Rabbi Yochanan Ben Nappaha
____ Ravina and Rav Ashi
____ The elders

5 Put the following literary works in the right order:

____ Gemara
____ Torah
____ Codes of law
____ Commentaries
____ The Prophets (*Nevi'im*) and
Writings (*Ketuvim*)
____ Mishnah
____ Responsa
____ Babylonian Talmud
____ Jerusalem Talmud

WHO WAS MOSES BEN MAIMON?

Moses Ben Maimon, also known as Maimonides, or Rambam, was born in Spain in 1135 but lived most of his life in Egypt, where he was physician to the court. He died in 1204. In his commentaries, his method was to give a short review of a talmudic treatise on the Mishnah, explain individual words, and determine the law so that the student would get a clear picture of the text. His objective was to define the actual law in the most concise manner. Rambam's theological views are concisely summed up in his Thirteen Articles of Faith, which have been included in the liturgy in poetic form.

Now that we've seen the official statement of the "chain of the tradition," let's look at how reading and understanding the Torah evolved through this progress.

1. TORAH

Traditional Judaism, as we have seen, is based on the belief that God gave the Torah to Moses on Mt. Sinai. (In the next module we'll learn that scientific scholars believe that the Torah was finished by 444 B.C.E.) In either case, the finished Torah is the starting point for Jewish biblical exegesis.*

---

* Exegesis is derived from the Greek word *exegeisthai* (to explain, interpret) = *ex* (out of) + *hegeisthai* (to lead). Thus, exegesis means an explanation/interpretation derived by leading or drawing out the meaning of a text.

2. THE BIBLE

The Torah is only the first part of the Bible.

[Bible = תַּנַ"ךְ / TANACH =
תּוֹרָה /TORAH
+ נְבִיאִים /NEVI'IM (Prophets)
+ כְּתוּבִים /KETUVIM (Writings)]

The last of the twenty-four books which make up the Bible were finished around 200 B.C.E. and the canonization of the Bible took place around 90 C.E. In Yavneh a group of rabbis known as the Council of Jamnia (Greek for Yavneh) decided which books would be included in the Jewish Bible. (You can find some of the records of their discussions on the Mishnah in *Yad* 3.)

We can even find commentaries on the Torah in the Prophets and Writings (*NaCh*). For example, in chapter 20 of Numbers, the people complain about the lack of water and Moses answers them (verse 10):

Listen, you rebels, shall we get water for you from this rock?

While it is not clear why Moses then strikes the rock, Psalm 106:33 adds some new information.

Because they rebelled against Him and he spoke rashly.

How does this expand our understanding? (Clue: Think about what happens to Moses because of this passage.)

3. EZRA

While we can find some examples of the Bible providing commentary on itself, when we look into the Book of Nehemiah we get our first clue as to how Jewish biblical commentary began. In 586 B.C.E., the Jews were exiled to Babylonia. Seventy years later, Jews were allowed to return. Around 458 B.C.E., Ezra the scribe led 1,800 Jews back to Israel and became the leader of the reconstruction. Nehemiah the prophet was his co-leader. Ezra took a number of actions that revived Jewish life—among these was starting the public reading of the Torah on Mondays and Thursdays. This was "prime-time" Torah because these were market days, so Torah reached the largest possible audience.

The Book of Nehemiah describes these public readings of the Torah like this:

Ezra the priest brought the Torah before the community, to both men and women, to all that could hear with understanding.
(Neh. 8:2)

And they read in the book, in the Torah of God, distinctly; and they gave the sense, and caused them to understand.
(Neh. 8:8)

The clue here is "gave the sense." In those days (c. 450 B.C.E.), the Jewish people spoke Aramaic—Hebrew was an ancient language which few people really understood. So "gave the sense" meant that they read it in Hebrew and gave the sense of the reading in Aramaic. It was simultaneous translation.

4. THE METURGEMAN

Around the time of Ezra, the synagogue began to evolve as a popular Jewish institution. We don't know for sure if synagogues began before, just after, or during the Babylonian Exile—but we do know that at this time Jews began building and going to synagogues. When the Torah was read in the synagogue the **meturgeman** "gave the sense" of the Hebrew text in Aramaic.

We learned in Module Five that every translation is a commentary.

5. THE TARGUMIM

It is almost a given rule in Judaism that oral traditions eventually get written down. The work of the **meturgeman** was no exception.

The Talmud (Meg. 3a) even tells us about the process. A number of Aramaic translations of the Torah (*targumim*) were created. The most famous is Targum Onkelos, by a convert to Judaism named Onkelos (pronounced Uncle Les).

Here is a literal translation of Genesis 22:2.

And He said: "Take your son, your only son, whom you love, Isaac, and go to the land of Moriah...."

Here is the way Targum Onkelos understands the passage.

And He said: "Please take your son, your only son, whom you love, Isaac, and go to the land of the Priestly Service [Jerusalem]...."

What does Onkelos add to the passage?

_____

_____

_____

(CLUE # I: There is no known place called Moriah.)

(CLUE # 2: If you want to see how he found his answer, turn to page 201.)

6. EZRA: PART II

So far, we've seen that one part of the beginning of Jewish exegesis was the need to translate the Torah so the public could understand it. If we go back to Ezra, we can see another process—**midrash**.

For Ezra had set his heart to דָּרַשׁ/DARASH (seek) the Torah of the Lord, and to do it, and to teach in Israel statutes and ordinances. (Ezra 7:10)

> −GESIS−Greek suffix: studying text
> EXEGESIS—Drawing meaning out of a text
> DARASH—To seek out/explore/investigate
> MIDRASH—Jewish biblical exposition

It would be an oversimplification to credit Ezra with beginning a process called **midrash**. To learn more of the story, we need to introduce a group of scholars called the **rabbis**.

7. THE RABBIS

Sometime after Ezra, a group of scholars called the "rabbis" emerged. We don't know the exact story, but we do know some of the pieces.

About 300 B.C.E., a young Macedonian named Alexander conquered the known world and then died. His conquest brought Greek culture to the Middle East and to Judea.

This meant (I) that Jews began moving to cities, (2) that in the cities Jews began to have trades rather than farms, and (3) that Jewish life had to change radically.

People now had leisure time, making gathering places like the synagogue and the *chavurah** important.

But, inevitably, change brings conflict.

First, a group called the Chasidim (no connection to the Eastern European followers of the Baal Shem Tov) emerged. These Jews objected to Greek culture and formed the backbone of the Hasmonean revolt, led by Judah Maccabee, against the Syrian king Antiochus. Chanukah is the festival commemorating the Maccabean victory.

Later, a group known as the Pharisees came into being. They brought new insights into the Jewish tradition. While we don't know the full connection, the Pharisees probably succeeded the Chasidim and preceded the "rabbis."

The Jews who moved to the "new" cities came from many locations and traditions. Some of these Jews were interested in preserving the Jewish tradition—following God's will and redeeming the world. Now that they worked at trades rather than the farms, they had some leisure time. While others used their leisure for "Greek pursuits"—athletics and the theater—some Jews used this time in Jewish activities. Various Jewish club houses—synagogues, *chavurot*, the *bet midrash*—became their centers and there they talked about Torah and the way it was understood and observed in their previous communities. One would tell how his town understood a given verse, and another would explain how the Torah was practiced in his region. Torah became dialogue.

Later, after the Romans conquered Jerusalem, formal academies were established, and these dialogues, the Oral Tradition, were written down and edited first by the early "rabbis," the **tana'im**, who lived and worked in Judea, and later by the **amora'im**, who worked both in Judea and Babylon. Together they produced the two Talmuds and many other important works, including many collections of midrashim.

---

* חָבֵר / *chaver* = friend/member
   חֲבוּרָה / *chavurah* = association

8. THE DARSHAN

Remember the **meturgeman**, the person who would "give the sense" of the Torah reading? After a while, the role of the **meturgeman** began to change. As the **meturgeman** began giving more and more of his own thoughts and insights on the passage, translation gave way to explanation. After a while, a form of public explanation evolved as part of the service. We know it as the "sermon." In Hebrew, the sermon is called a **derashah** (same root as **midrash**), and the person who gives it is called the **darshan**.

9. MIDRASH

If you've been following along, you've probably guessed that **midrash** is the written version of the sermons given by the **darshanim**.

If you thought that—you're half right. There are really two kinds of **midrashim**:

Homiletic midrash = written sermons.

Exegetical midrash = written explanations of individual problems in the text.

DARSHAN

ME TURGEMAN

TORAH READER

TORAH

Over the next few pages, you'll have a chance to tackle a few pieces of exegetical midrash. In each case, you'll find a piece of Torah text followed by one or two midrashim. Work them through using the accompanying questions. By the time you're done, you should have a good understanding of how midrash works.

EXEGETICAL MIDRASH
(Explanation of a Problem)

Exercise 7.2

Gen. 4:1-10

Here is the way the Torah tells the story of Cain and Abel. As you read it, see if you can figure out (1) why God rejected Cain's offering, and (2) why God didn't stop the fight between the brothers.

Now the man knew his wife Eve, and she conceived and bore Cain, saying, "I have gained a male child with the help of the LORD." She then bore his brother Abel. Abel became a keeper of sheep, and Cain became a tiller of the soil. In the course of time, Cain brought an offering to the LORD from the fruit of the soil; and Abel, for his part, brought the choicest of the firstlings of his flock. The LORD paid heed to Abel and his offering, but to Cain and his offering He paid no heed. Cain was much distressed and his face fell. And the LORD said to Cain,

"Why are you distressed,
And why is your face fallen?
Surely, if you do right,
There is uplift.
But if you do not do right
Sin couches at the door;
Its urge is toward you,
Yet you can be its master."

Cain spoke to his brother Abel...and when they were in the field, Cain set upon his brother Abel and killed him. The LORD said to Cain, "Where is your brother Abel?" And he said, "I do not know. Am I my brother's keeper?" Then He said, "What have you done? Hark, your brother's blood cries out to Me from the ground!"

1 Why do you think God accepted Abel's offering and not Cain's?

_____

_____

_____

2 Why do you think God started the fight between Cain and Abel and then didn't stop it?

_____

_____

_____

A Midrash (Gen. R. 22:7ff.)

The slaying of Abel by Cain wasn't a total surprise. The two brothers often fought. This is why Adam, their father, gave them different jobs. He made Cain a farmer and Abel a shepherd. This fight, however, started with their sacrifices. Adam told his sons that they had to offer the first of their new crops and herds to God. Abel selected the best of his flocks, but Cain offered that which was left over after his own meal. That is why God rejected Cain's offering.

Cain blamed his brother and told him: "Let's separate and divide our possessions." He told Abel: "Take the sheep and cattle and I will take the land." Abel agreed. The next day Cain told Abel: "Get yourself and your herd off my land—I own the earth." Abel answered: "Your clothing is made out of wool—take it off—I own it." This is the way the fight began.

(Text drawn from *Torah-Toons I*)

1 Underline the parts of this midrash which are not told to us in the Torah.

2 What facts from the Torah does this midrash use?

_____

_____

3 According to this midrash, what is the reason for God's rejection of Cain's offering?

_____

_____

4 What lesson does this midrash teach?

_____

Another Midrash (Gen. R. 22:8ff.)

You might think that God in this story was like a king watching two gladiators fighting. If one of the gladiators was killed, it would be the king's fault because he didn't stop the contest. Cain asked God: "Isn't it Your fault, because You did not command me to stop?" God answered: "I made you in My image with a brain and a soul. Were I to direct your every action you would be just like a puppet. You have a will of your own and you are responsible for your actions."

(Text drawn from *Torah-Toons I*)

1 Underline the parts of this midrash that can be found in the Torah. (Hint: It may not come from this story.)

2 According to the midrash, why didn't God stop Cain?

_____

_____

3 What moral is taught by this midrash?

_____

_____

Exercise 7.3

Gen. II:I-9

Here is the way the Torah tells the story of the Tower of Babel. As you read it, see if you can figure out why God wanted to stop people from building a tower.

All the earth had the same language and the same words. And as men migrated from the east, they came upon a valley in the land of Shinar and settled there. They said to one another, "Come, let us make bricks and burn them hard."—Brick served them as stone, and bitumen served as mortar.—And they said, "Come, let us build us a city, and a tower with its top in the sky, to make a name for ourselves; else we shall be scattered all over the world." The LORD came down to look at the city and tower which man had built, and the LORD said, "If, as one people with one language for all, this is how they have begun to act, then nothing that they may propose to do will be out of their reach. Let us, then, go down and confound their speech there, so that they shall not understand one another's speech." Thus the LORD scattered them from there over the face of the whole earth; and they stopped building the city. That is why it was called Babel, because there the LORD confounded the speech of the whole earth; and from there the LORD scattered them over the face of the whole earth.

1 Why was God angry that the people were building a tower and a city?

_____
_____
_____

2 Do you think that God was really afraid of what the people were doing?

_____
_____
_____

A Midrash (Pirke D'Rabbi Eliezer 24)

The tower was built with careful planning. On the east side were steps which were used to go up and on the west side was a down staircase. The tower got to be so high that it took a year to reach the top. People cared more about the bricks than they did about other people. If a person fell, no one cried. But if a brick was dropped, the workmen cried and tore out their hair— because it would take a year to replace it.

People lived all their lives on the tower. They married, had children, and raised them without setting foot on the ground. Nimrod, the leader of the group, cared only about finishing the tower. Often he would send up bricks but no food. Only when the workers refused to continue would the food be sent. (Adapted from *Torah-Toons I*)

1 What facts from the Torah does this midrash use?

_____
_____

2 What reasons does this midrash give for God's anger at the way the tower was being built?

_____
_____
_____

3 What is the message of this midrash?

_____
_____
_____

Exercise 7.4

Gen. 13:1-12

This is the way the Torah tells the story of the split between Abram and Lot. See if you can figure out the real reason for the split.

Now Abram was very rich in cattle, silver, and gold. And he proceeded by stages from the Negeb as far as Bethel, to the place where his tent had been formerly, between Bethel and Ai, the site of the altar which he had built there at first; and there Abram invoked the LORD by name. Lot, who went with Abram, also had flocks and herds and tents, so that the land could not support them staying together; for their possessions were so great that they could not remain together. And there was quarreling between the herdsmen of Abram's cattle and those of Lot's cattle.

—The Canaanites and Perizzites were then dwelling in the land.—

Abram said to Lot, "Let there be no strife between you and me, between my herdsmen and yours, for we are kinsmen. Is not the whole land before you? Let us separate: if you go north, I will go south; and if you go south, I will go north." Lot looked about him and saw how well watered was the whole plain of the Jordan, all of it—this was before the LORD had destroyed Sodom and Gomorrah—all the way to Zoar, like the garden of the LORD, like the land of Egypt. So Lot chose for himself the whole plain of the Jordan, and Lot journeyed eastward. Thus they parted from each other; Abram remained in the land of Canaan, while Lot settled in the cities of the Plain, pitching his tents near Sodom.

1 Why is there a quarrel between Abram's and Lot's shepherds?

_____

_____

2 When you read this story in the Torah, what is strange about the line: *"The Canaanites and Perizzites were then dwelling in the land"*?

_____

_____

_____

A Midrash (Gen. R. 41:5-6)

When Abram and Lot returned from Egypt, both of them had many sheep and cattle. Abram was very careful about his sheep and cattle, so he had them muzzled so that they would not eat from fields where they weren't welcome. Abram knew that allowing his flocks and herds to graze on someone else's fields was a kind of robbery. Lot didn't muzzle his cattle and sheep. He felt that it was too much bother, and he didn't really worry about what his animals ate. Abram told Lot: "It is wrong not to muzzle your flocks and herds—it is the same thing as stealing. This land belongs to the Canaanites and the Perizzites. These fields are theirs." Lot said to Abram: "If it is stealing—we are stealing from ourselves. God has already promised this land to us—here is no problem in our using it now."

Abram decided not to continue the argument. For the sake of *shelom bayit* (peace at home) he let the matter drop. Later the argument was picked up by the herdsmen. Lot's herdsmen said: "You are really stupid—doing all that extra work—putting on and taking off muzzles." Abram's herdsmen answered: "You are no better than thieves." Lot's men answered: "If we are stealing, it is only from ourselves. Abram has no son. After he is dead the land will belong to Lot. We are just using some of it now."

When Abram heard this, he decided that it was time to separate.

1 Underline the parts of this midrash which are taken directly from the Torah.

2 How does the midrash explain the fight between the herdsmen?

_____

_____

3 What is the message of this midrash?

_____

_____

Exercise 7.5

Exod. 3:1-4

After Moses fled from Egypt, he went to Midian and became a shepherd. The Torah tells only this short story about his experience as a shepherd. As you read, see if you can decide (1) why it was important training for Moses to be a shepherd, and (2) why he led his flock all the way from Midian to Mt. Horeb (a.k.a. Mt. Sinai).

Now Moses, tending the flock of his father-in-law Jethro, the priest of Midian, drove the flock into the wilderness, and came to Horeb, the mountain of God. An angel of the LORD appeared to him in a blazing fire out of a bush. He gazed, and there was a bush all aflame, yet the bush was not consumed. Moses said, "I must turn aside to look at this marvelous sight; why doesn't the bush burn up?" When the LORD saw that he had turned aside to look, God called to him out of the bush: "Moses! Moses!" He answered, "Here I am" [*Hineni*].

1 Why do you think it was good for Moses to spend time as a shepherd?

_____

_____

_____

2 Why would Moses take his flock as far as Sinai? (Hint: Think about what Abraham did with his sheep.)

_____

_____

_____

A Midrash (Exod. R. 2:2)

As soon as Moses took over Jethro's flocks they were blessed. Not a single animal was ever injured by a wild beast. Moses used to graze his flocks in ownerless land to insure that they would not steal from lands which were not Jethro's.

Once a lamb ran away from the flock. Moses followed it until it reached some bushes near a pond. It stopped to drink. Moses said: "I didn't know you ran all this way because you were thirsty. You must be tired too." He lifted the lamb on his shoulder and carried it back to the flock.

Another Midrash (Exod. R. 2:2)

God tested two people by making them shepherds. One of them was King David, who used to protect the smaller sheep from the attacks of the larger ones, and who would make sure that each animal got the food which was best for it. God said: "A man who cares for the needs of each individual sheep will do the same for My people, *B'nai Yisrael*."

Moses was also tested. God said: "A man who tends sheep with such mercy will be a compassionate leader for My sheep, *Yisrael*."

1 Underline the parts of these midrashim which are based on facts in the Bible.

2 How do these midrashim explain that it was good for Moses to be a shepherd?

_____

_____

3 How do these midrashim explain why Moses led his herd as far as Mt. Sinai?

_____

4 What lessons are taught by the two midrashim?

_____

_____

Exercise 7.6—THOUGHT SHEET

The six midrashim we've just worked through were written about four specific biblical passages. From these, we want you to draw your own conclusion about the nature of midrash.

1 Why are midrashim written? What in the biblical text "generates" the need for a midrash?

_____

_____

_____

_____

2 What is the relationship between a midrash and the biblical text?

_____

_____

_____

3 What else does a midrash try to do?

_____

_____

_____

4 What styles or forms are used in writing midrashim?

_____

_____

_____

_____

_____

From these examples, we've learned that midrashim tend to follow some basic rules.

1. A midrash is written because there is a problem/question in the biblical text which needs an answer/explanation/comment.

2. In answering the question, the midrash uses some facts/details from the biblical text and creates an explanation which fits the biblical text.

3. In addition to answering the question/problem, a midrash usually tries to teach a lesson, a moral, a value.

A GALLERY OF MIDRASHIC STYLES

1. Puns and Wordplays

And go to the land of Moriah....
(Gen. 22:2)

Here is how Rabbi Hiyya the Elder and Rabbi Jannai discussed this verse in Genesis Rabbah 55:7.

One said: Moriah means the place where teaching is done.

מוֹרִיָּה /Moriah =
מוֹרֶה /MOREH (teacher).

(This means the place in the Temple where the Sanhedrin studied and taught Jewish law.)

The other said: Moriah means the place where awe came into the world.

מוֹרִיָּה /Moriah =
יִרְאָה /YIRAH (awe).

(The Temple was the center of religious awe in the world.)

The rabbis said: Moriah means the place where incense would be offered (the Temple Mount in Jerusalem).

מוֹרִיָּה /Moriah =
מֹר /MOR/Myrrh
(a spice used in incense).

(This is the same as you find in Song of Songs 4:6: *"I will betake me to the mount of myrrh."*)

THE PROBLEM: Where is Moriah? (This is the only verse in which the name is used, and we know of no historical place called Moriah.)

THE ANSWER: Moriah = The Temple Mount in Jerusalem.

THE METHODOLOGY: Wordplays (and pseudo-etymologies) on the name Moriah.

THE PROOF-TEXT: Song of Songs 4:6 (the mount of myrrh).

THE MESSAGE: The Temple Mount is a unique Jewish location, the center of teaching, awe, and the national ritual.

2. Parables

When God was going to destroy Sodom, God decided to tell Abraham:

Now the Lord had said, "Shall I hide from Abraham what I am about to do...?" (Gen. 18:17)

Here is how Rabbi Joshua Ben Levi explains this verse in Genesis Rabbah 49:2.

This is like a king who presented an estate to his friend and later wanted to cut down five non-fruit-bearing trees from it. Said the king: "Even if I wished to cut them down from the land which was originally his—he would not refuse me. What can I lose by asking him?" And so he consulted him about it.

This is the same as the Holy One who is to be blessed saying: "I have already made a gift of this land to Abraham," as it says: *To your offspring I give this land.* (Gen. 15:18)

Now these five towns (Sodom, Gomorrah, Admah, Zeboiim, and Zoar) were indeed in My territory, yet even if I asked him for something which was ancestrally his—he would not refuse Me. And so God consulted him.

THE PROBLEM: Why does God tell Abraham about the plan to destroy Sodom and Gomorrah (and the other three towns)?

THE ANSWER: Because they are part of a land which has been promised to Abraham's offspring. While God expects Abraham to agree, God tells him because it is the right thing to do.

THE METHODOLOGY: Parable—Rabbi Joshua creates the story of a king and a friend to explain the situation.

THE PROOF-TEXT: Gen. 15:18 (God promised this land to Abraham).

THE MESSAGE: Property rights are important—even for God.

3. Analysis

The Lord said to Moses and Aaron in the land of Egypt: "This month shall mark for you the beginning of months...."

(Exod. 12:1-2)

Why did God speak to Moses and to Aaron? Because the consecration of a new month must be performed by three witnesses. When God wished to consecrate the month, God said to Moses and Aaron: "You and I will consecrate the month." (Exodus Rabbah 15:20)

THE PROBLEM: Why does God teach this mitzvah to both Aaron and Moses and not just to Moses (like most mitzvot)?

THE ANSWER: Because it takes three witnesses to start a new month.

THE METHODOLOGY: Analysis—The author of this midrash took a rule he knew and, through a process of reasoning, applied it to the situation.

THE PROOF-TEXT: None—but it does imply knowledge of a rule found in Mishnah about Rosh Chodesh.*

THE MESSAGE: Both God and people share in the maintenance of the Jewish calendar.

* In the Mishnah, Rosh Chodesh I:Iff., we are taught about the procedure for starting a new month. Before the Sanhedrin could declare a new month, at least three witnesses who had seen the new moon had to present themselves in Jerusalem and give testimony.

4. Connections

At Moses' first encounter with God at the burning bush, God tells him:

"I have come down to rescue them from the Egyptians...."
(Exod. 3:8)

Here is how this verse is explained in Exodus Rabbah 3:3.

God said to Moses: "I promised their ancestor Jacob: *I Myself will go down with you to Egypt, and I Myself will bring you back*, and now I have come here to take his children, as I promised their father Jacob." (Gen. 46:4)

Now the cry of the Israelites has reached Me. (Exod. 3:9)

Up to now, they have been crying out—but it has not reached Me—because the time set for their redemption had not passed. I did tell Abraham: *"And they shall be enslaved and oppressed for four hundred years."* (Gen. 15:13) Now the time has passed: *"Come, I will send you to Pharaoh."* (Exod. 3:10)

THE PROBLEM: Why does God choose this moment to hear Israel's cry after having ignored it for years?

THE ANSWER: The time fixed for slavery in Egypt wasn't up till now.

THE METHODOLOGY: Connecting verses—The author uses promises made to Jacob and Abraham to explain God's conversation with Moses. (The author also writes some additional dialogue for God.)

THE PROOF-TEXT: Gen. 46:4—God's promise to Jacob; and Gen. 15:13—God's promise to Abraham.

THE MESSAGE: God keeps promises—Israel's fate is secure—even when things seem darkest.

5. Insertions

And God blessed the seventh day.... (Gen. 2:3)

Here is what is done with that verse in Genesis Rabbah II:6.

Why did God bless the seventh day?

Rabbi Berekiah said: Because it has no mate. Sunday has Monday, Tuesday has Wednesday, and Thursday has Friday, but Shabbat has no partner.

Rabbi Simeon Bar Yohai taught: Shabbat pleaded to the Holy One blessed be He: "All the other days have a partner—but I have no partner!" God answered: "The community of Israel is your partner."

When Israel stood at Mt. Sinai, God said to them: "Remember what I said to Shabbat—that the community of Israel is your partner—So 'Remember the sabbath day and keep it holy.' " (Exod. 20:8)

THE PROBLEM: Why does God bless the seventh day?

THE ANSWER: The sabbath day is special.

THE METHODOLOGY: Insertions—Rabbi Simeon Bar Yohai creates a dialogue between Shabbat and God and then connects it to an original dialogue between God and Israel.

THE PROOF-TEXT: Exod. 20:8. This commandment is to remind Israel of their special relationship with Shabbat.

THE MESSAGE: Israel has a special relationship with Shabbat.

THOUGHT SHEET

Let's go back over the six exegetical midrashim on the previous pages.

1 Find out which uses each of these styles/tools:

Puns and wordplays _____
Connections _____
Analyses _____
Parables _____
Insertions _____

2 Underline all the places where the midrashim create new dialogue for biblical characters.

3 This is the first time we've really worked with "proof-texts." What do you think is their purpose?

_____

_____

_____

_____

4 What clues can you find in these midrashim showing that midrash was a dialogue—the product of Jews studying together?

_____

_____

_____

_____

HOMILETIC MIDRASH (Written Sermon)

Exercise 7.7

Moses went back to Jether [Jethro] his father-in-law. (Exod. 4:18)

Who shall ascend into the mountain of the Lord? (Ps. 24:3)

Thus is it written: *One who has clean hands and a pure heart, who has not taken My name in vain and has not sworn deceitfully.* (Ps. 24:4)

Who can ascend the mountain of the Lord?— one who has within him those virtues. All of these were found in Moses.

Clean hands: This applies to Moses, as it is said: *I have not taken the ass of any one of them.* (Num. 16:15)

Surely, if he had taken anything of theirs, he would have been a robber. What Moses meant was that he never even asked any of them to place any of their belongings on his ass. Here the word נְשִׂיאָה /Nisi'ah, which we usually translate as taken, should be understood as meaning "loading." This is the way it is used in Genesis 44:13, *"Each man loaded his pack animal...."*

Pure heart: (Pure = bar) Moses didn't begin his divine mission before he thoroughly investigated (נִתְבָּרֵר /Nitbarer) the matter, as it says: *and they ask me: "What is His name?"* (Exod. 3:13)

Who has not taken My name [the Hebrew says "*his soul*"] *in vain:* This refers to the soul of the Egyptian, whom Moses killed only after he had judged him and found him worthy of death.

Has not sworn deceitfully: This too applies to Moses. When he came to Jethro, he swore to him that he would not depart without his knowledge, and when he went on his divine mission, he went to ask Jethro's permission to leave— keeping his promise. This is why it says: **And Moses went and returned to Jethro his father-in-law.**

(Exodus Rabbah 4:1)

Unlike the other midrashim we have seen, this midrash was written as a sermon. It uses a number of tricks (some of which we've seen and some of which are new) and conforms to a basic style. Using what you've already learned, you'll be able to figure out what this midrash is saying and how it works.

The Torah texts below will help you by providing a context for many of the verses cited.

Exod. 4:18

Moses went back to his father-in-law Jether and said to him, "Let me go back to my kinsmen in Egypt and see how they are faring." And Jethro said to Moses, "Go in peace."

Ps. 24:3-4

Who shall ascend into the mountain of the Lord? And who shall stand in His holy place? One who has clean hands and a pure heart, who has not taken My name in vain, and has not sworn deceitfully.

Num. 16:15

Moses was very much aggrieved and he said to the LORD, "Pay no regard to their presentation. I have not taken the ass of any one of them, nor have I wronged any one of them."

Gen. 44:13

At this they rent their clothes. Each reloaded his pack animal and they returned to the city.

Exod. 3:13

And Moses said to God: "When I come to the Israelites and say to them 'The God of your fathers has sent me to you' and they ask me, 'What is His name?' what shall I say to them?"

STEP # 1: Underline the verse this midrash was written to explain. (Clue: It comes from Exodus.)

STEP # 2: In a proem (that is the formal name for this kind of sermon), the **darshan** picks a verse from *NaCh* (Prophets or Writings). The sermon is made up of the comparison of these two verses. This second verse is called the proem-verse. Put a star by it.

STEP # 3: Like the exegetical midrashim we've studied, this midrash too centers on solving one problem. Look at the full text of Exodus 4:18. What is strange about Moses' behavior? What problem is this midrash answering?

State the problem:

Why did Moses _____

_____?

STEP # 4: For our next step, we have to understand the relationship between the "proem-verse" and the "Torah-text."

For the **darshan**, how does the "proem-verse" apply to Moses?

_____

_____

_____

_____

STEP # 5: This midrash is trying to prove that Moses was chosen to go up to Mt. Sinai and receive the Torah because he had all the "virtues" listed in the Psalm 24:4. To prove the point, the **darshan** uses two *wordplays* and two *insertions*. How do they prove each of these four traits?

Moses had *clean hands*_____

_____

Moses had a *pure heart* _____

_____

Moses had not *taken a soul in vain* _____

_____

Moses had not *sworn deceitfully*_____

_____

STEP # 6: In the end, the proem verse provides the specific answer to our problem. How does the Psalm 24:4 explain why Moses went to Jethro?

_____

_____

_____

STEP # 7 What is the moral of this sermon? How should we be like Moses?

_____

_____

_____

CONCLUSIONS:

There are two sides to midrash. In much of this module we've worked with a technical literature that takes careful analysis before it becomes clear. Most midrashim need to be unpacked. It takes three steps to open up most midrashim.

First, we have to find the tracing, the connection between a given midrash and the Torah's text. This connection is always rooted in a problem. Once we understand what a midrash is solving, then the rest is easy. Through a quick comparison with the Torah, it is easy to find out which details are taken from the Torah and which have been invented for this midrash.

Second, we have to find the solution. We've seen that midrash can use many tools to evolve answers to difficulties in the biblical text.

Third, we go beyond the biblical solution to the central lesson of the midrash. Every midrash (be it homiletic or exegetical) is a mini-sermon. At the root of each there is a teaching about how we can become better people.

Along the way, we've had to figure out proof-texts, apply parables, follow wordplays, etc. For us, midrash becomes a puzzle which must be solved, for the rabbis (and especially the **darshanim**) it was an art form, the rules and techniques adding to the artistry. Compare it to gymnastics or figure-skating—the required moves give the stunts more meaning.

But midrash is also Jewish fantasy literature. It is a wonderful world of images and characters, a fabulous connection of stories. Midrash is much more than a simple set of answers to basic biblical questions: It is a wonderfully enriched view of the Bible with new stories and events embroidered between every line of text.

POST-TEST

This module has four objects. This time, we're going to make it easy. Our post-test will look only at the last two. (We'll trust you to master the first two on your own.)

7.1 Trace the "chain of the tradition" through the works which expound on the Torah's meaning.

7.2 Describe the evolution of midrashic literature.

7.3 Examine a piece of midrash and identify (1) the parts of that midrash which are taken from the Torah, (2) the answer given to the biblical problem, and (3) the message or moral of that midrash.

7.4 Identify the technique a given midrash uses to solve a biblical problem.

This is the line of Noah. Noah was a righteous man; he was blameless in his age; Noah walked with God. (Gen. 6:9)

Genesis Rabbah 30:9

In his age
Rabbi Judah and Rabbi Nehemiah disagreed.

Rabbi Judah said: Only in his age was he a righteous man. If he had lived in the time of Moses or Samuel, he would not have been called righteous.

In the street of the totally blind, a one-eyed man is called a visionary and the infant is called a scholar.

This can be compared to a man who had a wine vault and who opened one barrel and found it vinegar, then opened another and found it vinegar, but the third barrel had only begun to turn sour. People told him, "It is turning," but he said, "Is there any better?" This is the meaning of *in his age*.

Rabbi Nehemiah said: If he was righteous in his age, he would have been even more righteous in the age of Moses. Compare him to a tightly closed pail of perfume lying in a graveyard (full of the stench of rotting bodies) that still gave off a pleasant odor. It would smell even better outside the graveyard.

PROBLEM:_____

_____

SOLUTION:_____

_____

LESSON: _____

_____

METHODS OF SOLUTION:_____

_____

APPENDIX TO MODULE SEVEN

ANSWERS

Exercise 7.1

1. Maimonides (a.k.a. Rambam, or Moses Ben Maimon) was an important Jewish teacher, philosopher, and writer. He served as a doctor to the sultan and wrote important works on both Jewish law and philosophy.

2. The problem with Jewish education seems the same.

3. Moses = One who received the Torah from God

   Mishnah = Rabbinic Law Code (First Layer of Law)

   Prophets = People who were inspired by God to speak out for social justice

   Eli = A High Priest who taught Samuel

   Rabbi Judah = Compiler of the Mishnah

   Oral Law = All the literature which followed the Bible

   Geonim = Rabbinic scholars following the Talmud

   Ezra = A scribe and a leader of the return from Babylonia

   Talmud = Commentary on Mishnah (Second Layer of Law)

   Responsa = Questions and answers about Law

   Commentaries = Writings about the Torah, Talmud, etc.

   Midrash = explanations of the Torah's stories and laws

   Mishneh Torah = Maimonides' Code of Law

4. The right order is: 7, 9, 8, 2, 13, 14, 1, 3, 6, 10, 5, 11, 12, 4

5. The right order is: 4, 1, 7, 8, 2, 3, 9, 5, 6. The placement of responsa and commentaries is problematic because they overlap and interweave with one another.

Exercise 7.2

page 125

These are opinion questions.

Genesis Rabbah 22:7

1. Most of this midrash is not found in the Torah.

2. The fight and the occupations chosen by each.

3. Abel offered "the best." Cain offered "left-overs."

4. Selfishness leads to conflict, etc.

Genesis Rabbah 22:8

1. Just the fact of the fight and people being created in God's image.

2. Because people have "free will." God wants people to choose the right.

3. We have free will and must choose to do right, etc.

Exercise 7.3

1. Just the fact that there was a tower built from bricks.

2. The ethics of the way it was being built.

3. People are the most important human achievement, etc.

Exercise 7.4

1. The two herds, and the fact that the land belonged to the Canaanites and the Perizzites.

2. The two owners had different ethics—a contrast with the psychological interpretation we looked at earlier in the book.

3. A good person is completely responsible for all of his or her actions and guards against any kind of theft.

Exercise 7.5

1. Moses cared for sheep. Moses led his sheep far into the wilderness. Moses was a shepherd and David was also a shepherd.

2. Leading sheep teaches you to lead people.

3. To be like Abraham and keep his sheep from grazing on the lands of others.

4. Be ethical. Be sensitive to the needs of others.

MODULE EIGHT: READING THE TORAH WITH RABBINIC EYES

Whenever I enter a classroom crowded with boys who could be, as far as age is concerned, my grandchildren—I enter the classroom as an old man, with a wrinkled face and eyes reflecting fatigue and the sadness of old age, and sit down. Opposite me are rows of young boys with beaming eyes, beaming faces, clear eyes radiating the joy of being young. I enter in a very pessimistic mood, in despair.

And I ask myself can there be a dialogue between young students and an old teacher, between a rebbe in Indian summer and boys enjoying the spring of their lives?

Whenever I start the *shiur*, the door opens up and another old man comes in and sits down. He is older than I am. He is my grandfather. His name is Reb Chaim Brisker, without whom I cannot say my *shiur*.

Then the door opens quietly again and another old man comes in. He is older than Reb Chaim. He lived in the seventeenth century. His name is Shabbetai ben Meir Hacohen, the famous "Shakh" who might be present when you study Baba Kamma and Baba Metzia.

And then more visitors show up. Some of the visitors lived in the eleventh century and some lived in the twelfth century, some in the thirteenth century—some even lived in antiquity.

Rashi—Rabbenu Tam—Rava—Rashba

More and more come in. Of course, what do I do? I introduce them to my pupils and the dialogue commences. The Rambam says something; the Rava disagrees. A boy jumps up; he has an idea. The Rashba smiles gently. I try to analyze what the young boy meant.

Another boy intervenes. We call upon the Rabbenu Tam to express his opinion and suddenly a symposium of generations comes into existence. Young boys 18, 20, 23 years of age from one generation join with my generation, then the generation of Reb Chaim, then the generation of the Shakh, then the generation of the Rashba, the generation of the Rambam, the generation of Rashi, the generation of Rabbenu Tam—there is no end.

What about Rabbi Yochanan Ben Zakkai? What about Rabbi Akiba? We all speak one language. We all chat. We speak together. We discuss. We enjoy each other's company. We all pursue one goal. We are all committed to a common vision and we all operate under the same categories. There is a Masorah colleague-ality, a friendship, a comradeship—between young and old, between antiquity and Middle Ages and modern times.

Transcribed from a talk given on his birthday by Rabbi Joseph Soloveichik

(Part Two)
COMMENTARIES: *MIKRAOT GEDOLOT*

The full page of Hebrew opposite this one is a page taken from a book called: מִקְרָאוֹת גְּדוֹלוֹת /MIKRAOT GEDOLOT. It means "**THE BIG BIBLE**." When Jews sit down to learn Torah seriously, they use this book. In this module, we're going to see how this tradition of commentary evolved from the time of the Midrash down to Sforno, a commentator who lived in the 1500s.

In a sense, the מִקְרָאוֹת גְּדוֹלוֹת /MIKRAOT GEDOLOT is a timeline tracing the ways that Jews studied Torah. The page includes the work of the *targumim*, the Masoretes (a group you'll meet on the next page), commentators including Rashi, Rashbam, Rambam, Ibn Ezra, and Sforno. There is also a "super commentary" and a reference work called *Toledot Aharon*. In the course of working through this module, we'll trace this part of the history of Jewish biblical commentary.

In another sense, מִקְרָאוֹת גְּדוֹלוֹת /MIKRAOT GEDOLOT is an encyclopedia of insights and methodologies. Squeezed into this page is almost every insight the Jewish people have collected (up to 1550) on the five verses of the Torah reproduced here. We have a guide to copying, a translation, five commentaries, and one commentary on a commentary—plus an index of everywhere each of these verses is quoted in the Talmud.

Finally, this page provides us with a curriculum. By looking at the commentaries, we get a good sense of what it means to read Torah with rabbinic eyes. When you're done with this module, you'll be ready to learn (in English) all the material found on this and every other page of the מִקְרָאוֹת גְּדוֹלוֹת /MIKRAOT GEDOLOT.

קְרִיאָה /KERIAH (reading)
מִקְרָאָה /MIKRA'AH (the reading = Bible)
גָּדוֹל /GADOL (big)

By the time you've finished this module, you should be able to:

8.1 Trace the history of Jewish biblical commentary from the Masoretes through the commentators.
8.2 Identify by category *kusheyot* (difficulties/problems) in a biblical verse.
8.3 Give a brief explanation of the way Rashi comments on a verse.
8.4 Follow a commentary by Rashi, identifying (a) the question, (b) the solution, (c) the moral/message, and (d) the use of proof-texts.
8.5 Follow the work of other biblical commentators.
8.6 Express in your own words what can be gained from studying Torah "with rabbinic eyes."

On the left-hand side of the next page we have a copy of a section of the Torah as it is handwritten by a *sofer*. This was the original form of the Written Torah. On the right-hand side is a Masoretic text. In the next few pages we'll come to understand how their grammatical work was really a commentary.

BEFORE

Scribal Torah

בְּרֵאשִׁית בָּרָא אֱלֹהִים אֵת הַשָּׁמַיִם וְאֵת הָאָרֶץ
וְהָאָרֶץ הָיְתָה תֹהוּ וָבֹהוּ וְחֹשֶׁךְ עַל־פְּנֵי תְהוֹם וְרוּחַ
אֱלֹהִים מְרַחֶפֶת עַל־פְּנֵי הַמָּיִם וַיֹּאמֶר אֱלֹהִים יְהִי
אוֹר וַיְהִי אוֹר וַיַּרְא אֱלֹהִים אֶת־הָאוֹר כִּי טוֹב
וַיַּבְדֵּל אֱלֹהִים בֵּין הָאוֹר וּבֵין הַחֹשֶׁךְ וַיִּקְרָא
אֱלֹהִים לָאוֹר יוֹם וְלַחֹשֶׁךְ קָרָא לַיְלָה וַיְהִי עֶרֶב
וַיְהִי בֹקֶר יוֹם אֶחָד

וַיֹּאמֶר אֱלֹהִים יְהִי רָקִיעַ בְּתוֹךְ הַמָּיִם וִיהִי מַבְדִּיל
בֵּין מַיִם לָמָיִם וַיַּעַשׂ אֱלֹהִים אֶת הָרָקִיעַ וַיַּבְדֵּל
בֵּין הַמַּיִם אֲשֶׁר מִתַּחַת לָרָקִיעַ וּבֵין הַמַּיִם אֲשֶׁר
מֵעַל לָרָקִיעַ וַיְהִי כֵן וַיִּקְרָא אֱלֹהִים לָרָקִיעַ שָׁמַיִם
וַיְהִי עֶרֶב וַיְהִי בֹקֶר יוֹם שֵׁנִי

וַיֹּאמֶר אֱלֹהִים יִקָּווּ הַמַּיִם מִתַּחַת הַשָּׁמַיִם אֶל
מָקוֹם אֶחָד וְתֵרָאֶה הַיַּבָּשָׁה וַיְהִי כֵן וַיִּקְרָא אֱלֹהִים
לַיַּבָּשָׁה אֶרֶץ וּלְמִקְוֵה הַמַּיִם קָרָא יַמִּים וַיַּרְא
אֱלֹהִים כִּי טוֹב וַיֹּאמֶר אֱלֹהִים תַּדְשֵׁא הָאָרֶץ
דֶּשֶׁא עֵשֶׂב מַזְרִיעַ זֶרַע עֵץ פְּרִי עֹשֶׂה פְּרִי לְמִינוֹ
אֲשֶׁר זַרְעוֹ בוֹ עַל הָאָרֶץ וַיְהִי כֵן וַתּוֹצֵא הָאָרֶץ
דֶּשֶׁא עֵשֶׂב מַזְרִיעַ זֶרַע לְמִינֵהוּ וְעֵץ עֹשֶׂה פְּרִי
אֲשֶׁר זַרְעוֹ בוֹ לְמִינֵהוּ וַיַּרְא אֱלֹהִים כִּי טוֹב וַיְהִי
עֶרֶב וַיְהִי בֹקֶר יוֹם שְׁלִישִׁי

וַיֹּאמֶר אֱלֹהִים יְהִי מְאֹרֹת בִּרְקִיעַ הַשָּׁמַיִם לְהַבְדִּיל
בֵּין הַיּוֹם וּבֵין הַלָּיְלָה וְהָיוּ לְאֹתֹת וּלְמוֹעֲדִים וּלְיָמִים
וְשָׁנִים וְהָיוּ לִמְאוֹרֹת בִּרְקִיעַ הַשָּׁמַיִם לְהָאִיר עַל
הָאָרֶץ וַיְהִי כֵן וַיַּעַשׂ אֱלֹהִים אֶת שְׁנֵי הַמְּאֹרֹת
הַגְּדֹלִים אֶת הַמָּאוֹר הַגָּדֹל לְמֶמְשֶׁלֶת הַיּוֹם וְאֶת
הַמָּאוֹר הַקָּטֹן לְמֶמְשֶׁלֶת הַלַּיְלָה וְאֵת הַכּוֹכָבִים
וַיִּתֵּן אֹתָם אֱלֹהִים בִּרְקִיעַ הַשָּׁמָיִם לְהָאִיר עַל
הָאָרֶץ וְלִמְשֹׁל בַּיּוֹם וּבַלַּיְלָה וּלְהַבְדִּיל בֵּין הָאוֹר
וּבֵין הַחֹשֶׁךְ וַיַּרְא אֱלֹהִים כִּי טוֹב וַיְהִי עֶרֶב וַיְהִי
בֹקֶר יוֹם רְבִיעִי

וַיֹּאמֶר אֱלֹהִים יִשְׁרְצוּ הַמַּיִם שֶׁרֶץ נֶפֶשׁ חַיָּה
וְעוֹף יְעוֹפֵף עַל הָאָרֶץ עַל פְּנֵי רְקִיעַ הַשָּׁמַיִם
וַיִּבְרָא אֱלֹהִים אֶת הַתַּנִּינִם הַגְּדֹלִים וְאֵת כָּל נֶפֶשׁ
הַחַיָּה הָרֹמֶשֶׂת אֲשֶׁר שָׁרְצוּ הַמַּיִם לְמִינֵהֶם וְאֵת
כָּל עוֹף כָּנָף לְמִינֵהוּ וַיַּרְא אֱלֹהִים כִּי טוֹב וַיְבָרֶךְ
אֹתָם אֱלֹהִים לֵאמֹר פְּרוּ וּרְבוּ וּמִלְאוּ אֶת הַמַּיִם
בַּיַּמִּים וְהָעוֹף יִרֶב בָּאָרֶץ וַיְהִי עֶרֶב וַיְהִי בֹקֶר
יוֹם חֲמִישִׁי

וַיֹּאמֶר אֱלֹהִים תּוֹצֵא הָאָרֶץ נֶפֶשׁ חַיָּה לְמִינָהּ
בְּהֵמָה וָרֶמֶשׂ וְחַיְתוֹ אֶרֶץ לְמִינָהּ וַיְהִי כֵן וַיַּעַשׂ
אֱלֹהִים אֶת חַיַּת הָאָרֶץ לְמִינָהּ וְאֶת הַבְּהֵמָה לְמִינָהּ

AFTER

Masoretic Text

א בְּרֵאשִׁ֖ית בָּרָ֣א אֱלֹהִ֑ים אֵ֥ת הַשָּׁמַ֖יִם וְאֵ֥ת הָאָֽרֶץ׃ 2 וְהָאָ֗רֶץ
הָיְתָ֥ה תֹ֙הוּ֙ וָבֹ֔הוּ וְחֹ֖שֶׁךְ עַל־פְּנֵ֣י תְה֑וֹם וְר֣וּחַ אֱלֹהִ֔ים
מְרַחֶ֖פֶת עַל־פְּנֵ֥י הַמָּֽיִם׃ 3 וַיֹּ֥אמֶר אֱלֹהִ֖ים יְהִ֣י א֑וֹר וַֽיְהִי־
א֑וֹר׃ 4 וַיַּ֧רְא אֱלֹהִ֛ים אֶת־הָא֖וֹר כִּי־ט֑וֹב וַיַּבְדֵּ֣ל אֱלֹהִ֔ים בֵּ֥ין
הָא֖וֹר וּבֵ֥ין הַחֹֽשֶׁךְ׃ 5 וַיִּקְרָ֨א אֱלֹהִ֤ים ׀ לָאוֹר֙ י֔וֹם וְלַחֹ֖שֶׁךְ
קָ֣רָא לָ֑יְלָה וַֽיְהִי־עֶ֥רֶב וַֽיְהִי־בֹ֖קֶר י֥וֹם אֶחָֽד׃ פ
6 וַיֹּ֣אמֶר אֱלֹהִ֔ים יְהִ֥י רָקִ֖יעַ בְּת֣וֹךְ הַמָּ֑יִם וִיהִ֣י מַבְדִּ֔יל בֵּ֥ין
מַ֖יִם לָמָֽיִם׃ 7 וַיַּ֣עַשׂ אֱלֹהִים֮ אֶת־הָרָקִיעַ֒ וַיַּבְדֵּ֗ל בֵּ֤ין הַמַּ֙יִם֙
אֲשֶׁר֙ מִתַּ֣חַת לָרָקִ֔יעַ וּבֵ֣ין הַמַּ֔יִם אֲשֶׁ֖ר מֵעַ֣ל לָרָקִ֑יעַ וַֽיְהִי־
כֵֽן׃ 8 וַיִּקְרָ֧א אֱלֹהִ֛ים לָֽרָקִ֖יעַ שָׁמָ֑יִם וַֽיְהִי־עֶ֥רֶב וַֽיְהִי־בֹ֖קֶר
יוֹם שֵׁנִֽי׃ ישׂראל פ

9 וַיֹּ֣אמֶר אֱלֹהִ֗ים יִקָּו֨וּ הַמַּ֜יִם מִתַּ֤חַת הַשָּׁמַ֙יִם֙ אֶל־מָק֣וֹם אֶחָ֔ד
וְתֵרָאֶ֖ה הַיַּבָּשָׁ֑ה וַֽיְהִי־כֵֽן׃ 10 וַיִּקְרָ֨א אֱלֹהִ֤ים ׀ לַיַּבָּשָׁה֙ אֶ֔רֶץ
וּלְמִקְוֵ֥ה הַמַּ֖יִם קָרָ֣א יַמִּ֑ים וַיַּ֥רְא אֱלֹהִ֖ים כִּי־טֽוֹב׃ 11 וַיֹּ֣אמֶר
אֱלֹהִ֗ים תַּֽדְשֵׁ֤א הָאָ֙רֶץ֙ דֶּ֗שֶׁא עֵ֚שֶׂב מַזְרִ֣יעַ זֶ֔רַע עֵ֣ץ פְּרִ֞י
עֹ֤שֶׂה פְּרִי֙ לְמִינ֔וֹ אֲשֶׁ֥ר זַרְעוֹ־ב֖וֹ עַל־הָאָ֑רֶץ וַֽיְהִי־כֵֽן׃
12 וַתּוֹצֵ֨א הָאָ֜רֶץ דֶּ֗שֶׁא עֵ֣שֶׂב מַזְרִ֤יעַ זֶ֙רַע֙ לְמִינֵ֔הוּ וְעֵ֧ץ עֹֽשֶׂה־
פְּרִ֛י אֲשֶׁ֥ר זַרְעוֹ־ב֖וֹ לְמִינֵ֑הוּ וַיַּ֥רְא אֱלֹהִ֖ים כִּי־טֽוֹב׃ 13 וַֽיְהִי־
עֶ֥רֶב וַֽיְהִי־בֹ֖קֶר י֥וֹם שְׁלִישִֽׁי׃ פ

14 וַיֹּ֣אמֶר אֱלֹהִ֗ים יְהִ֤י מְאֹרֹת֙ בִּרְקִ֣יעַ הַשָּׁמַ֔יִם לְהַבְדִּ֕יל בֵּ֥ין
הַיּ֖וֹם וּבֵ֣ין הַלָּ֑יְלָה וְהָי֤וּ לְאֹתֹת֙ וּלְמ֣וֹעֲדִ֔ים וּלְיָמִ֖ים וְשָׁנִֽים׃
15 וְהָי֤וּ לִמְאוֹרֹת֙ בִּרְקִ֣יעַ הַשָּׁמַ֔יִם לְהָאִ֖יר עַל־הָאָ֑רֶץ וַֽיְהִי־
כֵֽן׃ 16 וַיַּ֣עַשׂ אֱלֹהִ֔ים אֶת־שְׁנֵ֥י הַמְּאֹרֹ֖ת הַגְּדֹלִ֑ים אֶת־הַמָּא֤וֹר
הַגָּדֹל֙ לְמֶמְשֶׁ֣לֶת הַיּ֔וֹם וְאֶת־הַמָּא֤וֹר הַקָּטֹן֙ לְמֶמְשֶׁ֣לֶת
הַלַּ֔יְלָה וְאֵ֖ת הַכּֽוֹכָבִֽים׃ 17 וַיִּתֵּ֥ן אֹתָ֛ם אֱלֹהִ֖ים בִּרְקִ֣יעַ
הַשָּׁמָ֑יִם לְהָאִ֖יר עַל־הָאָֽרֶץ׃ 18 וְלִמְשֹׁל֙ בַּיּ֣וֹם וּבַלַּ֔יְלָה
וּֽלֲהַבְדִּ֔יל בֵּ֥ין הָא֖וֹר וּבֵ֣ין הַחֹ֑שֶׁךְ וַיַּ֥רְא אֱלֹהִ֖ים כִּי־טֽוֹב׃
19 וַֽיְהִי־עֶ֥רֶב וַֽיְהִי־בֹ֖קֶר י֥וֹם רְבִיעִֽי׃ פ

כ וַיֹּ֣אמֶר אֱלֹהִ֔ים יִשְׁרְצ֣וּ הַמַּ֔יִם שֶׁ֖רֶץ נֶ֣פֶשׁ חַיָּ֑ה וְעוֹף֙ יְעוֹפֵ֣ף
עַל־הָאָ֔רֶץ עַל־פְּנֵ֖י רְקִ֥יעַ הַשָּׁמָֽיִם׃ 21 וַיִּבְרָ֣א אֱלֹהִ֔ים אֶת־
הַתַּנִּינִ֖ם הַגְּדֹלִ֑ים וְאֵ֣ת כָּל־נֶ֣פֶשׁ הַֽחַיָּ֣ה ׀ הָֽרֹמֶ֡שֶׂת אֲשֶׁר֩
שָׁרְצ֨וּ הַמַּ֜יִם לְמִֽינֵהֶ֗ם וְאֵ֨ת כָּל־ע֤וֹף כָּנָף֙ לְמִינֵ֔הוּ וַיַּ֥רְא
אֱלֹהִ֖ים כִּי־טֽוֹב׃ 22 וַיְבָ֧רֶךְ אֹתָ֛ם אֱלֹהִ֖ים לֵאמֹ֑ר פְּר֣וּ וּרְב֗וּ
וּמִלְא֤וּ אֶת־הַמַּ֙יִם֙ בַּיַּמִּ֔ים וְהָע֖וֹף יִ֥רֶב בָּאָֽרֶץ׃ 23 וַֽיְהִי־עֶ֥רֶב
וַֽיְהִי־בֹ֖קֶר י֥וֹם חֲמִישִֽׁי׃ פ

24 וַיֹּ֣אמֶר אֱלֹהִ֗ים תּוֹצֵ֨א הָאָ֜רֶץ נֶ֤פֶשׁ חַיָּה֙ לְמִינָ֔הּ בְּהֵמָ֥ה
כה וָרֶ֛מֶשׂ וְחַֽיְתוֹ־אֶ֖רֶץ לְמִינָ֑הּ וַֽיְהִי־כֵֽן׃ וַיַּ֣עַשׂ אֱלֹהִים֩ אֶת־
חַיַּ֨ת הָאָ֜רֶץ לְמִינָ֗הּ וְאֶת־הַבְּהֵמָה֙ לְמִינָ֔הּ

Exercise 8.1a

COPY THIS TEXT EXACTLY

You shall love the Lord your Your God with all your heart with all your soul and with all might. Take to heart these instructions with which I charge you this day. Impress them upon your children. Impress them upon your children. Recite them when you stay at home and when you are away, when you lie down, and when you get up. Bind them as a a sign upon your head and let them serve as a symbol upon your hand. Inscribe them on the door post of your house and on your gates. Deut. 6:5-9 (NJV)

_____

_____

_____

_____

_____

_____

_____

_____

_____

_____

_____

_____

_____

_____

_____

_____

_____

_____

_____

_____

Have a friend carefully check your work. What kinds of mistakes did you find?

_____

_____

_____

Official copies of the *Sefer Torah* are handwritten. They always have been. Until 1442, when the printing press was invented, that was the only way to reproduce a book. Copying something by hand is a very difficult process. Even if you are very careful, you will make some mistakes. People skip words, transpose letters or words, make small changes (by anticipating and not copying) by double-copying words and lines. When we read the word of ancient scribes, we find such mistakes. When teachers correct term papers, these are the kinds of mistakes they find. It is part of the process of copying.

These are the same kinds of mistakes you found in the previous column.

In an appendix to the Babylonian Talmud, Tractate Soferim 6:4, we find this passage:

Rabbi Shimon Ben Lakish said, Three copies of the Torah were found in the hall of the Temple. They were named:

The מְעֹנָה **Me'onah** Scroll,
The זָאֲטוּטֵי **Za'atutei** Scroll,
The הִיא **Hi** Scroll.

In one scroll, you find the word **Ma'on** מְעוֹן . In the two other scrolls this word was written as מְעֹנָה **Me'onah.** (Deut. 33:27)

In one scroll, the word which the other two scrolls showed as **Na'arei** נַעֲרֵי was written as **Za'atutei** זָאֲטוּטֵי . (Exod. 24:5)

And, in one scroll, the word **Hu** הוּא is written eleven times, and in the two others **Hi** הִיא appears eleven times.

The rabbis ruled that any reading which appeared in two out of the three scrolls would be considered correct. Therefore the accepted text reads הִיא and נַעֲרֵי, מְעֹנָה —Me'onah, Na'arei, and Hi.

Exercise 8.1b

What can we learn from this passage?

_____

_____

_____

22 טַפְּכֶם וְיִנַחֵם אוֹתָם וַיְדַבֵּר עַל־לִבָּם׃ וַיֵּשֶׁב יוֹסֵף בְּמִצְרַיִם הוּא וּבֵית אָבִיו וַיְחִי יוֹסֵף מֵאָה וָעֶשֶׂר שָׁנִים׃ וַיַּרְא יוֹסֵף לְאֶפְרַיִם בְּנֵי שִׁלֵּשִׁים גַּם בְּנֵי מָכִיר בֶּן־מְנַשֶּׁה יֻלְּדוּ

24 עַל־בִּרְכֵּי יוֹסֵף׃ וַיֹּאמֶר יוֹסֵף אֶל־אֶחָיו אָנֹכִי מֵת וֵאלֹהִים פָּקֹד יִפְקֹד אֶתְכֶם וְהֶעֱלָה אֶתְכֶם מִן־הָאָרֶץ הַזֹּאת אֶל־

25 הָאָרֶץ אֲשֶׁר נִשְׁבַּע לְאַבְרָהָם לְיִצְחָק וּלְיַעֲקֹב׃ וַיַּשְׁבַּע יוֹסֵף אֶת־בְּנֵי יִשְׂרָאֵל לֵאמֹר פָּקֹד יִפְקֹד אֱלֹהִים אֶתְכֶם

26 וְהַעֲלִתֶם אֶת־עַצְמֹתַי מִזֶּה׃ וַיָּמָת יוֹסֵף בֶּן־מֵאָה וָעֶשֶׂר שָׁנִים וַיַּחַנְטוּ אֹתוֹ וַיִּישֶׂם בָּאָרוֹן בְּמִצְרָיִם׃

v. 23. ס׳ רבתי

ח ז ק

סכום פסוקי דספר בראשית אלף וחמש מאות ושלשים וארבעה.

אֹ"ךְ ל"ד סימן: וחציו ועל חרבך תחיה: ופרשיותיו י"ב. זֶה שמי לעלם סימן: וסדריו מ"ג. נם ברוך יהיה סימן: ופרקיו נ'. יי' חנו לך קוינו סימן: מנין הפתוחות שלשה וארבעים והסתומות שמנה וארבעים. הכל תשעים ואחת פרשיות.

צֵא אתה וכל העם אשר ברגליך סימן:

What you see above is the end of the Book of Genesis in a Masoretic Bible. First the text ends, then you see the word חֲזַק /CHAZAK(Be strong), which we say whenever we finish a book of the Torah, and then down below you see notes for the scribes. These notes give the correct number of sentences, words, usages of God's name, columns, and paragraphs. They serve as a double check—a way for a scribe to make sure that his work is correct.

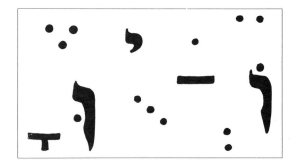

These are the **vowels** in the Hebrew language. As you can see (by comparing "BEFORE" and "AFTER"), these were added to the original Hebrew text in order to make it easier to understand and to read.

When the Torah is read in public, it is chanted. These symbols are the "notes" which are used to indicate the melodic patterns. In Hebrew they are usually called "**trope**"— though the correct Hebrew is טַעֲמֵי מִקְרָא/**ta'amei mikra**. These too were added to the text.

What you see below this line is another addition to the text which is found at the bottom of many biblical pages. It is another Masoretic marking. It is called קְרֵי וּכְּתִיב/**kerei uketiv** (spoken and written). It is an indication to the reader to pronounce something differently from the way it is written. It is an indication that we know that the correct understanding is different from the preserved text (but we can't change the text).

אִתּוֹ מֵעֲבָדֶיךָ וָמֵת וְגַם־אֲנַחְנוּ
י וַיֹּאמֶר גַּם־עַתָּה כְדִבְרֵיכֶם כֶּן־הוּא
11 לִי עָבֶד וְאַתֶּם תִּהְיוּ נְקִיִּם:
12 אַמְתַּחְתּוֹ אַרְצָה וַיִּפְתְּחוּ אִישׁ
הֵחֵל וּבַקָּטֹן כִּלָּה וַיִּמָּצֵא
18 וַיִּקְרְעוּ שִׂמְלֹתָם וַיַּעֲמֹס אִישׁ

מד v. 10. קמץ בזק

The *Masorah* is a protective fence around the Torah. (Pirke Avot 3:17)

Masorah is the name given to the body of work which includes the sentence breaks, the vowels, the "trope," the numerical countings for scribes, the marginal comments on the written nature of the biblical text.

We call the scholars who worked on the Masorah—Masoretes. But we don't know a lot about them. The earliest document found that shows their work is called the Leningrad Codex (because it's in a museum in Leningrad). It is believed to have been written circa 1009. We guess, however, (because of a number of external sources) that the majority of the Masoretic work took place between 700 and 800. Like the Talmud (where we have a Babylonian and a Jerusalem Talmud), the Masorah was developed interdependently in both Babylonia and Palestine. But, unlike the Talmud, the Palestinian school is usually given preference.

We do know that the Masoretic tradition culminated in the work of Aaron Ben Asher. His school was in Tiberias (in the Galilee), and he assembled a complete codex in 930. The Leningrad Codex is a copy of his work.

טו וַיֹּאמֶר לָבָן לְיַעֲקֹב הֲכִי־אָחִי אַתָּה וַעֲבַדְתַּנִי חִנָּם הַגִּידָה לִּי מַה־מַּשְׂכֻּרְתֶּךָ: טז וּלְלָבָן שְׁתֵּי בָנוֹת שֵׁם הַגְּדֹלָה לֵאָה וְשֵׁם הַקְּטַנָּה רָחֵל: יז וְעֵינֵי לֵאָה רַכּוֹת וְרָחֵל הָיְתָה יְפַת־תֹּאַר וִיפַת מַרְאֶה:

שלישי יח וַיֶּאֱהַב יַעֲקֹב אֶת־רָחֵל וַיֹּאמֶר אֶעֱבָדְךָ שֶׁבַע שָׁנִים בְּרָחֵל בִּתְּךָ הַקְּטַנָּה: יט וַיֹּאמֶר לָבָן טוֹב תִּתִּי אֹתָהּ לָךְ מִתִּתִּי אֹתָהּ לְאִישׁ אַחֵר שְׁבָה עִמָּדִי: כ וַיַּעֲבֹד יַעֲקֹב בְּרָחֵל שֶׁבַע שָׁנִים וַיִּהְיוּ בְעֵינָיו כְּיָמִים אֲחָדִים בְּאַהֲבָתוֹ אֹתָהּ: כא וַיֹּאמֶר יַעֲקֹב אֶל־לָבָן הָבָה אֶת־אִשְׁתִּי כִּי מָלְאוּ יָמָי וְאָבוֹאָה אֵלֶיהָ: כב וַיֶּאֱסֹף לָבָן אֶת־כָּל־אַנְשֵׁי הַמָּקוֹם וַיַּעַשׂ מִשְׁתֶּה: כג וַיְהִי בָעֶרֶב וַיִּקַּח אֶת־לֵאָה בִתּוֹ וַיָּבֵא אֹתָהּ אֵלָיו וַיָּבֹא אֵלֶיהָ: כד וַיִּתֵּן לָבָן לָהּ אֶת־זִלְפָּה שִׁפְחָתוֹ לְלֵאָה בִתּוֹ שִׁפְחָה: כה וַיְהִי בַבֹּקֶר וְהִנֵּה־הִוא לֵאָה וַיֹּאמֶר אֶל־לָבָן מַה־זֹּאת עָשִׂיתָ לִּי הֲלֹא בְרָחֵל עָבַדְתִּי עִמָּךְ וְלָמָּה רִמִּיתָנִי: כו וַיֹּאמֶר לָבָן לֹא־יֵעָשֶׂה כֵן בִּמְקוֹמֵנוּ לָתֵת הַצְּעִירָה לִפְנֵי הַבְּכִירָה: כז מַלֵּא שְׁבֻעַ זֹאת וְנִתְּנָה לְךָ גַּם־אֶת־זֹאת בַּעֲבֹדָה אֲשֶׁר תַּעֲבֹד עִמָּדִי עוֹד שֶׁבַע־שָׁנִים אֲחֵרוֹת:

ויעש

טו וַאֲמַר לָבָן לְיַעֲקֹב הֲמִדְאָחִי אַתְּ וְתִפְלְחִנַּנִי מַגָּן חַוִּי לִי מָה־אַגְרָךְ: טז וּלְלָבָן תַּרְתֵּין בְּנָן שׁוּם רַבְּתָא לֵאָה וְשׁוּם זְעֵרְתָא רָחֵל: יז וְעֵינֵי לֵאָה יָאֲיָן וְרָחֵל הֲוָת שַׁפִּירָא בְּרֵיוָא וְיָאֲיָא בְּחֶזְוָא: יח וּרְחֵם יַעֲקֹב יָת רָחֵל וַאֲמַר אֶפְלְחִנָּךְ שְׁבַע שְׁנִין בְּרָחֵל בְּרַתָּךְ זְעֵרְתָּא: יט וַאֲמַר לָבָן טָב דְּאֶתֵּן יָתַהּ לָךְ מִדְּאֶתֵּן יָתַהּ לִגְבַר אָחֳרָן תֵּב עִמִּי: כ וּפְלַח יַעֲקֹב בְּרָחֵל שְׁבַע שְׁנִין וַהֲווֹ בְעֵינוֹהִי כְּיוֹמִין זְעֵירִין בִּדְרָחֵים יָתַהּ: כא וַאֲמַר יַעֲקֹב לְלָבָן הַב יָת אִתְּתִי אֲרֵי אַשְׁלִימוּ יוֹמַי וְאֵיעוֹל לְוָתַהּ: כב וּכְנַשׁ לָבָן יָת־כָּל־אֱנָשׁ אַתְרָא וַעֲבַד מִשְׁתְּיָא: כג וַהֲוָה בְרַמְשָׁא וּדְבַר יָת־לֵאָה בְרַתֵּהּ וְאָעֵיל יָתַהּ לְוָתֵהּ וְעָל לְוָתַהּ: כד וִיהַב לָבָן לַהּ יָת־זִלְפָּה אַמְתֵהּ לְלֵאָה בְרַתֵּהּ לְאַמְהוּ: כה וַהֲוָה בְצַפְרָא וְהָא הִיא לֵאָה וַאֲמַר לְלָבָן מָה־דָא עֲבַדְתְּ לִי הֲלָא בְרָחֵל פְּלָחִית עִמָּךְ וּלְמָא שַׁקַּרְתְּ־בִּי: כו וַאֲמַר לָבָן לָא־אִתְעֲבֵד כְּדֵין בְּאַתְרָנָא לְמִתַּן זְעֵרְתָא קֳדָם רַבְּתָא: כז אַשְׁלֵים שְׁבֻעְתָּא דָא וְנִתֵּן לָךְ אַף־יָת־דָא בְּפָלְחָנָא

וְאַף עַל פִּי כֵן לֹא כֵן תּוֹעִיל שְׂכָרִי רַמָּזוּ: (כח) מָלְאוּ יָמָי. שֶׁאָמְרָה לִי אִמִּי. וְעוֹד מָלְאוּ יְמֵי שֶׁהֲרֵי אֲנִי בֶן פ"ד שָׁנָה וְאֵימָתַי אַעֲמִיד י"ב שְׁבָטִים חֲבוֹ שֶׁנֶּאֱמַר וַאֲבוֹאָה אֵלֶי' וַהֲלֹא קַל שֶׁבַּקַּלִים אֵינוֹ אוֹמֵר כֵּן אֶלָּא לְהוֹלִיד תּוֹלָדוֹת אָמַר כֵּן: (כה) וַיְהִי בַבֹּקֶר וְהִנֵּה הִוא לֵאָה. אֲבָל בַּלַּיְלָה לֹא הָיְתָה לֵאָה לְפִי שֶׁמָּסַר יַעֲקֹב סִימָנִים לְרָחֵל וּכְשֶׁרָאֲתָה רָחֵל שֶׁמַּכְנִיסִין לוֹ לֵאָה אָמְרָה עַכְשָׁיו תִּכָּלֵם אֲחוֹתִי עָמְדָה וּמָסְרָה לָהּ אוֹתָן סִימָנִים (מגילה יג:): (כז) מַלֵּא שְׁבֻעַ זֹאת. דְּנָק סוֹף שֶׁבַע נָקוּד בְּחָטָף (פי' נ"מ"א) שְׁבַע שֶׁל זֹאת וְהֵן שִׁבְעַת יְמֵי הַמִּשְׁתֶּה יְרוּשַׁלְמִי בְּמוֹעֵד קָטָן (וְא"ת לוֹמַר שְׁבוּעַ מַמָּשׁ שֶׁבַע שֶׁל לְגַּלְנֵי לֵינַקַּד בְּפַתַּח כַּשְׁ"ף). וְטוּ שֶׁטְּבוּעַ לְשׁוֹן שֶׁבַע כְּדִכְתִיב שֶׁבְעַת שָׁבוּעוֹת תִּסְפָּר לָךְ אֵין מִשְׁמַע שְׁבַע אֶלָּא שָׁבַע שְׁבֻעוֹת שְׁבִיעוֹת בְּלַעַ"ז נְקֵדָה וְנִגְבֶּלֶה אַף זֶה ל' וְנִתַּן: נִתְּנָה לָךְ: מִיַּד לְאַחַר שְׁבַע יְמֵי הַמִּשְׁתֶּה

לוֹ אֲבָל בְּנַקֶּה בְּכֻלָּם לֹא אָמַר אֲשֶׁר הַמַּכְשִׁיטִין אֲשֶׁר נָתְנוּ לוֹ בְמַתָּב הַנְּעָרוֹת: (סו) הֲכִי אָחִי אַתָּה וַעֲבַדְתַּנִי חִנָּם. לֹא אָמַר בַּכָּמַר שֶׁהָיָה כֵּן שֶׁהִיא יַעֲקֹב טוֹבֵד אוֹתוֹ וְיִתֵּן כִּי מֵעַת שֶׁאָמַר וְשָׁם אֵת לָבָן לֹא אָמַר לוֹ אָחִי לֹא יַלֵּד שֶׁלֹּאן מִידוֹ כִּי בְּכַמּוּתוֹ אִם רָאֵל כִּי כּוֹעֵס שֶׁיֵּא מַפֵּל עָלָיו שֶׁלֹּא תָּשׁוּב לְהַמֵּס לָהֶן עַל וְסִיס שׁוֹב כּוֹעֵס אוֹתָן בִּלְאֵנַת אוֹתָם וְאוֹמֵר עוֹד לֵיתוֹל עוֹד כִּי לָבָן דֶּגֶל בַּעֲרַמָּה אָחַב לוֹ מִתְהַלֵּל כִּי עֶלְמוֹ וְנַסְבַּר הוּא וִיסַפֵּל עָלָיו כְּאֲשֶׁר יִשְׁמֹאל סוֹדָם עַל עַלְמוֹ וְעַל בְּשָׂרוֹ וְכַאֲשֶׁר כָּלָה אֲשֶׁר שֶׁהָיָה יַעֲקֹב מִתְהַלֵּל שָׁם מִתְחַרְנֵם מֵאֲשֶׁר מַלְּאָן לְלָבָן אָמַר לוֹ הֲכִי אָחִי אַתָּה וַעֲבַדְתַּנִי חִנָּם כִּי יָדַעְתִּי כִּי מֵעַתָּה תַּעֲבוֹד אוֹתִי כִּי לֹא

Exercise 8.1c

Now, we know that the Masoretes did a lot of work on the biblical text—but we haven't established that they were commentators. To understand what they've added to the tradition, try this puzzle:

1 Make sense out of these letters:

andhecametohisfatherandsaidmyfathe
randhesaidhereamiandhesaidwhoareyo
umysonandjacobsaidtohisfatheriamesa
uyourfirstborn.

_____
_____
_____
_____
_____
_____

2 There is more than one way of breaking the same words (in the same order) into sentences.

ויאמר יעקב אל־אביו אנכי עשו בכרך

Here are two ways of breaking it into a sentence (with a translation of each).

ויאמר יעקב אל־אביו

אנכי עשו

בכרך

**And Jacob said to his father
"I am Esau,
your first-born."**

ויאמר יעקב אל־אביו

אנכי

עשו בכרך

**And Jacob said to his father
"I am.
Esau is your first-born."**

Clue: This verse is in response to the question: "Which of my sons are you?"

Explain the difference in meaning between the two versions.

_____
_____
_____
_____

Originally, the Torah was written without vowels, punctuation, or even spaces between words. The Masoretes added spaces, punctuation, and "trope." These were all added by the Masoretes. (What did they add to the tradition?)

_____
_____
_____
_____
_____

If you look at the next page, you should be able to identify four parts of this half page of *Mikraot Gedolot*.

1. The **Masoretic text** of the Torah.

2. On the left of the text, under the letters (Onkelos), is the **Targum**. Targum is the Aramaic translation of the Bible.

3. Below the Targum, you find the letters מְסוֹרָה (**Masorah**). These are the notes on the way the text is written.

4. Below the Masorah are the letters תא. These two letters stand for תּוֹלְדוֹת אַהֲרוֹן/**Toledot Aharon**. *Toledot Aharon* is an index of biblical passages that appears in the Babylonian Talmud. It was edited by Aaron of Pesaro, a sixteenth-century Italian scholar and businessman.

בראשית כט ויצא

טו וַיֹּאמֶר לָבָן לְיַעֲקֹב הֲכִי־אָחִי אַתָּה וַעֲבַדְתַּנִי חִנָּם הַגִּידָה לִּי מַה־מַּשְׂכֻּרְתֶּךָ: טז וּלְלָבָן שְׁתֵּי בָנוֹת שֵׁם הַגְּדֹלָה לֵאָה וְשֵׁם הַקְּטַנָּה רָחֵל: יז וְעֵינֵי לֵאָה רַכּוֹת וְרָחֵל הָיְתָה יְפַת־תֹּאַר וִיפַת מַרְאֶה: שלישי יח וַיֶּאֱהַב יַעֲקֹב אֶת־רָחֵל וַיֹּאמֶר אֶעֱבָדְךָ שֶׁבַע שָׁנִים בְּרָחֵל בִּתְּךָ הַקְּטַנָּה: יט וַיֹּאמֶר לָבָן טוֹב תִּתִּי אֹתָהּ לָךְ מִתִּתִּי אֹתָהּ לְאִישׁ אַחֵר שְׁבָה עִמָּדִי: כ וַיַּעֲבֹד יַעֲקֹב בְּרָחֵל שֶׁבַע שָׁנִים וַיִּהְיוּ בְעֵינָיו כְּיָמִים אֲחָדִים בְּאַהֲבָתוֹ אֹתָהּ: כא וַיֹּאמֶר יַעֲקֹב אֶל־לָבָן הָבָה אֶת־אִשְׁתִּי כִּי מָלְאוּ יָמָי וְאָבוֹאָה אֵלֶיהָ: כב וַיֶּאֱסֹף לָבָן אֶת־כָּל־אַנְשֵׁי הַמָּקוֹם וַיַּעַשׂ מִשְׁתֶּה: כג וַיְהִי בָעֶרֶב וַיִּקַּח אֶת־לֵאָה בִתּוֹ וַיָּבֵא אֹתָהּ אֵלָיו וַיָּבֹא אֵלֶיהָ: כד וַיִּתֵּן לָבָן לָהּ אֶת־זִלְפָּה שִׁפְחָתוֹ לְלֵאָה בִתּוֹ שִׁפְחָה: כה וַיְהִי בַבֹּקֶר וְהִנֵּה־הִוא לֵאָה וַיֹּאמֶר אֶל־לָבָן מַה־זֹּאת עָשִׂיתָ לִּי הֲלֹא בְרָחֵל עָבַדְתִּי עִמָּךְ וְלָמָּה רִמִּיתָנִי: כו וַיֹּאמֶר לָבָן לֹא־יֵעָשֶׂה כֵן בִּמְקוֹמֵנוּ לָתֵת הַצְּעִירָה לִפְנֵי הַבְּכִירָה: כז מַלֵּא שְׁבֻעַ זֹאת וְנִתְּנָה לְךָ גַּם־אֶת־זֹאת בַּעֲבֹדָה אֲשֶׁר תַּעֲבֹד עִמָּדִי עוֹד שֶׁבַע־שָׁנִים אֲחֵרוֹת:

ויעש

אונקלוס

טו וַאֲמַר לָבָן לְיַעֲקֹב הֲמִדְּאָחִי אַתְּ וְתִפְלְחִנַּנִי מַגָּן חַוִּי לִי מָה אַגְרָךְ: טז וּלְלָבָן תַּרְתֵּין בְּנָן שׁוּם רַבְּתָא לֵאָה וְשׁוּם זְעֶרְתָּא רָחֵל: יז וְעֵינֵי לֵאָה יָאֲיָן וְרָחֵל הֲוַת שַׁפִּירָא בְּרֵיוָא וְיָאֵא בְּחֶזְוָא: יח וּרְחֵם יַעֲקֹב יָת רָחֵל וַאֲמַר אֶפְלְחִנָּךְ שְׁבַע שְׁנִין בְּרָחֵל בְּרַתָּךְ זְעֶרְתָּא: יט וַאֲמַר לָבָן טַב דְּאֶתֵּן יָתַהּ לָךְ מִדְּאֶתֵּן יָתַהּ לִגְבַר אָחֳרָן תִּיב עִמִּי: כ וּפְלַח יַעֲקֹב בְּרָחֵל שְׁבַע שְׁנִין וַהֲווֹ בְעֵינוֹהִי כְּיוֹמִין זְעֵרִין בִּדְרָחֵם יָתַהּ: כא וַאֲמַר יַעֲקֹב לְלָבָן הַב יָת אִתְּתִי אֲרֵי אַשְׁלִימוּ יוֹמֵי פְלַחְנִי וְאֵעוֹל לְוָתַהּ: כב וּכְנַשׁ לָבָן יָת כָּל אֱנָשֵׁי אַתְרָא וַעֲבַד מִשְׁתְּיָא: כג וַהֲוָה בְרַמְשָׁא וּדְבַר יָת לֵאָה בְרַתֵּהּ וְאָעֵיל יָתַהּ לְוָתֵהּ וְעַל לְוָתַהּ: כד וִיהַב לָבָן לַהּ יָת זִלְפָּה אַמְתֵהּ לְלֵאָה בְרַתֵּהּ לְאַמְהוּ: כה וַהֲוָה בְצַפְרָא וְהָא הִיא לֵאָה וַאֲמַר לְלָבָן מָה דָא עֲבַדְתְּ לִי הֲלָא בְרָחֵל פְּלָחִית עִמָּךְ וּלְמָא שַׁקַּרְתְּ בִּי: כו וַאֲמַר לָבָן לָא אִתְעֲבֵד כְּדֵין בְּאַתְרָנָא לְמִתַּן זְעֶרְתָּא קֳדָם רַבְּתָא: כז אַשְׁלֵים שְׁבֻעֲתָא דְּדָא וְנִתֵּן לָךְ אַף יָת דָּא בְּפֻלְחָנָא דִי תִפְלַח עִמִּי עוֹד שְׁבַע שְׁנִין אָחֳרָנְיָן:

מסרה טז אחי, מלׄא. לֵאָה, י"ד זקפין [ז"ל מלעיל]. הגידה, מ"ל. לי, דנגה מדין ל"ם. משכרתך, לי קמן ומׄ משכרתך שלמה. יז ועיני, מ"ל ל"ף, רכות, ג' וכו' ב יעקב, כל אׄ מסק. כא הבה, כל אׄ מסק בנטעמא מלרע [נגד הכלל]. ימי, הכ"ס קנמ וכו' ואׄ מסק. כב מ"ל. כב ויעסף, כל אׄ מסק. כד ללאה, ג' בעניב, ברוב ספרׄ בֹקזמׄ. ויתל, נמֹ, כׄ מסק. כה כה הוא, ויו ומיקר, ללאה, ל"ז. זֹאת, דנגה מד"ד. לי, דנגה מדין ל"ם, מסק. הלֹא, מסק. כו לֹא מלֹא, כו זֹאת מלֹא, ה' זֹאת ל"ז ל"ו. במקומנו, ל' ולׄ [מ"ו ומׄ"ל]. הצעירה, מ"ל. הבכירה, מ"ל. כז מלֵּא, כל אׄ מסק, עֹד מסק. מ"ל. שבֻע, מסק. ונתנה, ג' בעניב, כ"ל ל"ף במׄ"ב. אשר, במונמ. מעבֹד, כל אׄ מסק מ"ל מ"ל.
ת"א ועיני לֵאָה בתכלא סס. ויהי בבקר מגילה יג בתכלא קנב.

רש"י

ואף על פי כן לא תועיל שכרי כמסו: (כ) מלאו ימי. שאמרה לי אמי. ועוד מלאו ימי שהרי אני בן פ"ד שנה ואימתי אעמיד י"ב שבטים וזהו שנאמר ותאמר רבקה אלי אנא כן זֹאת תולדות אמר כך: (כה) ויהי בבקר והנה היא לֵאה. אבל בלילה לֹא היתה לֵאה לפי שנתן יעקב סימנים לרחל וכשראתה וכל שמכניסין לֹא לֹאה עשתה עצמה כרחל מסרה לֹאה אותן סימנים (מגילה יג:): (יג) (כז) מלֹא שבע זֹאת. דבק סֹל מלֹא שבֹע שֹל זֹאת וזהן שבע ימי המשתה נדרשת בֹמֹועד קטן (וֹלׄא לֹומר שבוע ימים שהם כן סֹיב לֹריך לֹינקד בפתח בֹסׄ'. ועוד שבוֹע לֹשון זכר כדכתיב שבֹעה שבֹעות תספר לֹמיך אין מטמע מטנֹ אלֹא שבֹעה שהם שפייׄא גלֹעׄ"ן): ונתנה לך זה כ' רבים כֹמו ונשֹרֹפֹה נגדלה ונכלה אף זה כׄ רבים ומטֹקᵃ המשתה

רמב"ן

עוֹסק אֹתה ולֹא תִּטַמֹטֹגֹכֹ מִטֹל לאֹכֹרים וגם אֹני אֹני כֹולֹה אֹינֹי שֹתֹסֹיס סענוֹדֹ שֹעוֹבֹדֹנֹי בֹתֹגֹם בֹלׄא מֹטֹכֹורֹת טֹליֹטֹ וֹהֹגֹידֹה לֹי אֹני תֹנֹבֹם לׄאֹם בֹתֹמֹטֹכֹוֹרֹתֹך. וֹאֹתֹה אֹז טֹכֹיֹר יֹעֹקֹב דֹעֹתֹו בֹּתֹעֹבֹוֹד אֹוֹתֹו ז' טֹניֹם בֹכֹרֹ וֹטֹעֹנֹוֹדֹה מֹן הֹקֹמֹה הֹיֹה מֹכֹרֹם כֹלֹאֹן כֹי אֹני טֹרֹיֹס וֹנֹב כֹי הֹיֹו מֹדֹנֹכֹיֹם: (כ) כֹי מֹלֹאֹו יֹמֹי. שֹאֹמֹרֹה לֹי אֹמֹי. וֹעֹוֹד כֹי מֹלֹאֹו יֹמֹי כֹי הֹרֹי אֹני בֹן פ"ד שֹנֹה וֹתֹמֹתֹי תֹעֹמֹיֹד י"ב טֹבֹתֹים לֹטֹון כֹ"ד: (כו) מֹלֹא שֹבֹע זֹאת. דֹבֹק סֹל מֹלֹא שֹבֹע שֹל זֹאת וֹהֹן ז' יֹמֹי הֹמֹטֹתֹה גֹם זֹה לֹטֹון כֹ"ט וֹאֹ"ו כֹמֹה זֹה פׄ' הֹנֹא מֹלֹאֹו יֹמֹי עֹל שֹר סֹעֹוֹדֹה וֹהֹגֹידֹו כֹדֹנֹרֹי אֹנֹקֹלֹוס טֹלֹמֹ וֹהֹוֹ מֹטֹמֹעֹה

סכתֹט

עיקר שפתי חכמים

ד כמ"ש ויֹשֹב עֹטֹו חֹדֹט יֹמֹים. ה. וֹהֹתֹיֹמֹה הֹוֹא עֹל וֹעֹבֹדֹתֹנֹי חֹנֹם וֹלֹא עֹל אֹחֹי תֹנֹם. ו לֹכֹ"פ דֹכֹיֹיֹוֹס אֹחֹדֹים הֹיֹו כֹימֹים אֹחֹדֹים שֹאֹמֹרֹה לֹו אֹמֹי. ז שֹאֹין תֹדֹרֹך הֹכֹוֹסֹר תֹהֹכֹיר יֹעֹקֹב לֹאֹר כֹלֹוֹת
למרונׄה כׄ"פ. תֹוֹתֹח תֹחֹוֹטֹכֹה גֹ' לֹכֹ"פ דֹכֹיֹיֹוֹס אֹחֹדֹים הֹיֹו כֹימֹים אֹחֹדֹים. ח אֹבֹל לֹא יֹתֹפֹרֹט וֹנֹתֹנֹה הֹגֹ"ן לֹגֹפֹעֹל וֹיֹתֹפֹרֹט כֹי רֹחֹל עֹגֹר וֹרֹחֹל עֹדֹיֹן לֹא נֹתֹנֹה לֹו: עֹנֹוֹדֹתֹו אֹת טֹכֹרֹו כֹי וֹנֹתֹנֹה הֹוֹא פֹעֹל עֹגֹר וֹרֹחֹל עֹדֹיֹן לֹא נֹתֹנֹה לֹו:

Here we continue the history of how Torah learning evolved. Up to now, we've seen the effect of the Masorah, the Targum, and the Midrash.

What happens to the Jews has often been the result of what is happening in the rest of the world. To understand the work and life of the medieval commentators, we've got to know what has been happening in the rest of the world.

Starting back in the days of the Roman Empire, more Jews lived in the Diaspora than in *Eretz Yisrael.* Jewish communities existed just about everywhere in the Roman Empire—large ones in Egypt, Rome, and Babylonia. By 395 (just as the Palestinian Talmud was being finished), the Roman Empire was split in half—east and west. By 500, the western empire (including Rome) had declined while the eastern empire gained strength. Meanwhile, Jewish life in the eastern empire continued to flourish. The Talmud was completed, and a majority of the work on the Midrash, the Targumim, and the Masorah had been done.

By 650, a man named Muhammad had lived and died, and in his wake a new religion, Islam, began the process of conquering the known world. Muslims did this through a jihad—a holy war. Quickly, Muslim forces swept through the Middle East, taking Babylonia, Egypt, northern Africa, and crossing over into Europe got as far as Spain. Inside the Islamic Empire, Jews did fairly well (even though there were some restrictions) and Jewish culture continued to prosper. The Masorah was finished under Islamic influence. While the Goths, Visigoths, Vandals, and other barbarian hordes were busy destroying the Roman Empire and creating the "Dark Ages," the Islamic Empire was advancing in the fields of science, medicine, art, and literature.

Jews who lived under Islamic influence learned from the culture around them. Judaism began to prosper, and Jews began bringing linguistics, philosophy, science, and other skills from their general culture to their study of the Torah. Jews of the Iberian Peninsula, who were the core of Jews living under Islamic influence, became known as Sephardim.

Spain was known as *Eretz Sephardi* and was the center of Sephardic culture. This may seem strange, since Spain was the meeting ground between Islam and Christianity—and there were often wars, persecutions, and conflicts. Nevertheless, in Spain Jewish art and scholarship thrived. Yet, during this "Golden Age" of Spanish Jewry, almost every major Jewish scholar and poet had to flee either from his city or from Spain.

Meanwhile, the Jews who lived under Christian influence developed their first great cultural center on the banks of the Rhine River (in what is now Germany). Jews began to call this area *Eretz Ashkenaz*. Soon the Jews from that region became known as *Ashkenazim*. As with the term *Sephardim*, the name *Ashkenazim* soon came to apply to most Jews living under Christian influence.

Unlike Sephardic Jewry, *Ashkenazim* lived in an isolated cultural world. Their scholars and teachers were almost exclusively influenced by the talmudic tradition as it had been handed down to them.

To generalize, one can say that Ashkenazic Bible commentators spent most of their efforts explaining the biblical text in light of midrashic and talmudic literature. In contrast, Sephardic commentators spent much of their time applying linguistics, lexicography, and philosophical inquiry to the text.

Starting with the Crusades (1066), the economy of Europe began to change. As key trade items—silk, cinnamon, the movable tiller, and other Islamic innovations—were brought into Europe by the returning Crusaders, an international trade network was established. Christian Europe wanted the products acquired through trade with the Islamic infidels. Market centers and guilds emerged, and Jews began to play a unique role as international bankers and agents. (Ironically, Jews who were not accepted fully in any land were the only ones to have contacts in every land.) This not only added stability to the daily life of many Jews but also expanded the communications between the diverse Jewish communities.

These changes formed an important backdrop to the "golden age" of Jewish biblical scholarship. Bible study became a leading Jewish art form—because the outside world was still by and large closed to the Jew. But it also came to grow and flourish, in spite of—and perhaps because of—the conflict, and because of the economic and cultural growth of the world economy.

יונתן בן עוזיאל   ירושלמי

ירושלמי   יונתן בן עוזיאל   ירושלמי   קג

(טו) אמר לכן לעקב המדאה אנת חזה ... תתפלחינגי
מן תגי לי בן תהי אנגרך : (טז) וללכן הוו תרתין בנן שום רבתא לאה
ושום זעירתא רחל : (יז) ועיני לאה הוון צריגתין מבכא ומצליא דלא תיסב קדם יי
דלא חזן לד לעשו רשיעא ורחל הות שפירא ביחואה :
(יח) ועיני דלאה הוו רגיבן על דהות בבא ומצלא דלא תיסק בסליה
דעשו ורחל הות יאה ברבא ושפירא בחזוא :

(יח) ורחם יעקב ית רחל ואמר אפלחינך שב שנין בכן רחל ברתך זעירתא :
(יט) אמר לבן בריטי טב דאתין יתה לך מדאתין יתה לגבר אחרן תוב עמי :
(כ) ופלח יעקב בגין רחל שב שנין והוו בעינוי כיומין קלילין מדלחים לותה :
(כא) ואמר יעקב ללבן הב ית אנתתי ארום אשלמית יומי פולחני ואעול
לותה : (כב) וכנש לבן ית כל אנשי אתרא ועבד להן שירוי עני ואמר
להון הא שב שנין דאתא יעקב לותן בכין לא חסרו בית שקוות פנו
ודין אתו נתעשא עלה עשא דר יסתן ליה עשאדחסי
לאתגבא ליה לאה חלף רחל :

בעל הטורים

רמב"ן

(כו) אשלים שבעתי יומי משתותא דלאד ואתן :

יונתן   תעבד

אבן עזרא

פירוש על אבן עזרא

ספורנו

פירוש רשב"ם

This half of the מִקְרָאוֹת גְּדוֹלוֹת /*Mikraot Gedolot* page introduces us to five commentators.

RASHI = Rabbi Solomon Yitzchaki. The most important of Jewish biblical commentators, he lived in Troyes, France, from 1040 to 1105. (We'll learn a lot more about him later in this module.)

RASHBAM = Rabbi Samuel Ben Meir. The Rashbam, another French commentator, was born in Ramerupt, France, in 1085 and died circa 1174. He was Rashi's grandson and student. His work was famous both for his halachic insight and for his commitment to finding *peshat*—the literal exposition of the meaning of the text.

IBN EZRA = Rabbi Abraham Ibn Ezra. (Ibn is the Arabic equivalent of *Ben.*) Ibn Ezra was born in Tudela, Spain, in 1089 and died in 1164(?). Until 1140 he lived in Spain; afterward he traveled extensively, living the life of a wandering scholar. During his travels, he wrote the biblical commentaries for which he is best known. Based on linguistics and careful examination of the biblical text, these commentaries, written in Hebrew, reflect great depth, clarity of thought, and a remarkable understanding of human nature.

RAMBAN = Rabbi Moses Ben Nachman = Nachmanides. An important Spanish commentator, Ramban was born in Gerona, Spain, in 1194 and died in 1270 in *Eretz Yisrael*. Besides writing his own commentaries, the Ramban was famous for defending Rambam's (Maimonides) works and for participating in a religious disputation with Jewish apostate Pablo Christiani. His published account of this dispute was burned, and he was prosecuted, barely escaping to *Eretz Yisrael*.

SFORNO = Obadiah Ben Jacob Sforno. He was born circa 1475 and died in 1550. He was an Italian physician and Bible commentator whose commentaries rely on plain meaning (*peshat*) and on philosophy but include no linguistic observations.

רש״י

וּלֵּף על פי כן לא הועיל שהרי רמזו : (כח) מלאני ימי . שאמרה לי אמי . ועוד מלאו ימי שהרי אני ב' פ״ד שנה ואימתי אעמיד י״ב שבטים וזהו שנאמר ואבואה אלי׳ והלא קל שבקלים אינו אומר כן זאלא להוליד תולדות אמר כך : (כה) ויהי בבקר והנה היא לאה . אבל בלילה לא היתה לאה לפי שמסר יעקב סימנים לרחל וכשראתה רחל שמכניסין לו לאה אמרה עכשיו תכלם אחותי עמדה ומסרה לה אותן סימנים (מגילה יג) : (מז) מלא שבע זאת . דנוק הוא שהרי נקוד נחטף (פי׳ בש״א) שבוע של זאת וכן שבעת ימי המשתה בגמרא ירושלמית במועד קטן (וח״א לומר שבוע ממש שאם כן היה צריך לינקד בפתח הט״ו). ושני שבועות לשון זכר כדכתיב שבעת שבועות תספר לפיכך אין משמע מטע אלא שבעת שטי״נא בלע״ז) : ונתנה לך . ל׳ רבים חכמו ונשרפה נכרדה ונגלה אף זה ל׳ רבים : גם את זאת . מיד לאחר שבעת ימי המשתה

רמב״ן

מוכר אתה ולא התחלפנא מטל אחרים וגם אני איני רוצה שתהיה העבודה שתעבדני בחנם בלא משכורת שליהיה והגידה לי מה תנקש לאתה נמשכורתך ואתן לך הביר יעקב דעתו אמר לו שיעבוד אותו ז' שנים בעבל ובעבודה מן הכחס היה מרעה הבקשה כי לה היו לריכים וגם היו מדנבים : (כח) כי מלאו ימי . שאמרה לי אמי ועוד כי מלאו ימי הריני בן פ״ד שנה ואימתי אעמיד י״ב שבטים לשון כש״י : (כה) מלא שבוע זאת . דנק הוא נחטף שבוע של זאת וכן ז׳ ימי המשתה גם זה ל׳ שבי״י וח׳ב לחה לא פי׳ הנא מלאו ימי על שני העבודה שאמר לו בתחלה כי ידעתי גם כי מעתה תעבוד אותי כי איש לו אכי אפי אתה ותעבדני גם כי מעתה תעבוד אותי כי איש

Exercise 8.2

QUESTION: Why do you think that Torah study was so important in this period? Why was it probably the leading Jewish art form?

_____

_____

_____

_____

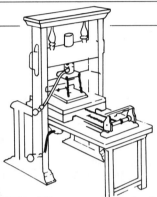

AN ANSWER: The great period of Jewish biblical commentary started with Rashi in the middle of the eleventh century and ended with Sforno in the mid-sixteenth century. The eleventh century was really the beginning of the growth of the great market centers and the beginning of guilds. The sixteenth century saw the growth of the printing press as a viable means of communication.

The printing press seemed to bring the "classical age" of Jewish commentary to an end. After Sforno, the world began changing rapidly through the application of new technologies. Changes in the economy brought the enlightenment through which Jews became full members of the communities in which they lived. As we will see in the next module, this new age brought new tools to the process of learning Torah.

קֹשִׁי /*koshi* (difficulty/problem)

קָשֶׁה /*kasheh* (hard)

קֻשְׁיָה /*kusheyah* (question)

אַרְבַּע קֻשְׁיוֹת /*arba kusheyot* (the four questions)

In a few pages we are going to begin to study Rashi's commentary on the Torah. Before we get there, we'll need to develop a new skill. In Module Three: "Close-Reading," we saw that the Torah was written. In Module Six: "Who Done It?" we learned that the assumption "God Wrote It" leads to a unique way of learning Torah. In Module Seven: "Reading the Torah with Rabbinic Eyes—Midrash" we learned how to learn midrash. We learned that a midrash starts with a question about the biblical text, and that in answering that question it often teaches an additional moral or message.

Before we get to Rashi, we're going to have to develop the skill of finding the problem in the verse (without looking at the answer). These questions or problems in the text are called קֻשְׁיוֹת /*kusheyot*.

In most Jewish commentaries on the Torah, five basic kinds of *kusheyot* are studied. These include some of the difficulties we defined in Modules Three, Four, and Five, as well as some new kinds of *kusheyot*.

The traditional commentators all assumed that God wrote the entire Torah. If God wrote it, then it must be *PERFECT*. That means that God would not have put anything extra into the Torah, that God would have arranged the Torah in a totally logical way.

REMEMBER, traditional Judaism believes that God intentionally put each of these *kusheyot* in the biblical text. Each difficulty is there to make us pause and learn something through struggling with it.

FIVE TYPES OF *KUSHEYOT*

CONTRADICTIONS

If God wrote the Torah, then there can be nothing written there which contradicts another part.

DIFFERING DETAILS BETWEEN TWO VERSIONS OF THE SAME STORY/LAW:

...male and female he created them. Gen. 1:27

and the Lord God formed the rib that He had taken from the man into a woman. Gen. 2:22

ONE STORY CONTRADICTS THE FACT OR PREMISE OF A PREVIOUS STORY:

And Cain knew his wife, and she conceived.... Gen. 4:17

(Where does she come from—Adam and Eve had only two sons?)

A BROKEN PATTERN OF SERIES:

(Once the Torah sets up a pattern, it must have a reason for breaking or changing it.)

In Gen. I, we have: one day... a second day... a third day... the sixth day.... (Why no "first day"? Why does day six rate a "the"?)

EXTRA LANGUAGE

If God wrote the Torah, everything in it must be there for a good reason. Nothing would be done just for emphasis or literary effect. Everything which seems to be extra, everything which is repeated, must be there to teach us something.

A PHRASE OR INCIDENT IS REPEATED:

In the beginning God created the heaven and the earth.... Gen. 1:1

When the Lord God made earth and heaven.... Gen. 2:4

(Once should have been enough. Notice also: heaven-earth/earth-heaven)

A SERIES OF PHRASES OR WORDS SAYING THE SAME THING:

Go from *your land*, from *your birthplace*, from your *father's house* to a land that I will show you.... Gen. 12:1

(God could have just said "Go to where I show you.")

EXTRA WORDS IN A SENTENCE:

And these are the days of the years of Abraham's life *which he lived*, a hundred threescore and fifteen years. Gen. 25:7

(Is "which he lived" needed?)

WORD REVERSALS:

Honor your father and your mother.... Exod. 20:12

You shall each revere his mother and father.... Lev. 19:3

(If we are going to repeat something, why change the order?)

NEXT TO EACH OTHER

If God wrote the Torah, then there must be a logic in the way it is put together. God must have had a reason to connect passages which don't immediately seem to follow one from the other.

TWO STORIES OR EVENTS ARE LINKED:

And it came to pass after these things.... Gen. 22:1

(Look it up and try to figure out after what things?)

TWO DISTINCT SUBJECTS JOINED INTO ONE SENTENCE:

You shall each revere his mother and his father, and keep My sabbaths.... Lev. 19:3

(What does revering mother and father have to do with Shabbat? If the two are next to each other, there must be a connection.)

BEHAVIOR

If God wrote the Torah, we would expect to find no limitations or evidence of human weakness in God. Similarly, biblical heroes should be the most righteous and law-abiding people imaginable.

SOMETIMES GOD SEEMS TO DO THINGS WE FEEL ARE "UNGODLIKE":

"And the Lord God called unto the man and said to him: "Where are you?" Gen. 3:9

(Shouldn't God know where he is? Does God need to ask?)

SOMETIMES BIBLICAL HEROES SEEM TO VIOLATE SOME OF THE COMMANDMENTS:

and he [Abraham] took cream and milk and the calf which he dressed, and he set it before them. Gen. 18:8

(Doesn't Abraham keep kosher? Biblical heroes are expected to follow all the commandments.)

GRAMMAR/MEANING

God should write Hebrew perfectly and clearly, but we find in some places obscure words or even bad grammar. There are some places where the meaning is confused or impossible to comprehend. (Many of these *kusheyot* are impossible to translate.)

SOMETIMES WE EXPECT ONE THING AND GET ANOTHER:

Let them make me a dwelling-place [sanctuary] that I may dwell in them. Exod. 25:8

(When God is talking about a sanctuary, we would expect that God, and not we, would dwell in it.)

SOMETIMES THE WAY A WORD IS USED IS INTERESTING:

Noah walked *with* God. Gen. 6:9

The Lord *before* whom I [Abraham] walk. Gen. 24:40

(Why does Noah walk with and Abraham walk before?)

Exercise 8.3

In the following quotations you'll find at least one *koshi*. They've all been put in *italics* for you. Your job is to:

a. Define these *kusheyot*. (What is the problem? What question does the text make us ask?)

b. Categorize the kind of *koshi*. (Contradiction, extra language, next to each other, behavior, or grammar/meaning.)

c. Identify where (what story or section) they come from.

d. Remember: Look for questions—we'll find answers later.

1 And you shall love the Lord your God with *all your heart*, with *all your soul*, and with *all your might*. Deut. 6:5

2 "Come and let us sell him to the *Ishmaelites*"...and there passed by *Midianites*, and they drew and lifted Joseph out of the pit, and sold Joseph to the *Ishmaelites*...and the *Midianites* sold him in Egypt. Gen. 37:27-36

3 And God said: "Let *Us* make man in **Our** image, *after our likeness*..." and God created man in *His own* image. Gen. 1:26-27

4 "How can *I, myself, alone,* bear *your* cumbrance, and *your* burden, and *your* strife." Deut. 1:12

5 And the Children of Israel were *fruitful,* and *increased abundantly,* and *multiplied,* and *waxed exceedingly mighty*....Exod. 1:7

6 And the Lord *called* unto Moses and *spoke* to him outside the Tent of Meeting, saying... Lev. 1:1

7 And you will say to Pharaoh: "Thus saith the Lord: '*Israel is My first-born....*'" Exod. 4:22

8 And the Lord said to Cain: "*Where is Abel your brother?*" Gen. 4:9

9 And *Jacob* was left alone, **and there wrestled with a man** until daybreak....And he said: "*Your name shall no longer be Jacob, but Israel,* **because you have struggled with God** and man and prevailed." Gen. 32:25-29

And God said to him: "Your name is *Jacob: your name shall not be called any more Jacob but* **Israel** *shall be your name.*" *And they called his name* **Israel**. Gen. 35:10

10 Now these are the names of the sons of *Israel* who came into Egypt with *Jacob*; every man came with his household. Exod. 1:1

_____

_____

11 And the servant took *ten camels, of the camels of his master,* and departed. Gen. 24:10

_____

_____

12 And *Jacob said* to his father: *"I am Esau, your first-born."* Gen. 27:19

_____

_____

13 And Isaac called Jacob and blessed him...and Isaac sent Jacob away and *he went to Paddan-aram....Now Esau saw...so Esau went to Ishmael and took wives....And Jacob went out of Beer-sheba and went towards* **Haran**. Gen. 28:1-10

_____

Exercise 8.4

In these selections you'll find hidden *kusheyot*:

a. Circle or underline these *kusheyot*.
b. Define/describe the *koshi*. Sometimes this involves comparing two quotes.
c. Remember—find questions, not answers.

1 Cursed be everyone who curses you and blessed be everyone who blesses you. Gen. 27:29

Blessed be everyone who blesses you and cursed be everyone who curses you. Num. 24:9

2 And Sarah laughed to herself, saying: "Now that I am withered, am I to have enjoyment with my husband so old?" Then the Lord* said to Abraham, "Why did Sarah laugh, saying: 'Shall I in truth bear a child, old as I am?'" Gen. 18:12-13

*Up to now, Abraham was talking to three visitors.

3 I will bring you out from under the burden of the Egyptians, and I will deliver you from their bondage, and I will redeem you with an outstretched arm. ...And I will take you to Me for a people. Exod. 6:6-7

4 Honor your father and your mother, that your days may be long upon the land which your God gave you. Exod. 20:12

Honor your father and your mother, as the Lord commanded you, that your days may be long, and that it may go well of you upon the land that the Lord your God gave you. Deut. 5:16

5 And if a man shall open a pit, or if a man shall dig a pit and not cover it, and an ox or an ass fall into it, the owner of the pit must make good, he shall give money to their owner and the dead beast shall be his. Exod. 21:33-34

6 And the angel of the LORD appeared to him in a flame of fire out of the midst of the bush...and when the LORD saw that he turned aside, God called to him out of the midst of the bush.... Exod. 3:4

7 And God spoke unto Israel in the visions of the night, and said: "Jacob, Jacob...." Gen. 46:2

8 The LORD, the LORD God, is merciful and gracious, long-suffering and abundant in goodness and truth, keeping mercy unto the thousandth generation, forgiving iniquity, transgression, and sin. Exod. 34:6-7

9 And Abraham said of Sarah his wife: "She is my sister." Gen. 20:2

10 Abraham buried Sarah his wife in the cave of the field of the Machpelah before Mamre—the same is Hebron—in the land of Canaan. Gen. 23:19

11 And the LORD said: "Shall I hide from Abraham that which I am doing, seeing that Abraham shall surely become a great and mighty nation...?" Gen. 18:17-18

12 מִי־כָמֹכָה בָּאֵלִם יהוה
מִי כָּמֹכָה נֶאְדָּר בַּקֹּדֶשׁ

Mi chamochah ba'elim Adonai Mi kamochah ne'edar ba-kodesh. Exod. 15:11

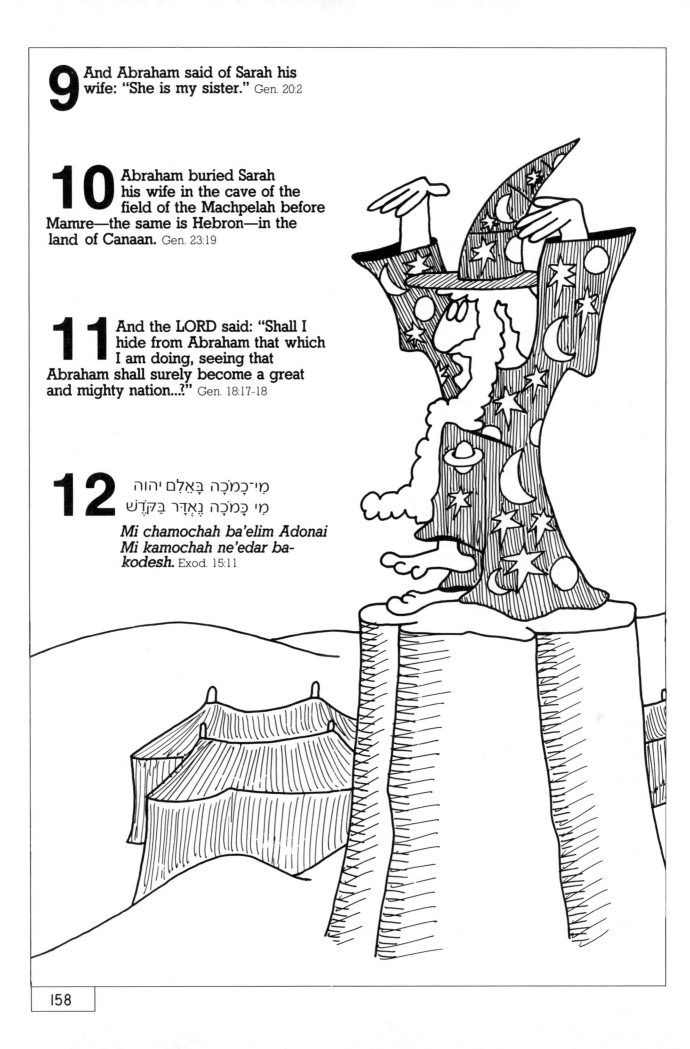

Exercise 8.5

a. Find the *kusheyot* in each of the pairs of quotes.
b. Then find the *koshi* discovered by comparing the quotations.

1 Remember the sabbath day to keep it holy...for in six days the LORD made heaven and earth...and on the seventh He rested....The Lord blessed the sabbath day and hallowed it. Exod. 20:8-11

Observe the sabbath day to keep it holy. For you shall remember that you were a slave in the land of Egypt and the Lord your God brought you out of there with a mighty hand and an outstretched arm; therefore the Lord your God commanded you to keep the sabbath day. Deut. 5:12-15

_____

2 The Lord spoke unto Moses, saying, "Send men to scout the land of Canaan which I am giving to the Children of Israel. Send one man from each of their ancestral tribes, each one a chieftain among them." Num. 13:1-2

Then all of you came to me [Moses] and said: "Let us send men ahead to explore the land for us and bring back word on the route we shall follow and the cities we shall come to." I approved the plan, so I selected twelve of your men, one from each tribe. Deut. 1:22-23

_____

3 And the Lord spoke unto Moses, saying: "Speak unto the Children of Israel, saying...." (Over a hundred times in the Torah)

And the Lord spoke unto Moses, saying: "Speak unto all the congregation of the Children of Israel, and say unto them ..." Lev. 19:1-2

_____

4 And Abraham rose early in the morning and took bread and water and gave it to Hagar and put it on her shoulder and the child, and sent her away. Gen. 21:14

And Abraham rose early in the morning, and saddled his ass, and took two of his young men with him, and Isaac his son; and he cleaved the wood for the burnt-offering, and rose up, and went unto the place that God had told him. Gen. 22:3

_____

Exercise 8.6

GENESIS 22

Now try to find the *kusheyot* in a real chapter of Torah. Define the *koshi* in the appropriate place in the right-hand column.

And it came to pass *after these things*, that *God tested* Abraham, and said to him: "Abraham"; and he said: "Here I am." And He said: "Take—please, *your son, your only son, whom you love—Isaac*, and go to the land of Moriah, and *offer him there for a burnt-offering upon one of the mountains which I will show you*." **Abraham** rose early in the morning, and **saddled his ass, and took two of his young men, and he chopped wood for the burnt-offering**, and rose up, and went to the place that God had told him of. *On the third day*, Abraham lifted up his eyes and saw the place in the distance, and Abraham said to his young men: "Wait here with the ass, and I and the lad will go yonder, *and we will worship and come back to you*." And Abraham took the wood of the burnt-offering, and laid it upon Isaac his son; and he took in his hand the fire and the knife, and they went both of them together, and Isaac spoke to his father and said: "My father" and he said "Here I am, my son." And he said: "Here is the fire and the wood, but where is the lamb for the burnt-offering?" and Abraham said: "*God will provide for Himself the lamb* for the burnt-offering, my son." So they went, both of them together. **And they came to the place which God had told him of,** and

1. After these things.

2. God tested.

3. Your son, your only son, whom you love—Isaac.

4. Offer him...

5. Abraham...saddled his ass...

6. And took two of his young men...

7. On the third day.

8. And we will worship and come back to you.

9. God will provide...the lamb (or God will see for Himself the lamb).

10. Place which God had told him of.

11. And the angel of the Lord.

12. Abraham, Abraham.

13. Lay not your hand...nor do anything...

14. Now I know.

15. Your son, your only son.

Abraham built the altar there, and bound Isaac his son, and laid him on the altar, on the wood. And Abraham stretched forth his hand, and took the knife to slay his son. *And the angel of* **the Lord** called to him out of heaven, and said: *"Abraham, Abraham."* And he said: "Here I am." And he said: *"Lay not your hand upon the lad, nor do anything to him,* for **now I know** that you are a God-fearing man, seeing you have not withheld *your son, your only son, from Me."*

AND NOW—INTRODUCING RASHI

When Jews sat down weekly to read *parashat hashavua* (the weekly Torah portion), twice in Hebrew and once in translation, the volumes and volumes of Talmud and Midrash were too much to go through, so along came the commentators, who excerpted chunks from the Talmud and the Midrash to make things easier. The pressing need for an adequate and complete commentary on the Bible and the Talmud prompted Rashi to write his interpretation of these two works.

Rashi's style is simple and concise. His object was to present learners with a path to the direct and rational meaning of the text. At the same time, he wanted to provide his readers with access to the major midrashim on a given passage, and to significant talmudic law which was drawn from the passage. Rashi didn't write sermons; he wrote a tool from which Jews could work their way through the text and extract its meaning. His commentaries were a guidebook, providing direction for learners struggling with the text's meaning.

At twenty-five he founded an academy which attracted many students. Many halachic questions were addressed to him and his decisions have been preserved in the works of his students. Rashi's commentary is a work of art, providing direction and clarity without over-teaching or drifting into polemic.

אונקלוס

א בְּקַדְמִין בְּרָא יְיָ יַת שְׁמַיָּא וְיַת אַרְעָא: ב וְאַרְעָא הֲוָת צַדְיָא

בראשית א

א בְּרֵאשִׁית בָּרָא אֱלֹהִים אֵת הַשָּׁמַיִם וְאֵת

רש"י

אבן עזרא

רמב"ן

A LOOK AT THE WAY RASHI WORKS

אֵלֶּה תּוֹלְדֹת נֹחַ נֹחַ אִישׁ צַדִּיק תָּמִים הָיָה בְּדֹרֹתָיו אֶת־הָאֱלֹהִים הִתְהַלֶּךְ־נֹחַ

This is the line of Noah—Noah was a righteous man; he was blameless in his age [generation]; Noah walked with God. (Gen. 6:9)

We examined this verse as part of the post-test in Module Seven. Do you remember the *koshi* or can you work out what Rashi finds difficult? Write what you think is Rashi's question.

_____

_____

_____

(Or read Rashi's commentary. He doesn't state the problem because he assumes you can find it on your own. If you are clever, you can work out the problem from the answer.)

RASHI'S COMMENTARY ON GEN. 6:9

In his generation: Some of our rabbis explain *in his generation* to Noah's credit—it follows that had he lived in a generation of righteous people he would have been even more righteous.

Others, however, explain *in his generation* to discredit Noah. In the context of his own generation, he was considered righteous but, had he lived in the generation of Abraham, he would not have been considered as important.

Explain Rashi's two answers to this *koshi* in your own words.
In his generation means _____
In his generation means _____
Where do you think that Rashi got these two answers? (Remember our midrash?)

_____

_____

_____

Rashi didn't invent these comments on this verse. He merely "brings" them to the learner. They can be found in the Talmud (San. 108a) and the Midrash (Gen. R. 30:9).

Rabbi Judah and Rabbi Nehemiah disagreed.

Rabbi Judah said: Only in his age was he a righteous man. If he had lived in the time of Moses or Samuel, he would not have been called righteous.
In the street of the totally blind, a one-eyed man is called a visionary and the infant is called a scholar.
This can be compared to a man who had a wine vault and who opened one barrel and found it vinegar, then opened another and found it vinegar, but the third barrel had only begun to turn sour. People told him, "It is turning," but he said, "Is there any better?" This is the meaning of *in his age*.

Rabbi Nehemiah said: If he was righteous in his age, he would have been even more righteous in the age of Moses.
Compare him to a tightly closed pail of perfume lying in a graveyard (full of the stench of rotting bodies) that still gave off a pleasant odor. It would smell even better outside the graveyard. (Gen. R. 30:9)

Underline in this text those portions Rashi utilized in his commentary. See if you can figure out the guidelines Rashi uses in drawing from the sources.

_____
_____
_____
_____
_____
_____

Based on what you've learned so far, how does Rashi work, both as a teacher and as a commentator?

_____
_____
_____
_____
_____
_____
_____

Exercise 8.8a

1

And [Joseph's brothers] took him, and cast him in the pit. The pit was empty; there was no water in it. (Gen. 37:24)

RASHI: The pit was empty; there was no water in it: Since it states "the pit was empty," do I not know that "there was no water in it"? Why then does the Torah say "there was no water in it"? Not only did it not contain water, but also there were no snakes or scorpions in it. (Shab. 22a)

A. What is the *koshi*? (State both the type and the question.)

_____

_____

_____

B. How does Rashi solve this *koshi*?

_____

_____

_____

C. Is there a proof-text? (If so—what does it prove?)

_____

_____

D. From where does Rashi learn this explanation?

_____

_____

E. Is there a message being taught? (If so, what is the moral?)

_____

_____

_____

_____

2

These are the words that Moses addressed to all Israel on the other side of the Jordan.— Through the wilderness, in the Arabah near Suph, between Paran and Tophel, Laban, Hazeroth, and Di-zahab.
(Deut. 1:1)

RASHI: Between Paran and Tophel: Rabbi Yochanan said: We have gone through the whole Bible and we have found no place where the name of Tophel or Laban is mentioned. But the meaning here is that he rebuked them because of the תֹפֶל tophel/calumnious statements they made about the manna, which was לָבָן /lavan—white in color. And they said: Our souls hate this light bread.... (Num. 21:5; cf. Sifre; Ber. 32a)

A. What is the *koshi*? (State both the type and the question.)

_____

_____

_____

B. How does Rashi solve this *koshi*?

_____

_____

C. Is there a proof-text? (If so—what does it prove?)

_____

_____

D. From where does Rashi learn this explanation?

_____

E. Is there a message being taught? (If so, what is the moral?)

_____

_____

_____

3 These are the offspring of Aaron and Moses at the time that the Lord spoke with Moses on Mt. Sinai. And these are the names of Aaron's sons: Nadab, the first-born, and Abihu, Eleazar, and Ithamar.... (Num. 3:1-2)

RASHI: And these are the offspring of Aaron and Moses: But it mentions only the sons of Aaron! But they are also called the sons of Moses because he taught them Torah. This teaches us that whoever teaches Torah to the son of his neighbor is considered as though she/he is the child's parent. (San. 19b)

At the time that the Lord spoke with Moses: The children of Aaron became Moses' because then was the first time that he taught them what he had learned from God.

A. What is the *koshi*? (State both the type and the question.)

_____

_____

_____

B. How does Rashi solve this *koshi*?

_____

_____

_____

C. Is there a proof-text? (If so—what does it prove?)

_____

_____

D. From where does Rashi learn this explanation?

_____

_____

E. Is there a message being taught? (If so, what is the moral?)

_____

_____

_____

_____

4 So the LORD said to him, "Go down, and come back together with Aaron; but let not the priests break through to come up to the LORD, lest He break out against them." And Moses went down to the people and spoke to them.

God spoke all these words, saying: I am the LORD your God who brought you out of the land of Egypt, the house of bondage. (Exod. 19:24-20:2)

RASHI: God spoke all these words: The name אֱלֹהִים /*Elohim* (God) is the term for a judge. These chapters of the Torah are material where if a person obeys these *mitzvot,* she/he will receive a reward, and if she/he does not observe them, there is no punishment. However, to show that the Ten Commandments are different from the surrounding material, the Torah says: **"God spoke,"** meaning *God who is judge*, and who will exact punishment. (Mechilta)

A. What is the *koshi*? (State both the type and the question.)

_____

_____

_____

B. How does Rashi solve this *koshi*?

_____

_____

_____

C. Is there a proof-text? (If so—what does it prove?)

_____

_____

D. From where does Rashi learn this explanation?

_____

_____

E. Is there a message being taught? (If so, what is the moral?)

_____

_____

Exercise 8.8b

For each of these comments by Rashi, find the following:

1. The *koshi*.
2. The solution.
3. The proof-text (if one is used).
4. The message being taught.
5. Rashi's source.

1 If any man insults his father or mother, he shall be put to death; he has insulted his father and his mother—his bloodguilt is upon him. (Lev. 20:9)

RASHI: If any man insults his father or mother: These words seem to repeat themselves, but their intent is that anyone who insults his parents after they are dead or while they are alive is subject to the death penalty. (Sifra; San. 85b)

A. What is the *koshi*? (State both the type and the question.)

_____

_____

_____

B. How does Rashi solve this *koshi*?

_____

_____

_____

C. Is there a proof-text? (If so—what does it prove?)

_____

_____

D. From where does Rashi learn this explanation?

_____

_____

E. Is there a message being taught? (If so, what is the moral?)

_____

_____

2 The Lord God called out to the man and said to him, "Where are you?" (Gen. 3:9)

RASHI: Where are you?: God knew where he was but asked the question in order to start a conversation—so that he should not be confused in his reply—as if God were beginning by punishing him. Similarly, in the case of Cain, God said to him, "**Where is your brother Abel?**" (Gen. 4:9)

Similarly with Balaam: "**What do these people want of you?**" (Num. 22:9) —to begin a conversation with them....

A. What is the *koshi*? (State both the type and the question.)

_____

_____

_____

B. How does Rashi solve this *koshi*?

_____

_____

_____

_____

C. Is there a proof-text? (If so—what does it prove?)

_____

_____

D. From where does Rashi learn this explanation?

_____

_____

E. Is there a message being taught? (If so, what is the moral?)

_____

_____

_____

3 Then, whenever Moses held up his hand, Israel prevailed; but when he let down his hand, Amalek prevailed. (Exod. 17:11)

RASHI: When Moses held up his hand—But could Moses' hands win the battle? To understand this, see the whole passage in Rosh Hashanah 29a.

A. What is the *koshi?* (State both the type and the question.)

_____

_____

_____

B. How does Rashi solve this *koshi?*

_____

_____

_____

_____

C. Is there a proof-text? (If so—what does it prove?)

_____

_____

_____

D. From where does Rashi learn this explanation?

_____

_____

_____

E. Is there a message being taught? (If so, what is the moral?)

_____

_____

_____

_____

4 But Moses changed the name of Hosea son of Nun to Joshua. (Num. 13:16)

RASHI: Changing his name was part of praying for him—"May God save you from the evil counsel of the spies." (Sotah 34b)

His name, הוֹשֵׁעַ/*Hosea*, which means "saving," became יְהוֹשֻׁעַ/**Yehoshua**, which means "May God save ..."

A. What is the *koshi?* (State both the type and the question.)

_____

_____

_____

B. How does Rashi solve this *koshi?*

_____

_____

_____

C. Is there a proof-text? (If so—what does it prove?)

_____

_____

D. From where does Rashi learn this explanation?

_____

_____

E. Is there a message being taught? (If so, what is the moral?)

_____

_____

_____

_____

5 **Keep and hear all the words that I command you; thus it will go well with you and with your descendants after you forever, for you will be doing what is good and right in the sight of the LORD your God.** (Deut. 12:28)

RASHI: Keep and hear [understand] **all these words which I command you:** The word שְׁמֹר/*shemor* (keep) refers to the study of the Oral Law—that you must keep it within you. This is what is taught in Proverbs 22:17-18, *"And apply your heart to my knowledge...for it is a pleasant thing if you keep...[it] within you."* Because, only if you learn, is it possible to understand and act correctly. (Sifre, cf. Rashi on 4:6)

All the words: This teaches that a "light" commandment should be considered as carefully as a "heavy" commandment.

What is good: This refers to that which is proper in God's eyes.

And right: This refers to what is proper in people's eyes. (Sifre)

A. What are the three *kusheyot*? (State both the type and the question.)

_____
_____
_____
_____
_____
_____
_____
_____
_____

B. How does Rashi solve them?

_____
_____
_____

C. Is there a proof-text? (If so—what does it prove?)

_____
_____

D. From where does Rashi learn this explanation?

_____
_____
_____

E. Is there a message being taught? (If so, what is the moral?)

_____
_____
_____
_____

RASHI AS A TEACHER

Learning with Rashi's commentary is like having a private tutor sitting by your side. His work isn't "user-friendly"; in fact, it's often quite demanding, but, as you learn his tricks, Rashi is there holding your hand, helping you over the hard points, and making you a better Torah learner.

Obviously, I've never met Rashi, and little biographic material is available, but his personality comes through in his work. First, he is quiet and patient. He doesn't shout out—"You are going to learn three things from this passage." Rather, he sits waiting in the margins. As I'm reading the text and something isn't clear, I turn to him. Usually, he is waiting with an answer which begins, "I thought you might have a problem with this verse." Then, rather than giving a full answer, he begins with a few cryptic words—a hint and gentle sigh...."Now go work it out for yourself." Sometimes I scream in anger, "Why can't you just tell me what you're trying to teach me." But Rashi doesn't say anything. His commentary just echoes—"Look at the text again; think; you'll find it." And in the end, with satisfaction like that of the mountain-climber who has reached the top, my understanding of the text has brought me the satisfaction of owning this small piece of Torah. Rashi just smiles and says: "I knew you could figure it out." He's that kind of teacher.

Other times, when I'm reviewing or skimming, I look directly at Rashi. He's always one up on me. He'll review all the problems he's found in a passage, and I'll think—I should have seen that one, or how could I have missed that connection. Even so, Rashi is never loud or dramatic. His words work like a road sign, pointing the direction towards the next under-standing.

Clearly, Rashi has a vision of Torah learning as a way of life. For him, Torah isn't just knowledge or value statements, it isn't just rules and connections; it is a way of thinking and communicating. Rashi lived in the twelfth century, yet we talk regularly. He is that kind of teacher.

Rashi has a second objective too. For him, the Torah has to be read in context. It doesn't stand alone. As we read a passage, he will tell me to remember that this rule in the Talmud comes from this idea, or in the Midrash there is another idea which is like this. Jewish learning requires the making of connections, and Rashi is a master at reminding us how the rest of rabbinic literature grew from the Torah. For me, it is impossible to talk about Rashi in the past tense.

POST-TEST

This module has four objectives:

8.1 Trace the history of Jewish biblical commentary from the Masoretes through the commentators.
8.2 Identify *kusheyot* (difficulties/problems) by category in a biblical verse.
8.3 Follow a commentary by Rashi, identifying (a) the question, (b) the solution, (c) the moral/message, and (d) the use of proof-texts.
8.4 Express in your own words what can be gained from studying Torah "with rabbinic eyes."

The first of these (8.1) we are not going to test; you'll have to decide on your own competency.

If you completed Exercise 8.6, the identification of problems in chapter 22 of Genesis, you've fulfilled the second part.

Now for objective 8.3, here are Rashi's comments on the "Binding of Isaac." Your job is to identify the problem, solution, and moral.

PREPARATION

In Module Four: "Five Patterns" we talked a lot about "motivation." We understood that the "back-story" of characters helped us to understand the "sub-text" of many of their speeches. Often, the Torah makes us fill in both the back-story and the sub-text. Midrash often does that for us—and Rashi draws on midrash.

Fill this chart twice. First, before you begin this exercise, answer these questions from your own experience with this text; then, after you've completed it, fill in Rashi's answers.

	Your Opinion	Rashi's Opinion
1. Why does God need to "test" Abraham?		
2. By "testing" Abraham, is God cruel?		
3. Does Abraham just "go along" with God's request?		
4. Does Abraham know what he is doing?		
5. Does Isaac know what is happening?		
6. Did God "trick" Abraham?		
7. What is the "message" of this story?		

And it came to pass after these things, that God tested Abraham,

RASHI: After these things [words]: Some of our rabbis teach (San. 89b) that this means after the words of Satan who denounced Abraham (to God). He said: "Abraham prepares lots of banquets for people, but he never sacrifices anything to You." God said, "Everything he does is for the sake of his son [Isaac]; yet, if I asked him, 'Sacrifice him to Me,' he would not refuse."

Other rabbis teach that it was after the words of Ishmael, who boasted to Isaac that he had been circumcised when he was thirteen and had not resisted. Isaac said, "If God were to tell me, 'Sacrifice yourself to Me,' I would not refuse." (Cf. Gen. R. 55 and San. 89b)

Koshi:

Answer:

Lesson:

God tested: (Notice how Rashi deals with this koshi in his first comment.)

and said to him: "Abraham"; and he said: "Here I am."

Here I am: This is the answer given by a pious person; it shows meekness and **readiness.** (Tanch.)

Koshi:

Answer:

Lesson:

Take—please: The word נָא/na (please) is used to show that this is a request. God said: "I beg of you, stand firm for Me in this trial, so people may not say that the previous trials were not real tests."

Koshi:

Answer:

Lesson:

your son: Abraham said to God, "I have two sons [Ishmael and Isaac]." God said, "**Your only son.**" Abraham said, "Each is the 'only' son of his mother" [Sarah and Hagar]. Then God said, "**The one whom you love.**" Abraham said, "I love them both." Then God said, "**Isaac.**"

Koshi:

Answer:

Lesson:

and offer him [literally—bring him up]: God did not say, "Kill him," because the Holy One who is to be blessed did not want him killed; rather, God says to "bring him up" to the mountain and prepare him as a burnt-offering. So once he had been brought up, God said to him, "Bring him down."

Koshi:

Answer:

Lesson:

And He said: "Take—please, your son, your only son, whom you love—Isaac, and go to the land of Moriah,

and offer him there for a burnt-offering upon one of the mountains which I will show you."

Abraham rose early in the morning, and saddled his ass, and took two of his young men, and he chopped wood for the burnt-offering, and rose up, and went to the place that God had told him of.

Abraham rose early in the morning: He was alert to fulfill the command. (Pes. 4a)

Koshi:

Answer:

Lesson:

and saddled his ass: He did this himself and did not order one of his servants to do it, because love (of God) causes one to ignore the normal order of things.

Koshi:

Answer:

Lesson:

On the third day, Abraham lifted up his eyes and saw the place in the distance, and Abraham said to his young men: "Wait here with the ass,

On the third day: Why did God delay and not show it to him at once? So that people should not say, "God confused and confounded Abraham and bewildered his mind. This shows that with time for consideration he still obeyed God's command." (Tanch.)

Koshi:

Answer:

Lesson:

and I and the lad will go yonder, and we will worship and come back to you."

yonder: meaning a short distance (specifically the place in front of us). There is a midrashic explanation of כֹּה/*koh* (yonder)—"That I will see where it will be, and what will happen there, about the promise God made to me." (Gen. 15:5) *"Thus (כֹּה/koh), shall your seed be."* (Gen. R. 56)

and come back: He prophesied that they both would return.

Koshi: [blank box]	
Answer: [blank box]	
Lesson: [blank box]	

and they went both of them together: Abraham was aware that he was going to slay his son and walked along with the willingness and joy of Isaac, who had no idea of the matter.

Koshi: [blank box]

Answer: [blank box]

Lesson: [blank box]

And Abraham took the wood of the burnt-offering, and laid it upon Isaac his son; and he took in his hand the fire and the knife, and they went both of them together,

God will provide: The meaning is just as it seems—God will look out for and choose a lamb for Himself, and, if there will be no lamb for a burnt-offering, then **my son** will be the offering.

Koshi: [blank box]

Answer: [blank box]

Lesson: [blank box]

and Isaac spoke to his father and said: "My father" and he said: "Here I am, my son." And he said: "Here is the fire and the wood, but where is the lamb for the burnt-offering?" and Abraham said: "God will provide for Himself the lamb for the burnt-offering, my son."

So they went, both of them together: It was at this moment that Isaac understood that he was on his way to be killed, and yet they still both went with the same ready heart.

Koshi: [blank box]

Answer: [blank box]

Lesson: [blank box]

So they went, both of them together.

And they came to the place which God had told him of, and Abraham built the altar there, and bound Isaac his son, and laid him on the altar, on the wood. And Abraham stretched forth his hand, and took the knife to slay his son. And the angel of the Lord called to him out of heaven, and said: "Abraham, Abraham." And he said: "Here I am."

And he said: "Lay not your hand upon the lad, nor do anything to him,

for now I know that you are a God-fearing man, seeing you have not withheld your son, your only son, from Me."

Koshi:

Answer:

Abraham, Abraham: The repetition of the name is an expression of affection. (Gen. R. 56)

Koshi:

Answer:

Lesson:

Lay not your hand upon the lad: To slay him. Then Abraham said to God, "If this be so, I have come here for nothing; let me at least inflict a wound on him and draw some blood." Then God said: "**Nor do anything to him.**"

Koshi:

Answer:

Lesson:

for now I know: Rabbi Aba said: Abraham said to God, "I will lay my complaint before You. Before You told me (Gen. 17:21), 'But my covenant I will maintain with Isaac,' and then again You said, 'Take your son,' and now You tell me, 'Lay not your hand upon the lad!'" The Holy One who is to be praised said to him (using the words of Ps. 79:35), *"My Covenant I will not profane, nor will I alter that which has gone out of My lips.* When I told you, 'Take your son,' I did not alter the promise that My covenant would be with Isaac. I did not tell you, 'Kill him,' but to bring him up to the mountain. You have brought him up—take him down again." (Gen. R. 56)

for now I know: From now on I have an answer to give to Satan and to the nations who wonder at the love I show you: I have a reason because all can see that you are God-fearing.

Lesson:

How did Rashi use small problems in the text to confront the "whole" meaning of the story?

_____

_____

_____

_____

_____

_____

What can you tell about the way Rashi tries to teach?

_____

_____

_____

_____

_____

_____

_____

_____

EVALUATION

There are four types of students: the sponge, the funnel, the strainer, and the sieve. The sponge absorbs all; the funnel receives at one end and spills out the other; the strainer lets the wine through and retains the dregs; and the sieve lets out the flour and dust and retains the fine flour. Pirke Avot 5:18

Rate yourself.

Sieve	Sponge	Strainer	Funnel
I	I	I	I

Create your own metaphor for the kind of student you are:

_____

_____

_____

APPENDIX TO MODULE EIGHT

ANSWERS
Exercise 8.1a

No additional answers are needed.

Exercise 8.1b

This text shows us that even the written form of the Torah is something we are unsure of. Even the very written form we use is an interpretation, the first layer of interpretation.

Exercise 8.1c

1. And he came to his father and said, "My father." And he said, "Here am I." And he said, "Who are you, my son?" And Jacob said to his father, "I am Esau, your first-born."
2. In the first (the normative reading) Jacob lies to his father, claiming to be Esau. In the second, reading with Rashi (and a midrash), Jacob first answers the question with "I am," meaning "It's I." Then he states a fact: "Esau is your first-born."

Exercise 8.2

This is an opinion question.

Exercise 8.3

1. Extra Language. What is the difference between "heart," "soul," and "might"? From the V'ahavta.
2. Contradiction. Are we talking about Ishmaelites or Midianites? From the Joseph story.
3. Behavior. Who is the "Us"? —there is only supposed to be one God. From the story of Creation.
4. Extra Language. Why does it say "I," "myself," and "alone"? Aren't they all the same thing? Also: What is the difference between "cumbrance," "burden," and "strife"? The text is Moses complaining about Israel after the Golden Calf.
5. Extra Language. What is the difference between "fruitful," "increased abundantly," "multiplied," and "waxed exceedingly mighty"? This verse introduces the story of the Exodus.
6. Extra Language. Why does God both "call" and "speak"? What is the difference? This is the beginning of the Book of Leviticus. There is nothing exceptional in the quotation to tell you that. Rather, you have to learn it from the citation.
7. Behavior. Why does God want Moses to lie? Jacob (a.k.a. Israel) was not the first-born. This is part of the setup of the plagues.
8. Behavior. God already knows where Abel is; why does God play games with Cain? The story of Cain and Abel.
9. Repetition. Contradiction. Why is this story told twice? Which are the correct details—did God or a messenger change the name? Finally, in the first text, who does the talking—is it God, an angel, or a man? This is the story of Jacob wrestling the angel (or whatever).
10. Extra Language. Contradiction. Why does it say both Jacob and Israel? What do we learn from names being used? And, if God changed the name (twice), why does the Torah still use the old name? This is the first verse in the Book of Exodus, the transition between the story of the patriarchs and matriarchs and the story of the Exodus.
11. Extra Language. Why does it say camels twice? Why give us both the number and owner of the camels in two different clauses? What is so important about camels? This begins the story of Rebekah at the well. In that story, Rebekah becomes the second mother of Israel by drawing water for all ten of those camels.
12. Behavior. How could Jacob lie to his father? This is from the story of Jacob stealing Esau's blessing.
13. Behavior. Contradiction. Where does Jacob go—Paddan-aram or Haran (or are they both the same)? Also, why does Esau copy Jacob? This comes right after the stolen blessing.

Exercise 8.4

1. Extra Language. Why is this blessing repeated? What is learned by the reversal? The first is God's blessing to Jacob; the second is Balaam's blessing of Israel.
2. Contradiction. Who is speaking—God, the men, or angels? This is the story of Sarah laughing at the announcement of Isaac's birth.
3. Extra Language. Why does God make four different versions of the same promise—why not just one big promise? What is added by each of the four elements? These are God's promises to Moses.
4. Contradiction. Why does the repetition of this commandment differ? How can the two sets of the Ten Commandments be different? Obviously, this comes from the Ten Commandments. It is number four.
5. Extra Language. What is the difference between opening and digging, etc.? This comes from a law code given right after the Ten Commandments in parashat mishpatim.
6. Contradiction. The name switches from "the Lord" to "God" in the middle of the passage. The text comes from the incident of the Burning Bush.
7. Contradiction. Extra Language. Why doesn't the name-change stick? Why call "Israel," whose name has been changed, by his old name, "Jacob"? Then, why repeat the name? Wouldn't once be enough—especially if God is calling? The call introduces God's assurance that it is okay to join Joseph in Egypt.
8. Extra Language. The passage, which is a speech that Moses uses to calm God down after rebellions in the desert, is a series of parallel repetitions.
9. Behavior. Abraham lies—the first father of Israel shouldn't do that.
10. Extra Language. Why are we given two names for the same place, "Mamre" and "Hebron"? Why do we need the old name? This is obviously the burial of Sarah.
11. Behavior. Why does God feel the need to consult with Abraham? Also, who is God talking to? This divine monologue begins the destruction of Sodom and Gomorrah.
12. Grammar/ Meaning. Why is there a chaf in the first mi chamochah and a kaf in the second mi kamochah? This comes from Balaam's blessing of Israel.

Exercise 8.5

1. Contradiction. Why do these two versions of the fifth commandment differ?
2. Contradiction. Why do these two accounts of the spies' visit and report differ?
3. Extra Language. Why is the phrase "all the congregation of" added to the beginning of the Holiness Code?
4. Extra Language. Behavior. Why does Abraham take both sons out "early in the morning"?

Exercise 8.6

1. **After these things:** Next to. We don't know what things are being referenced. When you check back to the previous passage, the logical connection, there seems to be no reason to refer to it. We need to know the connection.
2. **God tested:** Behavior. Testing does not seem to be a God-like thing to do. Also, God should not need to test; God should already know.
3. **Your son, your only son, whom you love—Isaac:** Extra Language. Behavior. Why three extra sets of descriptors before he gets to the name—why not ask for Isaac right away? Also, God is being dishonest: Abraham has two sons. He has shown love to both of them.
4. **Offer him:** Behavior. God should not demand human sacrifice.

5. **Abraham . . . saddled his ass:** Behavior. In the next verse we learn that Abraham takes two servants with him. If he is rich enough to have servants, why does he saddle the ass himself? This behavior seems illogical.

6. **And took two of his young men:** Behavior. Next to. Again, if he is taking the servants, why does Abraham chop his own wood? Also, why is the order inverted—why not chop the wood before taking the servants?

7. **On the third day:** Next to. What happened to the other two days? Where is the missing part?

8. **And we will worship and come back to you:** Behavior. This is a lie. God has ordered a human sacrifice. Abraham does not expect them both to return.

9. **God will provide . . . the lamb:** Meaning. We don't know what these words actually mean.

10. **Place which God had told him of:** Meaning. Where are we? What hill is this? Also, when did God tell him?—we must have missed that, because God said "upon one of the mountains which I will show you." We missed the show-and-tell. It isn't in the text.

11. **And the angel of the Lord:** Behavior. Why the angel? God set up the test directly; why does God use an angel to deliver the test scores?

12. **Abraham, Abraham:** Extra Language. Why repeat the name?

13. **Lay not your hand . . . nor do anything:** Extra Language. Why two commands, "lay not your hand," and "nor do anything"? One should have been enough.

14. **Now I know:** Behavior. God should have known before. We again must ask, Why did God need the test?

15. **Your son, your only son:** Extra Language (this is the second time for this extra repetition).

Exercise 8.7

There are several problems in this verse: the most significant centers on "blameless in his age." It concerns the qualifier "in his age." Had we been told "he was blameless," the meaning would have been clear. The "in his age" confuses things more. "In his age" could mean "that he was righteous for his age," but not absolutely righteous. Or, it could mean that he was so righteous that he could even remain righteous in his very unrighteous age.

Exercise 8.8a

1. A. Extra Language. Why does the Torah include both "empty" and "no water"?

   B. He explains that "no water" means "no water," and "empty" means "no snakes or scorpions."

   C. There is no proof-text. It is established by logic.

   D. He learns it in Shabbat 22a. Because of the form of the citation—a page number followed by "a" or "b"—we know that this is a page of the Gemara.

   E. Yes. Even in selling their brother into slavery, the brothers took care not to hurt or kill him.

2. A. Meaning. Where are Paran and Tophel?

   B. He reports a passage where the Talmud states that nowhere in the entire Torah are these places mentioned. So, he looks for similar words, explaining the location in terms of the kind of place it must be.

   C. The place name is derived from a story found in Numbers 21.5. The two verses recall places where Israel rebelled.

   D. Rashi finds this explanation in both Sifre, a collection of midrash, and the Talmud, Berachot 32a.

   E. Even though God rewarded us with the Land of Israel, we are a people who are prone to rebellion. (Therefore, we must learn to discipline ourselves—because God never forgets.)

3. A. Behavior. The Torah seems to make a mistake. The children who are listed belong only to Aaron, yet the Torah credits both Moses and Aaron.

   Next to. Why is God's speech connected to listing this geneaology?

   B. He cites a rabbinic principle: "A person who teaches Torah to a child is like that child's parent."

C. There is no proof-text, but it is stated with the authority of the tradition.

D. The explanation comes from the Talmud, Sanhedrin 19b.

E. Yes. Torah teaching (and study) is a very meritorious activity.

4. A. Contradiction. The passage has the Lord as the active deity. Then, all of a sudden, when the commandments are given, it switches to "God." Why?

   B. Rashi explains that each God-name teaches a lesson. The name "The Lord" (*Adonai*) represents mercy; the name "God" (*Elohim*) God the judge. The Ten Commandments intentionally are spoken by God the judge.

   C. No.

   D. This one comes from the Mechilta, another collection of midrashim.

   E. Yes. Following God's commandments is a serious obligation. We will be judged for our actions.

Exercise 8.8b

1. A. Extra Language. Why does the Torah give this commandment twice in a row?

   B. He explains that one of the times is for insulting living parents (the death penalty) and the other time is for dead parents (bloodguilt).

   C. No proof-text.

   D. It is found both in Sanhedrin 85b (the Talmud) and Sifra (a collection of midrash).

2. A. Behavior. Why is God asking? God should know.

   B. Rashi compares it with the story of Cain and Abel, where God does the same thing. Rashi explains that God likes to begin conversations with questions.

   C. Yes. Genesis 4.9. It shows that God's actions are consistent. Also, Numbers 22.9.

   D. There is no source for this insight. It may be one that Rashi created himself.

   E. God asks questions. Also, God is careful not to push people or threaten them: we should be too.

3. A. Behavior. How could Moses' hand affect a war?

   B. Rashi says, "There is one, but I can't shorten it or make it easy for you."

   C. Probably, but it is the Talmud, not Rashi.

   D. The Talmud, Rosh Hashanah 29a.

   E. Yes, not everything Jewish can be made simple and easy.

4. A. Behavior. Usually, God changes people's names. It is unusual for Moses to do it. What does Moses accomplish by changing Joshua's name?

   B. He shows that what Moses did and what God did were different. He shows two different ways that the name-change was really Moses asking for God's blessing on Jacob.

   C. No.

   D. The first explanation comes from the Talmud, Sotah 34b. The second explanation has no source.

   E. God blesses and insures people's fates: people can only ask for that blessing.

5. A. There are three problems: Extra Language. Why does the Torah say both "keep" and "hear"? What is the meaning of each? Extra Language. Why does the Torah say "all the words," when just "words" would have been enough? The "all the" is extra. Extra Language. Why does the Torah include both "what is good" and "right"? They seem redundant.

   B. Rashi shows how each clause has its own meaning. (By now you don't need me to work out each one.)

   C. Proverbs 22.17-18. It shows that keeping and hearing are both important.

   D. They evolve from the midrash collection, Sifre.

   E. There are three lessons taught: It is important both to perform and understand the commandments. All commandments are important (not just some). We have to be responsible both to God and to other people.

The Post-Test

You are ready to work out these answers on your own.

As he stood that morning on top of the *tel* whose secrets he must probe, he was no ordinary man, come to the Holy Land with enthusiasm and a shovel; he had won the title archeologist only at the end of a long period of subtle training. At Harvard he had learned to read Aramaic, Arabic, and ancient Hebrew scripts.

During graduate work with Professor Albright at Johns Hopkins he had mastered Mesopotamian cuneiform and Egyptian hieroglyphs until he could read them as an average man reads a newspaper. He had taken off a year to attend  Carnegie Tech for advanced work in metallurgy, so that he would be able to identify with some certainty the provenience and smelting processes of local metals and their alloys. Later he had spent three winter terms at Ohio State University, taking advanced ceramics, precisely as if he intended making cups and saucers for the rest of his life, and from this experience had trained himself to guess within a hundred degrees centigrade the furnace heat at which any given piece of ancient pottery had been fired; he knew less of the historical relationships of ceramics than a real specialist like Dr. Bar-El, but in technical analysis he excelled her.

MODULE NINE: EXCAVATING THE BIBLE

Following these scientific courses he had lived for a year in New York, studying costume and armor at the Metropolitan Museum, and for another year—one of the best of his life—in the little French university town of Grenoble, specializing in prehistory and the cave art of France. Coincident with his work among the Indians of Arizona he had attended summer sessions at the state university, working on problems of dendrochronology, whereby time sequences in desert areas could be established by comparing the wide rings left in wood by growing seasons which had enjoyed heavy rainfall and the narrow ones left by years of drought. This was followed by a full year at Princeton, enrolled in the Presbyterian Seminary, where he worked with experts on problems of Bible research; but, as often happens, one of his most valuable skills he had picked up by himself. As a boy he had found pleasure in collecting stamps; perhaps he was now an archeologist because of this accident of his childhood, but his Irish father used to growl, "What are you doin' with them stamps?" He did not know, but when he became a man he vaguely sensed that he ought not to be fooling around with bits of paper and in some fortunate way he shifted to coins, which seemed more respectable, and this field of specialization was to prove of great value in biblical research. He had written one of the papers which had helped prove that there had been two issues of Jewish shekels: one used in the initial Jewish revolt led by Judah the Maccabee, 166 years before Christ; and a second minted during the final revolt of Bar Kochba, 135 years after Christ. As a result of this paper he was known as a numismatic expert. All these skills, plus others like ancient architecture and the conduct of war in biblical times, which he had acquired pragmatically during his various digs, he was now ready to apply to Tel Makor, but the location of his two trenches was so important that he intuitively postponed the decision. When the others left the *tel*, he remained alone, walking aimlessly across the mound, kicking idly at the topsoil to determine its construction.

A plateau only two hundred yards by a hundred and thirty wide doesn't sound like much, he mused. Two ordinary football fields. But when you stand looking at it with a teaspoon in your hand and somebody says, "Dig!" the damned thing looks immense. He prayed to himself: So much depends on this. God help me to pick the right spot; but his attention was diverted from this problem when he noticed protruding from the earth a small object which did not look like a pebble. Bending over to inspect it, he found a small piece of lead, slightly flattened on one side. It was a spent bullet and he started to throw it away, but reconsidered.

"*Voilà!* Our first find on Tel Makor," he said to himself.

James A. Michener, *The Source*

Rx

In Module Six: "Who Done It?" we realized that one's views of biblical authorship determine the methodology one uses learning the Bible. In the last two modules, we've been working with the assumption that God (in one way or another) authored the biblical text. In this module we are going to reverse that assumption and look at the kind of methodologies and assumptions which result when we assume that people wrote it. Our first impression of archeologists may come from "mummy" movies, where the scientist breaks into the hidden tomb and then decodes the mummy's curse; in reality, archeology is a meticulous science. Archeologists dig through soil with a toothbrush, unearth and catalog artifacts in carefully marked squares, and record the exact location of every piece they find. They are uncovering fragments of the past to reconstruct daily life in antiquity.

Scientific study of the biblical text, usually called "biblical criticism," works in much the same way. We use small clues found in individual passages to try to "reconstruct" the world of the biblical authors. We try to find out when the book was written, by whom, in what context, in an effort to understand what the author intended the words to mean (in contrast to their meaning today). Just as the archeologist always tries to examine an artifact *in situ* (in the exact location, layer, and setting in which it was found), the biblical critic tries to understand the *sitz im leben*—the contextual meaning of the verse as it was understood when it was written.

In the course of this module, we will take you on four biblical excavations. Each one will teach you a different process for exploring the biblical text.

EXCAVATION # 1: BEHIND THE BLESSINGS.
EXCAVATION # 2: TEXT AND ARTIFACT.
EXCAVATION # 3: THE NOAH PARALLELS.
EXCAVATION # 4: THE D-SOURCE.

Then we will look at how "critical" commentaries are read.

Before we go any further, it is important to point out that "criticism" doesn't mean finding what's wrong with the text. Criticism refers to the tools used to study the text (like literary criticism). It means using a critical eye.

By the time you're done with this module you will be able to:

9.1 Explain how history can be reconstructed from biblical texts.
9.2 Describe how archeology helps us to understand the Bible, and how the Bible helps archeologists explain what they've uncovered.
9.3 Describe the similarities and differences between the Noah story and an ancient Near Eastern parallel.
9.4 Explain why scholars think that the source of the Book of Deuteronomy differs from that of other Torah texts.
9.5 Decode the "notes" found in a critical commentary.

Twice in the Torah, we find long poetic pieces in which a major figure blesses the twelve tribes. In a biblical context, blessings are used to predict the future.

When biblical critics read these passages, they assume that these blessings are linked historically to an earlier prediction. Read these two blessings of Zebulun and Issachar and see if "history" emerges. (One clue: The story which we seem to be able to find isn't told elsewhere in the Torah.)

1

Zebulun shall dwell by the seashore;
He shall be a haven for ships,
And his flank shall rest on Sidon.
Issachar is a strong-boned ass,
Crouching among the sheepfolds.
When he saw how good was security,
And how pleasant was the country,
He bent his shoulder to the burden,
And became a toiling serf.

(Gen. 49:13-15)

2

Rejoice, O Zebulun, on your journeys,
And Issachar, in your tents.
They invite their kin to the mountain,
Where they offer sacrifices of success.
For they draw from the riches of the sea
And the hidden hoards of the sand.

(Deut. 33:18-19)

A. One blessing reminds us of the other. When we put the two together, what story seems to emerge?

_____

_____

_____

_____

B. How did two biblical verses allow us to reconstruct a piece of history which we hadn't previously known about?

_____

_____

_____

EXCAVATION # 2: TEXT AND ARTIFACT

Archeology requires detective work: uncovering clues, reconstructing events on the basis of evidence, and creating theories. Biblical archeologists work in two worlds—they need to balance the evidence gathered in archeological excavations with the biblical text, each shedding light on the other. Here are a number of examples of the intersection of text and artifact. Match the archeological finds with the verses they help to clarify. Notice how each helps us to understand the other.

(Note: This material was originally prepared for the Museum Utilization for School Education Project of HUC-JIR, Los Angeles.)

FROM THE BIBLE

1 In Genesis II: 4 we read:

And they said, "Come, let us build a city, and a tower with its top in the sky..."

Question: What did the Tower of Babel look like?

2 In the Bible, people are always making trips from the land of Canaan to Egypt. We never knew if this really happened.

In the Bible, Jacob gave his son Joseph a coat of many colors.

Is there a historical basis for the visits and for the coat of many colors?

3 In I Kings I:50 we find:

Adonijah, in fear of Solomon, went at once [to the Tent] and grasped the horns of the altar.

How can an altar have horns?

4 In the Bible, we find the following in I Samuel 13:20-21:

So all the Israelites had to go down to the Philistines to have their plowshares, their mattocks, axes, and colters sharpened. The charge for sharpening was a *pim*....

What is a *pim*?

5 In Ezekiel 21:26 we find a very strange passage:

For the king of Babylon has stood at the fork of the road, where two roads branch off, to perform divination: he has shaken arrows, consulted teraphim, and inspected the liver.

Why a liver? How can you "inspect" a liver?

6 The prophet Jeremiah curses in Jeremiah 19:10-11:

Then you shall smash the jug in the sight of the men who go with you, and say to them: "Thus said the Lord of Hosts: So will I smash this people and this city, as one smashes a potter's vessel, which can never be mended....

Where did Jeremiah get the metaphor of a smashed jug?

7 In the Book of Exodus 21:23-25 we find:

But if other damage ensues, the penalty shall be life for life, eye for eye, tooth for tooth, hand for hand, foot for foot, burn for burn, wound for wound, bruise for bruise.

Where did the Bible get the idea of an eye for an eye?

8 At the beginning of the Book of Exodus (I:II, 14), we read:

So they set taskmasters over them to oppress them...and they built garrison cities for Pharaoh: Pithom and Raamses. They made life bitter for them with harsh labor at mortar and bricks....

Was this real history?

FROM ARCHEOLOGY

A Archeologists found a stela inscribed with a law code referred to as the Code of Hammurabi. Among the inscriptions, we find statements concerning the following:

If a person destroys the eye of another person, the other shall destroy his eye.

If he has broken the bone of another, the other shall break his bone.

B Discovery of an incense altar at Megiddo shows that this altar had horns. It was made between 800 and 900 B.C.E.

Look up Psalms 118:27, Jeremiah 17:1, and Amos 3:14.

Then look up Leviticus 8:15, 9:9, and 16:18.

C A clay model of a liver was found at Megiddo. This clay liver was covered with omens and magical formulas.

It was crafted around 1830 B.C.E.

What was the purpose of this clay liver?

D In the ancient city of Ur, archeologists uncovered a temple tower.

We call this kind of temple tower by its Babylonian name—a *ziggurat*.

E These paintings were found on the walls of the tomb of Pharaoh Khnum-Hotep III, which is in Beni Hasan. They were painted around 1890 B.C.E.

Who is being represented?

Look up Genesis 4:21-23. How do these verses relate to the Egyptian tomb-paintings?

F Archeologists working at a place called Tel En-Nasbeh found a circular stone with the word *pim* written on it.

What is this stone?

G Clay statue of a bound prisoner.

Curses on the enemies of Egypt covered the figure, which had been smashed.

It was made around 1700 B.C.E.

What was the significance of this statue?

H The tomb-paintings of Rech-Mire in Thebes.

These pictures of brick-making in Egypt were painted around 1400 B.C.E.

A. What did the archeological finds cited above teach us about the "truth" and accuracy of the Bible?

_____

_____

_____

B. How did the Bible help the archeologists to understand their discoveries?

_____

_____

_____

_____

185

EXCAVATION # 3: THE NOAH PARALLELS

On the following pages you'll find excerpts from the EPIC OF GILGAMESH matched up with excerpts from the story of NOAH. (Gen. 5-8)

The GILGAMESH EPIC is a Babylonian myth which is basically a hero story. Compare it with the NOAH story.

THE EPIC OF GILGAMESH	THE STORY OF NOAH
A. The god (Enlil) became disturbed by their gatherings. The god heard their noise And said to the great gods: "Great has become the noise of mankind; With their tumult they make sleep impossible."	A. The Lord saw how great was man's wickedness on earth, and how every plan devised by his mind was nothing but evil all the time. And the Lord regretted that He had made man on earth, and His heart was saddened. (6:5-6)
B. Utnapishtim said to him, to Gilgamesh: "I will reveal to you, Gilgamesh, a hidden matter And a secret of the gods will I tell you: Shuruppak—a city which you know, (And) which on Euphrates' [banks] is situated— That city was ancient, (as were) the gods within it, When their hearts led the great gods to produce the flood.	B. But Noah found favor with the Lord. (6:8) God said to Noah, "I have decided to put an end to all flesh, for the earth is filled with lawlessness because of them: I am about to destroy them with the earth." (6:13)
C. Tear down (this) house, build a ship! Give up possessions, seek you life. Forswear (worldly) gods and keep the soul alive! Aboard the ship take you the seed of all living things. The ship that you shall build, Her dimensions shall be to measure.	C. Make yourself an ark of gopher wood; make it an ark with compartments, and cover it inside and out with pitch. This is how you shall make it.... (6:14-15)
D. Whatever I had of all the living beings I [laded] upon her. All my family and kin I made go aboard the ship. The beasts of the field, the wild creatures of the field.	D. "... But I will establish My covenant with you, and you shall enter the ark, with your sons, your wife, and your sons' wives. And of all that lives, of all flesh, you shall take two of each into the ark to keep alive with you; they shall be male and female. From birds of every kind, cattle of every kind, every kind of creeping thing on earth, two of each shall come to you to stay alive. For your part, take of everything that is eaten and store it away, to serve as food for you and for them." Noah did so; just as God commanded him, so he did. (6:18-22)

In this column, write down all the items these two stories have in common. Include use of images, actions, plot, language, words, phrases, order, etc.

In this column, write down new things the biblical story adds to the Babylonian myth. Include new ideas, concepts, values, and images.

187

E. I watched the appearance of the weather. The weather was awesome to behold. I boarded the ship and battened up the entrance.	E. And on the seventh day the waters of the Flood came upon the earth. In the six hundredth year of Noah's life, in the second month, on the seventeenth day of the month, on that day All the fountains of the great deep burst apart, And the flood-gates of the sky broke open. (7:10-11) They came to Noah into the ark, two each of all flesh in which there was breath of life. Thus they that entered comprised male and female of all flesh, as God had commanded him. And the LORD shut him in. (7:15-16)
F. Gathering speed as it blew [submerging the mountains], Overtaking the [people] like a battle, No one can see his fellow, Nor can the people be recognized from heaven. The gods were frightened by the deluge, And, shrinking back, they ascended to the heaven of Anu.	F. The Flood continued forty days on the earth, and the waters increased and raised the ark so that it rose above the earth. The waters swelled and increased greatly upon the earth, and the ark drifted upon the waters. When the waters had swelled much more upon the earth, all the highest mountains everywhere under the sky were covered. Fifteen cubits higher did the waters swell, as the mountains were covered. (7:17-20)
G. Six days and [six] nights Blows the flood wind, as the south-storm sweeps the land. When the seventh day arrived, The flood (—carrying) south-storm subsided in the battle, Which it had fought like an army. The sea grew quiet, the tempest was still, the flood ceased. I looked at the weather: stillness had set in, And all of mankind had returned to clay.	G. And all flesh that stirred on earth perished—birds, cattle, beasts, and all the things that swarmed upon the earth, and all mankind. All in whose nostrils was the merest breath of life, all that was on dry land, died. All existence on earth was blotted out—man, cattle, creeping things, and birds of the sky; they were blotted out from the earth. Only Noah was left, and those with him in the ark. (7:21-23)
H. On Mount Nisir the ship came to a halt. Mount Nisir held the ship fast, Allowing no motion.	H. ...At the end of one hundred and fifty days the waters diminished, so that in the seventh month, on the seventeenth day of the month, the ark came to rest on the mountains of Ararat. (8:3-4)
I. When the seventh day arrived, I sent forth and set free a dove. The dove went forth, but came back; Since no resting-place for her was visible, she turned round.	I. At the end of forty days, Noah opened the window of the ark that he had made and sent out the raven; it went to and fro until the waters had dried up from the earth. (8:6-7)

In this column, write down all the items these two stories have in common. Include use of images, actions, plot, language, words, phrases, order, etc.	In this column, write down new things the biblical story adds to the Babylonian myth. Include new ideas, concepts, values, and images.

J. Then I sent forth and set free a raven.
The raven went forth and, seeing that the waters had diminished,
She eats, circles, caws, and turns not around.
Then I let out (all) to the four winds....

J. Then he sent out the dove to see whether the waters had decreased from the surface of the ground. But the dove could not find a resting place for its foot, and returned to him to the ark, for there was water over all the earth. So putting out his hand, he took it into the ark with him. He waited another seven days, and again sent out the dove from the ark. The dove came back to him toward evening, and there in its bill was a plucked-off olive leaf! Then Noah knew that the waters had decreased on the earth. He waited still another seven days and sent the dove forth; and it did not return to him any more. (8:8-12)

K. And I offered a sacrifice, I poured out a libation on the top of the mountain.
Seven and seven cult vessels I set up.
Upon their pot-stands I heaped cane, cedarwood, and myrtle.
The gods smelled the savor;
The gods smelled the sweet savor.
The gods crowded like flies about the sacrificer.

K. Then Noah built an altar to the LORD and, taking of every clean animal and of every clean bird, he offered burnt-offerings on the altar. The Lord smelled the pleasing odor, and the Lord said to Himself: "Never again will I doom the earth because of man, since the devisings of man's mind are evil from his youth; nor will I ever again destroy every living being, as I have done...." (8:20-21)

A. Give as much evidence as you can that the biblical author(s) of the Noah story knew the Epic of Gilgamesh.

_____

_____

_____

_____

_____

_____

B. Compare Noah to Gilgamesh. What are and aren't we told?

_____

_____

_____

_____

_____

_____

C. Compare the gods in Gilgamesh to God in the Noah story. How, when, and why do they act?

_____

_____

_____

_____

_____

D. In reworking the Flood story, what do the biblical authors add?

_____

_____

_____

_____

_____

A REMINDER ON SOURCE CRITICISM

In Module Six: "Who Done It?" we introduced "source criticism"—J, E, P, and D—in a very simple manner. Here is the way Gunther Plaut describes the present state of biblical source scholarship.

Doubts that the Torah was a book set down by one author, Moses, developed some centuries ago, but it was not until the nineteenth century that extensive investigations made the critical study of the biblical text a highly specialized discipline. The early critics noted the differential use of the names of God in various parts of the Torah, the discrepancies of certain accounts and figures, and different literary styles. Later scholars further analyzed the text so that they could discern many authors and several editors, and they theorized about the times and events when these sources and documents were created and finally combined into the Torah as we have it now.

The theory which continues to command general scholarly adherence is called the Documentary Hypothesis and is often referred to by two of its most prominent expositors, Karl Graf and Julius Wellhausen. In substance it says that there are four major sources or documents (called J, E, P, and D), the combination of which during the fifth century B.C.E. resulted in the creation of a single book, the Torah, which was declared a sacred text by official canonization about the year 400.

J is the name given by biblical critics to the author who used the divine name יהוה (YHVH or YHWH) and...was responsible for most of Genesis. E uses אֱלֹהִים (Elohim) and authored the binding of Isaac and other passages of Genesis.... D is the author of Deuteronomy, which is said to be the book found by King Josiah in 621 B.C.E.... P is the author of the first chapter of Genesis, the Book of Leviticus, and other sections characterized by interest in genealogies and priesthood....

There are critics who find additional major sources—S (for Seir, believed to be an author of southern, possibly non-Israelite origin); K (originating with the tribe of Kenites); and L (a lay writer). Others detect several subsources in J, E, P, and D; and then there is R (the redactor/editor of the final text). There is no agreement on when these documents were composed, but most adherents of the critical schools would give 950 through 450 B.C.E. as the years during which this literary process took place—that is, from the days of the divided kingdom of Israel and Judah to their destruction and the time of the exile and return.

Since Moses lived in the thirteenth century B.C.E., he had, in that view, nothing to do with the writing of the complete Torah. His name was attached to it as author at the time of the book's canonization. This whole analysis is vigorously disputed by those who attempt to show that Moses was indeed the author. They consider much or all higher literary criticism as erroneous and some of its foundations as infected by Christian bias. [Footnote: "In general, it is probably true that much Jewish scholarship, even that which was not totally traditionalistic, was initially, and to a degree still remains, rather cool toward the standard results of German biblical scholarship, well aware of the subtle anti-Judaism, if not anti-Semitism, which by no means necessarily... accompanies any depreciation of the Old Testament...." (H.D. Hummel, *Encyclopaedia Judaica*, Vol. 4, col. 907.)] More recently, increasing numbers of critical scholars have denied the basic validity of the Graf-Wellhausen approach. They say that the difference in the divine names in the text is not traceable to different sources, but rather represents a largely intentional, stylistic alteration. They see the first four books of the Torah to be one basic unified collection which comes from a "traditionalist circle," which they are willing to call P (for the priestly school). These scholars assign the Book of

Deuteronomy to a second collection (which reaches all the way to 2 Kings) which they ascribe to a "Deuteronomic circle." In this view, the distinctions introduced by Wellhausen, who spoke of P, J, E, and similar sources, can no longer be maintained.

W. Gunther Plaut from *The Torah: A Modern Commentary* (UAHC), pp. xxi-xxiii.

EXCAVATION # 4: THE D-SOURCE

Over the next few pages, we are going to see the way scholars work with "source criticism" to try to "reconstruct" history.

This passage from the Book of Deuteronomy (11:26-28) is part of one of the last speeches that Moses delivered to the Jewish people just before his death.

See, this day I set
before you blessing and curse:
blessing, if you obey the commandments
of the Lord your God
which I enjoin upon you this day;
and curse, if you do not obey the commandments
of the Lord your God,
but turn away from the path
which I enjoin upon you this day
and follow other gods,
whom you have not experienced.

1. A THEOLOGICAL IDEA

Theology deals with ideas about God. The theology of the above passage is tied to two words: blessing and curse.

You get בְּרָכָה /berachah (blessing)
if_____.

You get קְלָלָה /kelalah (curse)
if_____.

In other words, it says:
God rewards people who_____.

God punishes people who_____.

Simply put, this is a Deuteronomic theology.

Do you have any problems with this theology? If so, what?

_____

_____

2. DEUTERONOMY

Look at the following passages. All of them deal with the idea of covenant (God's promise to Israel). Mark the ones that express a Deuteronomic theology. Circle their letters.

a See, I place the land at your disposal. Go, take possession of the land that the Lord swore to your fathers, Abraham, Isaac, and Jacob, to give to them and to their offspring after them. (Deut. 1:8)

b And now, O Israel, give heed to the laws and rules which I am instructing you to observe, so that you may live to enter and occupy the land that the Lord, the God of your fathers, is giving you. (Deut.4:1)

c And this is the Instruction—the laws and the rules—that the LORD your God has commanded [me] to impart to you, to be observed in the land which you are about to cross into and occupy, so that you, your son, and your son's son may revere the LORD your God and follow, as long as you live, all His laws and commandments which I enjoin upon you, to the end that you may long endure. Obey, O Israel, willingly and faithfully, that it may go well with you and that you may increase greatly [in] a land flowing with milk and honey, as the LORD, the God of your fathers, spoke to you. (Deut. 6:1-3)

d I am the Lord. I will free you from the burdens of the Egyptians and deliver you from their bondage. I will redeem you with an outstretched arm and through extraordinary chastisements. And I will take you to be My people, and I will be your God. And you shall know that I, the LORD, am your God who freed you from the labors of the Egyptians. I will bring you into the land which I swore to give Abraham, Isaac, and Jacob, and I will give it to you for a possession, I the LORD. (Exod. 6:6-8)

A. What ideas do all these passages have in common?

_____

_____

_____

B. What idea is unique to the theology we are discussing?

_____

_____

_____

3. THE D-SOURCE

To continue our exploration of the Deuteronomic theology, we need to look at the following materials from 2 Kings, chapters 22 and 23.

Josiah was eight years old when he became king, and he reigned thirty-one years in Jerusalem.... He did what was pleasing to the LORD and he followed all the ways of his ancestor David; he did not deviate to the right or to the left.

In the eighteenth year of King Josiah, the king sent the scribe Shaphan...to the House of the LORD, saying, "Go to the high priest Hilkiah and let him weigh the silver which has been deposited in the House of the LORD...that they in turn may pay it out to the workmen that are in the House of the LORD, for the repair of the House....

Then the high priest Hilkiah said to the scribe Shaphan, "I have found a scroll of the Teaching in the House of the LORD." And Hilkiah gave the scroll to Shaphan....

And Shaphan read it to the king. When the king heard the contents of the scroll of the Teaching, he rent his clothes. And the king gave orders to the priest Hilkiah...: "Go, inquire of the LORD on my behalf, and on behalf of the people, and on behalf of all Judah, concerning the words of this scroll that has been found...." So the priest Hilkiah...went to the prophetess Huldah....She responded: "Thus said the LORD, the God of Israel: Say to the man who sent you to me: Thus said the Lord: I am going to bring disaster upon this place and its inhabitants, in accordance with all the words of the scroll which the king of Judah has read. Because they have forsaken Me and have made offerings to other gods and vexed Me with all their deeds...." (22:1-5, 8, 10-17)

At the king's summons, all the elders of Judah and Jerusalem assembled before him. The king went up to the House of the LORD, together with all the men of Judah and all the inhabitants of Jerusalem, and the priests and prophets—all the people, young and old. And he read to them the entire text of the covenant scroll which had been found in the House of the LORD. The king stood by the pillar and solemnized the covenant before the LORD: that they would follow the LORD and observe His commandments, His injunctions, and His laws with all their heart and soul; that they would fulfill all the terms of this covenant as inscribed upon the scroll. And all the people entered into the covenant.

Then the king ordered the high priest Hilkiah...to bring out of the Temple of the LORD all the objects made for Baal and Asherah....

He suppressed the idolatrous priests... and those who made offerings to Baal, to the sun and moon and constellations.... He brought out the [image of] Asherah from the House of the LORD....

He brought all the priests from the towns of Judah [to Jerusalem] and defiled the shrines where the priests had been making offerings....Josiah also did away with the necromancers and the mediums, the idols and the fetishes—all the detestable things that were to be seen in the land of Judah and Jerusalem. Thus he fulfilled the terms of the Teaching recorded in the scroll which the priest Hilkiah had found in the House of the LORD. There was no king like him before who turned back to the LORD with all his heart and soul and might, in full accord with the Teaching of Moses; nor did any like him arise after him. (23:1-6, 8, 24-25)

In two or three sentences, write down your version of this story.

_____

_____

_____

_____

_____

_____

Now go back and mark any portions of this text which express a Deuteronomic theology. For comparison you may want to look at Deuteronomy 6:1-9, 29:9-28, and 34:10.

LET'S SUM UP WHAT WE'VE JUST READ:

a. A king named Josiah orders the Temple to be fixed.
b. While fixing it, "a lost book of the Law" is found.
c. This book becomes the center of a "renewal" of the covenant.
d. As part of this renewal, Josiah destroys:
   1. All idols and non-Jewish worship practices.
   2. All forms of Jewish worship outside the Temple.

4. CONNECTIONS

a. All of the Torah sees the covenant between God and Israel as the central core of Jewish theology.
b. All of the Torah discusses Israel as a land promised to the Jewish people.
c. In the Book of Deuteronomy we get the concept of a "conditional covenant." When Israel does "good," things will be "good." When Israel does "bad," things will be "bad."

NOW ANSWER THE FOLLOWING QUESTIONS.

1. We know that there are some theological connections between Deuteronomy and the Josiah story in 2 Kings. List a few.

_____

_____

_____

2. We know that there are some linguistic (language) similarities between Deuteronomy and the Josiah story. List a few.

_____

_____

_____

3. Josiah's destruction of Jewish worship outside of Jerusalem seems to be following this law found only in Deuteronomy (12:2-6). Draw a conclusion.

You must destroy all the sites at which the nations you are to dispossess worshiped their gods, whether on lofty mountains and on hills or under any luxuriant tree. Tear down their altars, smash their pillars, put their sacred posts to the fire, and cut down the images of their gods, obliterating their name from that site.

Do not worship the LORD your God in like manner, but look only to the site that the LORD your God will choose amidst all your tribes as His habitation, to establish His name there. There you are to go, and there you are to bring your burnt-offerings and other sacrifices, your tithes and contributions, your votive and freewill offerings, and the firstlings of your herds and flocks.

_____

_____

_____

_____

4. Below is a passage from a midrash. Draw your conclusion.

When Hilkiah discovered the scroll, he found that it was rolled open to: "Cursed be he who will not uphold the terms of this Teaching and observe them. " (Deut. 27:26) **When Josiah heard this verse read and found that the scroll was open to it, he tore his clothes.** (Midrash Hagadol)

_____

_____

_____

_____

5. There is little doubt that Deuteronomy and the reformation of Josiah are connected. What is your theory about this? (Use all the evidence we've collected.)

_____

_____

_____

_____

_____

_____

SUMMING UP

You've now been introduced to two complex and very different ways of learning the Bible.

1. Describe "rabbinic" study of the Torah.

_____

_____

2. Describe "scientific text" study.

_____

_____

_____

3. What are we trying to learn when we study the Torah through "rabbinic eyes"?

_____

_____

4. What are we trying to learn when we study the Torah with "critical" tools?

_____

_____

_____

5. What do the two "methodologies" have in common?

_____

_____

_____

6. What is your "chosen" method of learning a biblical text?

_____

_____

_____

_____

A CONFESSION FROM YOUR AUTHOR

I prefer the rabbinic reading of texts to critical commentaries though I believe fully in the value of both methodologies. While my own theology of the text reflects the view that "they both wrote it," I believe that, in settings where Jews are learning Torah, we have more to gain from mastering the rabbinic tradition. (I won't explain why here, though you may want to debate this in class.) Thus far, we have devoted two modules to learning how to work with rabbinic sources and commentaries; in the next few pages we're going to concentrate on critical commentaries.

MEET THE ANCHOR BIBLE

There are many different sources for critical commentaries. Almost all of the state-of-the-art work is found in journal articles or in very difficult technical books. Biblical criticism is a scholastic discipline, not a popular literature. Probably the best source of "popular" pieces is a collection called the Anchor Bible.

The ANCHOR BIBLE is a fresh approach to the world's greatest classic. Its object is to make the Bible accessible to the modern reader; its method is to arrive at the meaning of biblical literature through exact translation and extended exposition, and to reconstruct the ancient setting of the biblical story, as well as the circumstances of its transcription and the characteristics of its transcribers.

The ANCHOR BIBLE is a project of international and interfaith scope: Protestant, Catholic, and Jewish scholars from many countries contribute individual volumes. The project is not sponsored by any ecclesiastical organization and is not intended to reflect any particular theological doctrine....

Here is a familiar text (Genesis 22). We've worked with the *Akedah* before, though this will be significantly different from reading it with Rashi.

The Anchor Bible provides a translation of the text, followed by two commentaries. The first is called "Notes" and it explains (on a word-to-word basis) the decisions made by the translator. The second is called "Comment" and deals with a more general view of the passage. We'll start with the comment, but first the translation.

---

162   GENESIS   § 28

ham! Abraham!" "Here I am," he answered." 12 And he said, "Lay not your hand upon the boy, nor do the least thing to him! Now I know how dedicated you are to God, since you did not withhold from me your own beloved son." 13 As Abraham looked up, his eye fell upon a⁴ ram snagged in the thicket by its horns. Abraham went and took the ram and offered it up as a burnt offering in place of his son. 14 And Abraham named that site Yahweh-yireh,ᵉ hence the present saying, "On Yahweh's mountain there is vision."ᶠ

15 Yahweh's angel called to Abraham a second time from heaven, 16 and said, "'I swear by myself,' declared Yahweh, 'that because you have acted thus, and did not withhold your beloved son from me, 17 I will therefore bestow my blessing upon you and make your offspring as numerous as the stars in heaven and the sands on the seashore; and your descendants shall take over the gates of their enemies. 18 All the nations of the earth shall bless themselves by your descendants—all because you obeyed my command.'"

19 Abraham then returned to his servants, and they left together for Beer-sheba. And Abraham stayed in Beer-sheba.

ᵈ MT "behind"; see NOTE.
ᵉ "Yahweh sees/finds"; cf. vs. 8.
ᶠ Last two words *yhwh yr'h* in Heb. text; see NOTE.

NOTES

xxii 1. *God put Abraham to the test.* Heb. is inverted for emphasis, and the effect is heightened by the definite article with Elohim. The idea is thus conveyed that this was no ordinary procedure, but that God had a particularly important objective in mind. But the precise shading is difficult to determine. It might be that God chose to do so, or that it was an exceptional test.

Ready. Literally "here I am," a courteous response to a call, which should not be stereotyped in translation. Here the effect is that of our "Sir?" or "At your service, at once," much the same as the actual "Ready" of Arabic; cf. especially xxvii 13. In vs. 7 we obviously need something like "Yes?" (cf. also xxvii 18). In vs. 11, on the other hand, "Here I am" is not out of place.

xxii 1–19   163

2. *beloved.* Heb. uses a term that is not the regular adjective for "one," but a noun meaning "the unique one, one and only." Isaac, of course, was not an only son (xxi 11). The correct rendering is already found in LXX, and the meaning is reinforced in Heb. by the phrase that immediately follows.

land of Moriah. LXX gives "lofty," the same translation as for Moreh in xii 6; Syr. "of the Amorites"; other versions operate with *mr'h* "sight, vision"; elsewhere only in II Chron iii 1, referring to Temple Hill, cf. vs. 14 below.

3. *started out for.* Literally "rose and went to"; when so construed with another verb, Heb. presents a hendiadys in which *q-m* indicates the start or speed of action; cf. xxxi 22.

4. *sighted.* Literally "lifted up his eyes and saw"; for this function of the verb *nś'*, cf. NOTE on xxi 16.

5. *worship.* Literally "bow low."

6. *firestone.* Heb. "fire," but the flame would scarcely have been kept going throughout the long journey. What is evidently meant here is equipment for producing fire, other than the wood itself, which is separately specified: Akk. uses analogously *(aban) išāti* "fire (stone)."

cleaver. The pertinent Heb. noun (see also Judg xix 29 and Prov xxx 14) is used expressly for butcher knives.

together. Same Heb. term as in vs. 8, with singular possessive suffix in adverbial use. Here the point is that Abraham and Isaac left the servants behind; there the picture is that of two persons walking together in oppressive silence.

7. *broke the silence and said.* Literally "said . . . and said."

8. *will see to.* Literally "will see for himself," in anticipation of the place name Yahweh-yireh "Yahweh will see," vs. 14.

my son. Also in vs. 7, both times as a mark of great tenderness.

9–10. For the somnambulistic effect of these successive steps described in staccato sentences, see the sensitive comment by von Rad.

12. *how dedicated you are to God.* Literally "that you fear God, that you are a God-fearing man." But the manifest stress is not so much on fear, or even awe, as on absolute dedication.

13. *his eye fell upon a ram.* Text literally "he saw, and behold, a ram after," which is syntactically no better in Heb. than in word-for-word translation; nor would the ungrammatical "behind him/after" suit the context. Not only the ancient versions but many Heb. manuscripts read *'hd* for *'hr* (for the common misreading of Heb. letters R/D, cf. x 4), which makes immediate sense.

14. This parenthetical notice embodies two separate allusions. One, Yahweh *yir'ê*, points back to Elohim *yir'ê* in vs. 8; the other is connected with Temple Hill in Jerusalem. As now vocalized, the verb in the

GENESIS 22

(1) Some time afterwards, God put Abraham to the test. He said to him, "Abraham!" "Ready," he answered. (2) And He said: "Take your son, your beloved one, Isaac, whom you hold so dear, and go to the land of Moriah, where you shall offer him up as a burnt offering on one of the heights that I will point out to you."

(3) Early next morning, Abraham saddled his ass, took two of his servant boys along with his son Isaac, having first split some wood for the burnt offering, and started out for the place that God had indicated to him. (4) On the third day Abraham sighted the place from afar. (5) Then Abraham said to his servants, "You stay here with the ass while the boy and I go on yonder; we will worship and then come back to you."

(6) Abraham then took the wood for the burnt offering and put it on Isaac his son; the firestone and the cleaver he carried in his own hand. And the two walked off together. (7) Isaac broke the silence and said to his father Abraham, "Father!" "Yes, my son," he answered. "There is the firestone," he said, "and the wood, but where is the sheep for the burnt offering?" (8) Abraham replied, "God will see to the sheep for His burnt offering, my son." And the two of them walked on together.

(9) They came to the place that God had spoken of to him. Abraham built an altar there. He laid out the wood. He tied up his son Isaac. He laid him on the altar on top of the wood. (10) He put out his hand and picked up the cleaver to slay his son. (11) But an angel of Yahweh called to him from heaven, "Abraham! Abraham!" "Here I am," he answered. (12) And he said, "Lay not your hand upon the boy, nor do the least thing to him! Now I know how dedicated you are to God, since you did not withhold from Me your beloved son." (13) As Abraham looked up, his eye fell upon a ram snagged in the thicket by its horns. Abraham went and took the ram and offered it up as a burnt offering in place of his son. (14) And Abraham named that site Yahweh-yireh, hence the present saying, "On Yahweh's mountain there is vision."

(15) Yahweh's angel called to Abraham a second time from heaven, and said, " 'I swear by Myself,' declared Yahweh, 'that because you have acted thus, and did not withhold your beloved son from Me, I will therefore bestow My blessing upon you and make your offspring as numerous as the stars in heaven and the sands on the seashore; and your descendants shall take over the gates of their enemies. (18) All the nations of the earth shall bless themselves by your descendants—all because you obeyed My command.' "

(19) Abraham then returned to his servants, and they left together for Beer-sheba. And Abraham stayed in Beer-sheba.

THE COMMENT

We will quote only that passage that is relevant to our analysis.

The narrative is attributed to E with scarcely a dissenting voice and with only a few minor reservations. Nor can the consensus be held at fault, in view of the repeated mention of Elohim (1,3,8,9,12) and the seemingly theological tenor of the narrative. Yet Yahweh is also mentioned further down, vss. 11, 15, 16; and if the last two occurrences are credited to R(edactor), the same is not the case with the two etiological references to Yahweh in vs. 14. Furthermore, the style of the narrative is far more appropriate to J than to E, and the ability to paint a vivid scene in depth, without spelling things out for the reader, is elsewhere typical of J. What this amounts to, therefore, is that, on external grounds, J was either appended to E, or E was superimposed upon J. There was admittedly some fusion in any case (cf. the perplexed comment by Noth, Uberlieferungsgeschichte..., 38., n. 132).

On internal evidence, however, based on the style and content, the personality behind the story should be J's. Since the crystallized version was such as to be cited and copied more often than most accounts, it is possible that a hand which had nothing to do with E (conceivably even from the P school) miswrote Elohim for Yahweh in the few instances involved, sometime in the long course of written transmission. The issue is thus not a closed one by any means.

1. What is the key question of the comment?

_____

_____

_____

_____

2. What name is used in a J document?

_____

What is the style of a J document?

_____

_____

3. What name is used in an E document?

_____

What is the style of an E document?

_____

_____

_____

_____

4. Why should this be an E document?

_____

_____

_____

_____

5. Why might this be a J document?

_____

_____

_____

_____

6. What do we gain from this argument? What makes it important to us?

_____

_____

_____

_____

THE NOTES

Below you will find one section of "Notes" from the Anchor Bible. To understand it, you have to know a number of things: (I) They are talking about the translation of the Hebrew text into English (and often about the Hebrew); (2) they use a lot of abbreviations—we'll help you out, but they do list all the abbreviations at the front of each volume; and (3) they write in a terse scientific style, which means they skip a lot of the words we'd normally put in sentences.

Read the verse, then the note, and then answer the questions below.

(2) And He said: "Take your son, your beloved one, Isaac, whom you hold so dear, and go to the land of Moriah, where you shall offer him up as a burnt offering on one of the heights that I will point out to you."

land of Moriah. LXX gives "lofty," the same translation as for Moreh in I2: 6; Syr. "of the Amorites"; other versions operate with *mr'h*, "sight, vision"; elsewhere only in 2 Chron. 3: I, referring to Temple Hill, cf. vs. I4 below.

LXX = The Septuagint, which was the first translation of the Bible (from Hebrew into Greek).

Give the meaning of the first phrase:

LXX gives "lofty"— _____

Open a Bible and copy Genesis I2:6 here:

_____
_____
_____
_____

Now explain this phrase: LXX gives "lofty," the same translation as for Moreh in I2: 6;

_____
_____
_____

Notice the semicolon (;) at the end of this phrase. It means that this idea is over and another one is starting. Circle all the semicolons in the note.

Syr. = The Peshitta, which is the Syriac translation of the Bible (another important early translation).

Explain this phrase: Syr. "of the Amorites";

_____
_____
_____

---

mr'h = The three letters of the Hebrew root מ-ר-ה which form the core of the word Moriah.

Explain: other versions operate with **mr'h**, "sight, vision";

_____
_____
_____

Open a Bible and copy 2 Chron. 3:I here.

_____
_____
_____

Explain this phrase: elsewhere only in 2 Chron. 3:I, referring to Temple Hill,

Elsewhere only = The only other place in the Bible.

_____
_____
_____

---

cf. = Also found in...

(14) And Abraham named that site Yahweh-yireh, hence the present saying, "On Yahweh's mountain there is vision."

Explain: cf. vs. I4 below. (Below indicates location. This is verse 2; verse I4 is "below" in the text.)

_____
_____
_____

EXTRA CREDIT # 1

Here is the note on verse 14. Explain it.

This parenthetical notice embodies two separate allusions. One, *Yahweh yir'ê,* points back to *Elohim yir'ê* in vs. 8; the other is connected with Temple Hill in Jerusalem. As now vocalized, the verb in the descriptive clause is pointed as a passive, i.e., *yērā'ê* "(YAHWEH) is seen, appears," which accords with Mount Moriah, but obscures the allusion to vs. 8. If we repoint the verb to *yir'e,* the balance will shift the other way. The translation given is intentionally neutral.

EXTRA CREDIT # 2

Here are Rashi's notes on these two passages. Compare them. Do they notice the same *kusheyot* (problems)? Do they find answers in the same way?

(2) *THE LAND OF MORIAH*—This is Jerusalem, and so we find in 2 Chron. 3:1 *"To build the House of the Lord in Mount Moriah."*

Our rabbis explained that it is called *Moriah,* meaning "instruction," because it was from here that *Hora'ah* (Torah instruction) was given to the Jewish people. (Gen. R. 55)

In the Targum Onkelos it is translated as *"in accordance with the offering of incense."* The author understands that מֹר (*mor*, myrrh), the name of the spice in the incense used on the altar, is the root of *Moriah.*

(14) *Adonai-Yireh*—Its real meaning is the way the Targum translates it: *The Lord selects and sees for Himself this place to make His Shechinah reside in it and for sacrifices to be offered there.*

Now that you've completed Module Nine, you should be able to answer the following.

9.1 Explain how history can be reconstructed from biblical texts.

_____

_____

9.2 Describe how archeology helps us to understand the Bible, and how the Bible helps archeologists explain what they've uncovered.

_____

_____

9.3 Describe the similarities and differences between the Noah story and an ancient Near Eastern parallel.

_____

_____

9.4 Explain why scholars think that the Book of Deuteronomy comes from a source different from other Torah texts.

_____

_____

9.5 Decode the "notes" found in a critical commentary:

> _Eden_. Heb. _eden_, Akk. _edinu_, based on Sum. _eden_, "plain, steppe." The term is used here clearly as a geographical designation which came to be associated, naturally enough, with the homonymous but unrelated Heb. noun for "enjoyment."

> (Clues: Heb. = Hebrew, Akk. = Akkadian, Sum. = Sumerian.)

> A. Explain: Heb. _eden_, Akk. _edinu_, based on Sum. _eden_, "plain, steppe."

> (Homonymous comes from the word _homonym_—homonyms are words that sound alike but have different meanings.)

_____

_____

> B. Explain the rest of this note:

_____

_____

FINAL THOUGHTS

Both rabbinic text study and scientific text study involve close-reading of the biblical text as well as much work and reasoning. What is the value of each discipline? How do they fit together (or do they)?

APPENDIX TO MODULE NINE

ANSWERS

Excavation # 1

A. At some point the tribe of Zebulun seems to have conquered Issachar and turned his tribe into serfs. We don't know the exact story, but we do know from both accounts that Issachar wound up in Zebulun's tent. It suggests that they had some kind of land or territory that was rich enough to draw Issachar into servitude.

B. One story confirms the other. It shows us that there is clearly a tradition which has been preserved. Something happened to influence the writing of both blessings. Combining the clues from both texts, we take a guess at what happened.

Excavation # 2

1. D
2. E
3. B
4. F
5. C
6. G
7. A
8. H

Excavation # 3

A. In both texts, the god is angry at people. In the Epic of Gilgamesh it is over "noise"; in the Torah it is over "ethics."

B. In both texts, one man is told about the forthcoming flood. In the Torah, this is ethical; in the Epic of Gilgamesh, the god reveals a secret to a favorite.

C. Both texts instruct the man to build a boat.

D. Both men took all kinds of animals and provisions aboard. In the Torah, we introduce the idea of a covenant.

E. In both texts the flood comes. In the Epic of Gilgamesh, people are alone; in the Torah, God is a partner—God helps.

F. In both texts the flood covers the earth. Where the Torah is silent about God's reaction, the Epic of Gilgamesh informs us that the gods were scared.

G. In both texts the flood does its damage.

H. In both texts the ark rests on a mountain.

I. In both texts the man lets a bird go. In the Epic of Gilgamesh it is a dove. In the Noah story it is a raven. In both texts, the bird goes back and forth because there is no place to land.

J. The birds are reversed; this time Noah releases the dove and the hero of the Epic of Gilgamesh releases the raven. Both birds fly away.

K. Both men offer sacrifices. Both the gods and the Lord like the smell. In the Torah, the story ends with a covenant.

When you see the overlapping details in the story, it is fairly clear that they are related. It looks like the Torah rewords the Gilgamesh materials. The reversal of the dove and the raven is a telltale sign. The Torah often uses chaism, a reversal of details, to emphasize a repetition.

The reworking, however, represents major changes. There is one God, not many. This God is both ethical and concerned about people rather than capricious. And, finally, the Flood story becomes one of transformation, introducing to the world the idea of a covenant between God and people.

Excavation # 4

1. You get *berachah* if you **do good**.

   You get *kelalah* if you **do bad**.

   In other words, it says:

   God rewards people who **do good**.

   God punishes people who **do bad**.

2. A. They all share the idea that our actions have direct and specific consequences. If we do good, we are rewarded. If we do bad, we are punished. In the Deuteronomic world, reward and punishment are tied to the mitzvot— these are the criteria by which God judges our keeping of the covenant.

   B. This depicts God as being very directly in-volved in each of our lives. It shows that God really watches and responds to each of us.

3. A "lost scroll" is suddenly found, made public, and its "refound" laws are used to change Jewish life, purging all "non-Jewish" forms of worship.

The key word here is "covenant." The phrase "I am going to bring disaster...because they have forsaken Me" is pure Deuteronomy.

The Book of Deuteronomy was probably written as a document to allow Josiah to reform Jewish life. Taking this new book and suddenly finding it (as a very old text) gives him the authority to begin the reformation.

The Anchor Bible

1. The core issue here is who wrote this text: Is it a J, E, P, or D source?

2. The name *Adonai*, the Lord, is used in a J document.

   J documents are closer to folktales. God usually is directly involved (no angels), and the action is told directly without much editorial material. J tells stories from an earthly perspective. We look over the biblical characters' shoulders at God. The stories are rooted in human emotions, pain, conflict, love, joy, etc. J's people have free will.

3. The name *Elohim*, God, is used in an E document.

   E documents are more formal. They see God as more distant, and they see the universe precisely following rules. E stories have God contact people with angels and messengers. In E stories we look from heaven down at people. In these stories, God is in complete control.

4. Because the text uses *Elohim*.

5. Because the style of storytelling is much more J-like.

6. Knowing the source of a document helps us understand its meaning. In the case of this story, and the "test of faith" God uses on Abraham, understanding the God-view and culture of the authors helps us extrapolate the difficult lesson.

The Notes

LXX gives "lofty," the same translation as for Moreh in 12:6

This means, in the Septuagint, we find the name Moreh translated as lofty, meaning upon a lofty hill, rather than a specific hill. The same occurs in Genesis 12:6: "Abram passed through the land as far as the site of Shechem, at the terebinth of Moreh." Moreh is a similar place-name. The problem here is that there is no real place named Moriah which we can identify; therefore, everyone is trying to explain the name.

Syr. "of the Amorites"

In the Peshitta, the Syriac translation (another very early source), we find the word Moriah explained as "of the Amorites." This would make Mt. Moriah an Amorite mountain.

other versions operate with mr'h, "sight, vision"

In other sources, the word Moriah is connected to the Hebrew root *mem, reish, alef*, which means "sight" or "vision." This interpretation makes Mt. Moriah a place of insight, or a place where God is "seen."

elsewhere only in 2 Chron. 3:1, referring to Temple Hill

The only other place in the Bible where Mt. Moriah is found is in 2 Chron. 3:1, where the Temple Mount is clearly being referred to. The idea that the place of the Binding of Isaac is the Temple Mount is a midrashic tradition which is still held strongly today. The Muslims built the Dome of the Rock over a rock on the Temple Mount because they believe that rock is the precise site.

MODULE TEN: THE REAL THING

...For those of us who see in the Torah a people's search for and meeting with God the answer is self-evident. The search and the meeting provide a record which by its very nature has something to say about the essentials of human existence.

But even for those who see in the book only the human quest, with all its strengths and weaknesses, there ought to be something special about it....

...[The Torah] may be said to mirror the collective memory of our ancestors, and in the course of centuries this record became a source of truth for the Children of Israel. The reader will do well to keep in mind that the Torah not only speaks of history but has made history by helping to shape human thought.

The origins of the Torah are one thing, its life through the centuries another, and its ability to speak to us today yet a third....

W. Gunther Plaut—Introduction to *The Torah: A Modern Commentary* (UAHC)

Rx

When you study Torah seriously, working space can be a problem. You never sit alone, just yourself and the "naked" text. You sit with a whole collection of tools and guides—dictionaries and lexicons, various translations, commentaries, reference guides, an atlas. I always have trouble knowing how to stack and arrange the volumes. Something important is always getting buried.

These stacks of open books are much more than sources of information; they are voices from the past and present, differing insights and opinions, representing various methodologies. When you sit down to unpack a passage, you gather as many guides as possible. None of these references will tell you exactly what the passage will come to mean to you, but all of them provide trails for you to follow and clues to meanings which you can extract.

In Module Eight we were introduced to *Mikraot Gedolot*, "the Big Bible." We saw that a single page carried versions of all the different sources Bible students in the sixteenth century would stack on their desks. We also saw that it was "formatted" to make the established pattern of Torah study easier. In turn, its format has kept this process alive and trained us in an evolving dialogue of close-reading.

In this module, "The Real Thing," we will update this process by adding the critical (scientific) sources which are also part of our background. For nine modules you've been gaining the background, insights, and skills necessary to decode the biblical text and make it personally meaningful. In this module, we are going to put those skills to work. We are past the training process— we're into the real thing.

In this module you'll find three texts to consider:

TEXT ONE: ESTHER 2:5-11

(The Introduction of Mordecai and Esther)

TEXT TWO: LEVITICUS 19:1-18

(Part of the Holiness Code)

TEXT THREE: DEUTERONOMY 34:1-12

(The Death of Moses)

TEXT ONE: ESTHER 2:5-11

(The Introduction of Mordecai and Esther)

THE GAME PLAN

The first chapter of the Book of Esther introduces King Ahasuerus and tells the story of Queen Vashti refusing to appear before the king as ordered. At the end of the first chapter, she is presumed to be executed and, at the beginning of the second chapter, the king begins the search for a new queen. This is where our passage begins. We are introduced to Mordecai and then Esther, and then we see Esther's entrance into the harem.

In trying to figure out what this passage "means to you," you are going to work with the following tools:

1. Three different copies of the text: the Masoretic text, the 1916 JPS translation of the text (SJV), and the 1979 Anchor Bible translation.
2. Two sets of commentaries: Rashi and Carey A. Moore's "critical" commentary from the Anchor Bible.
3. Some additional midrashic insights.
4. A blank page for you to draw conclusions.
   We'll work with these sources in order—and now on to the first quarter.

STEP ONE: COMPARATIVE TRANSLATIONS

The first step in reading a biblical text is figuring out the *peshat*, the plain meaning of the text. Even traditional rabbis (like Rashi) checked out their understanding of the text by using translations. That is why the Targum is part of *Mikraot Gedolot* and is placed right alongside the Masoretic text.

If you can read and understand the Hebrew text, you can directly check out the "decisions" made by a translator in the English rendering. If you don't know that much Hebrew, you can often figure out the same thing by comparing two or more translations. (Think back to Module Five.)

In comparing translations (and looking for the *peshat*) we are trying (1) to find what places in the text aren't clear. (We already know that some places in the biblical text are difficult or almost impossible to understand. Before we try to interpret the symbolic meaning of a verse, we want to make sure that the literal understanding is clear. We want to know if the translator is "commenting" in the rendering.) And (2) we want to identify the "slant" used by the translator. (If there is an ideology behind the translation, which makes it a commentary, we want to be aware of it. That is why we practiced sorting out ornamental and stylistic differences in translation, in opposition to differences in actual understanding.)

In this text, there are no difficult words and no differences in understanding (so you don't have to look for them). What we have is a stylistic distinction. What makes this important is the fact that Carey Moore, the scholar who prepared the critical commentary we will use, supervised the Anchor translation, and understanding his translation will clarify his commentary.

אִישׁ יְהוּדִי הָיָה בְּשׁוּשַׁן הַבִּירָה וּשְׁמוֹ מָרְדֳּכַי בֶּן יָאִיר בֶּן־שִׁמְעִי בֶּן־קִישׁ אִישׁ יְמִינִי.

(5)There was a certain Jew in Shushan the castle, whose name was Mordecai the son of Jair the son of Shimei the son of Kish, a Benjaminite.

אֲשֶׁר הָגְלָה מִירוּשָׁלַיִם עִם־הַגֹּלָה אֲשֶׁר הָגְלְתָה עִם יְכָנְיָה מֶלֶךְ־יְהוּדָה אֲשֶׁר הֶגְלָה נְבוּכַדְנֶצַּר מֶלֶךְ בָּבֶל.

(6)who had been carried away from Jerusalem with the captives that had been carried away with Jeconiah king of Judah, whom Nebuchadnezzar the king of Babylon had carried away.

וַיְהִי אֹמֵן אֶת־הֲדַסָּה הִיא אֶסְתֵּר בַּת־דֹּדוֹ כִּי אֵין לָהּ אָב וָאֵם וְהַנַּעֲרָה יְפַת־תֹּאַר וְטוֹבַת מַרְאֶה וּבְמוֹת אָבִיהָ וְאִמָּהּ לְקָחָהּ מָרְדֳּכַי לוֹ לְבַת.

(7)And he brought up Hadassah, that is, Esther, his uncle's daughter; for she had neither father nor mother, and the maiden was of beautiful form and fair to look on; and when her father and mother were dead, Mordecai took her for his own daughter.

וַיְהִי בְּהִשָּׁמַע דְּבַר־הַמֶּלֶךְ וְדָתוֹ וּבְהִקָּבֵץ נְעָרוֹת רַבּוֹת אֶל־שׁוּשַׁן הַבִּירָה אֶל־יַד הֵגָי וַתִּלָּקַח אֶסְתֵּר אֶל־בֵּית הַמֶּלֶךְ אֶל־יַד הֵגַי שֹׁמֵר הַנָּשִׁים.

(8)So it came to pass, when the king's commandment and his decree was published, and when many maidens were gathered together unto Shushan the castle, to the custody of Hegai, that Esther was taken into the king's house, to the custody of Hegai, keeper of the women.

וַתִּיטַב הַנַּעֲרָה בְעֵינָיו וַתִּשָּׂא חֶסֶד לְפָנָיו וַיְבַהֵל אֶת־תַּמְרוּקֶיהָ וְאֶת־מָנוֹתֶהָ לָתֵת לָהּ וְאֵת שֶׁבַע הַנְּעָרוֹת הָרְאֻיוֹת לָתֶת־לָהּ מִבֵּית הַמֶּלֶךְ וַיְשַׁנֶּהָ וְאֶת־נַעֲרוֹתֶיהָ לְטוֹב בֵּית הַנָּשִׁים.

(9)And the maiden pleased him, and she obtained kindness of him; and he speedily gave her her ointments, with her portions, and the seven maidens, who were meet to be given her out of the king's house; and he advanced her and her maidens to the best place in the house of the women.

לֹא־הִגִּידָה אֶסְתֵּר אֶת־עַמָּהּ וְאֶת־מוֹלַדְתָּהּ כִּי מָרְדֳּכַי צִוָּה עָלֶיהָ אֲשֶׁר לֹא־תַגִּיד.

(10)Esther had not made known her people nor her kindred; for Mordecai had charged her that she should not tell it.

וּבְכָל־יוֹם וָיוֹם מָרְדֳּכַי מִתְהַלֵּךְ לִפְנֵי חֲצַר בֵּית־הַנָּשִׁים לָדַעַת אֶת־שְׁלוֹם אֶסְתֵּר וּמַה־יֵּעָשֶׂה בָּהּ.

(11)And Mordecai walked every day before the court of the women's house, to know how Esther did, and what would become of her.

(5)Now there was in the acropolis of Susa a Jew whose name was Mordecai the son of Jair, son of Shimei, son of Kish, a Benjaminite;

(6)he had been carried away from Jerusalem with the exiles who had been deported with Jeconiah king of Judah, whom Nebuchadnezzar king of Babylon had taken into exile.

(7)And he had reared his cousin Hadassah (Esther, that is) since she had neither father nor mother. The girl was shapely and had a beautiful face. After her father and mother had died, Mordecai adopted her.

(8)Later on, when the king's edict was promulgated and when many young girls were brought to the acropolis of Susa and placed in Hegai's custody, Esther was also taken to the palace and was entrusted to Hegai, who had charge of the women.

(9)The girl pleased him and gained his support so that he promptly gave her beauty treatment and her delicacies, and he provided her with seven special maids from the palace and transferred her and her maids to the best quarters of the harem.

(10)Esther had not said anything about her origins because Mordecai had forbidden her to do so;

(11)and every day Mordecai used to walk about in front of the court of the harem so as to find out about Esther's well-being and progress.

Before you go on to the next page, make some notes on the differences between these translations here.

_____

_____

_____

_____

_____

_____

_____

_____

_____

These phrases come from the JPS (SJV) translation. Find the matching terms used by the Anchor translation.

Shushan_____

the castle_____

his uncle's daughter _____

keeper of the women _____

house of the women_____

Let's state the obvious. The SJV translation uses "classical" English while the Anchor translation reflects a more modern use of English. Also, the SJV tries to follow the syntax (order) of the Hebrew words while the Anchor translation rearranges the phrases into a more logical English. This makes the Anchor Bible similar to the NJV (1962 JPS translation). There is another big difference.

When we introduced the Anchor Bible in Module Nine, we quoted from their statement of purpose:

> THE ANCHOR BIBLE is a fresh approach to the world's greatest classic. Its object is to make the Bible accessible to the modern reader; its method is to arrive at the meaning of biblical literature through *exact translation and extended exposition, and to reconstruct the ancient setting of the biblical story, as well as the circumstances of its transcription* and the characteristics of its transcribers.

How do the examples of Anchor "renderings" of Hebrew words express this objective?

_____

_____

What is the parallel commitment of the SJV? (Check back in Module Five if you need help.)

_____

_____

_____

STEP TWO: TWO SETS OF COMMENTARIES

In comparing the two translations we saw a major difference in purpose. In the SJV, Hebrew words were translated into the closest possible English word. In a sense, it is Hebrew written in English. The Anchor Bible has a different purpose in mind. Its style is more modern, but, more than "updating," it is extrapolating. So the Hebrew בֵּית הַנָּשִׁים / *bet hanashim*, house of the women or women's house, is translated as "harem," and the Hebrew שׁוּשָׁן / *Shushan* is changed to Susa—the historical name of the Persian capital. Perhaps the clearest example demonstrating the differences comes in the first verse of the book. Just about every translation of the Book of Esther refers to the king in the story as Ahasuerus (a transliteration of the Hebrew name). In the Anchor Bible, the king is called Xerxes. Carey Moore gives this explanation:

The author of Esther apparently knew of several Persian kings by the name of *ahasweros*, "the chief of rulers"...since the nineteenth century it has been clear from both the linguistic and archeological evidence that *ahswrws* is Xerxes I (485-465 B.C.E.), son of Darius and Atossa, the Persian king whose defeats at the hands of the Greeks at Thermopylae (480 B.C.E.), Salamis (480), and Plataea (479) have been immortalized by Herodotus in his *History of the Persian Wars*, VII-IX....

In other words, the Anchor Bible's translation is an expression of its objective: *to reconstruct the ancient setting of the biblical story*. In other words: Ahasuerus and women's house represent the Hebrew understanding of the period; Xerxes and harem reflect the "real culture" which the Hebrew author was observing.

This is all-important, because it explains the two commentaries we are going to study.

Carey Moore is a modern (Christian) Bible scholar. In working on his Anchor Bible translation and commentary, he was primarily answering two questions:

1. Is the Book of Esther a true story, a piece of fiction, or a piece of historical fiction—carefully using historical detail?

2. What did the author of the Book of Esther want to teach us? How did the author understand this work? In other words, Carey Moore is concerned with the *real meaning*. For him—*real meaning* reflects the historical reality.

Rashi, a traditional Jewish commentator who believed that God "wrote" the Book of Esther and that there is a religious message in the book, focused on different issues.

1. Esther seems to "do wrong" by marrying a non-Jew. Mordecai seems to encourage her. Rashi wants to learn why it was acceptable (or even commendable) to do "wrong" in order to save the Jewish people.

2. Rashi wants to learn the ultimate meaning of this story. While Esther's story is a historical event (for him), it is also a model for the way the Jewish people will again be saved and redeemed. Rashi wants to learn how this single moment of redemption teaches the pattern for the final redemption.

In other words, he, too, is concerned with the *real meaning* of the story. His "reality" concerns what one can learn about being a Jew.

Let's get into the passage.
For each one, explain (1) the question and (2) the explanation.

ANCHOR	SJV

ANCHOR

(5) Now there was in the acropolis of Susa a Jew whose name was Mordecai the son of Jair, son of Shimei, son of Kish, a Benjaminite;

Moore:

A Jew. In the Masoretic text, the phrase "a Jewish man" is put in an emphatic position; this is probably because the following verse introduces the hero and heroine to the reader.

Question _____

Explanation _____

Mordecai. A good Babylonian name, *mordakay.* It is a hebraized form of *marduka,* which is based on the god name—Marduk....That a religious Jew should have had such an unhebraic, not to say idolatrous, name has been of some concern to scholars. D. C. Siegfried insisted that the name is Aramaic and means "pure myrrh."...

Question _____

Explanation _____

The son of Jair. Unlike his son, Mordecai's father had a good Hebrew name. For proof, see Num. 32:41, Deut. 3:14, Josh. 13:30, Judg. 10:3.

Question _____

Explanation _____

SJV

(5) There was a certain Jew in Shushan the castle, whose name was Mordecai the son of Jair the son of Shimei the son of Kish, a Benjaminite,

Rashi:

A Jew. He is called יְהוּדִי / *Yehudi,* "a Judean" (the word could be understood as either "a Jew" or a "person from Judea") because he went into exile with the Judean exiles. All those who went into exile with the kings of Judea were called יְהוּדִים / *Yehudim,* Jews.

Koshi: _____

Answer: _____

Lesson: _____

RASHI

A Benjaminite. He came from the tribe of Benjamin. This is the *peshat* (plain meaning) but you can find other explanations in the Talmud: Meg. 12b, 13a.

*Koshi:*_____

Answer: _____

Lesson: _____

MOORE

Son of Shimei, son of Kish, a Benjaminite. Most commentators (following the lead of Josephus and the Targum) believe that these names are distant, well-known ancestors of Mordecai and not his grandfather and great-grandfather.

This genealogy tends to suggest that the character of Mordecai was a real historical figure. Kish's son King Saul fought Agag the Amalekite—the ancient enemy of the Jewish people. Haman is introduced as *Haman, the son of Hammedatha the Agagite.* Thus the ancient rivalry between Israel and Amalek (Saul and Agag) is continued with Mordecai and Haman. Had the author of the Book of Esther wanted to invent Mordecai, it would have been logical to make him a direct descendant of Saul. Here, they have only a common relative: Kish.

Question _____

Explanation _____

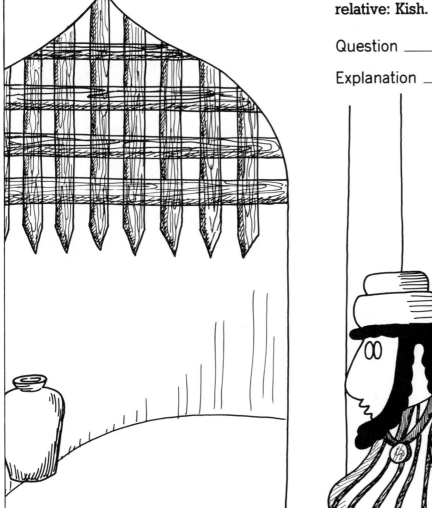

ANCHOR

(7) And he had reared his cousin Hadassah (Esther, that is) since she had neither father nor mother. The girl was shapely and had a beautiful face. After her father and mother had died, Mordecai adopted her.

Moore

Hadassah. P. Jensen thought that the name was related to *hadassatum,* a synonym of *kallatu,* "a bride." But, most scholars follow the Targum,which interprets it to mean "myrtle" (as in Isa. 41:19, etc). The II Targum explains "Because, as the myrtle spreads fragrance in the world, so did she spread good works...."

Some scholars have tried to match Hadassah with Atossa the daughter of Cyrus and wife of Darius, but Bardtke is correct that these efforts have been useless.

There is, of course, no great difficulty in believing that a Jewish girl could be part of a Persian king's harem. When it came to foreign wives, kings could be quite broad-minded; for example, the Assyrian king Sennacherib had in his harem a Palestinian wife, the famous Zakutu-Naqiya.

Question _____

Explanation _____

Esther. Esther had two names, one Hebraic and one non-Hebraic. The non-Hebrew name "Esther" was derived from either the Persian *"stara"* or Ishtar, the Babylonian goddess of love.

Question _____

Explanation _____

SJV

(7) And he brought up Hadassah, that is, Esther, his uncle's daughter; for she had neither father nor mother, and the maiden was of beautiful form and fair to look on; and when her father and mother were dead, Mordecai took her for his own daughter.

Rashi

To himself as a daughter. Our rabbis explained *"levat"* (like a daughter) as similar to *"levayit"* (like a house), which means "like a wife." (Meg.13a)

CLUE: Notice that Rashi only reports this insight as the rabbi's explanation. He doesn't underline it as correct, and he doesn't argue against it.

*Koshi:*_____

Answer:_____

Lesson: _____

MOORE

Adopted her. Literally "took her to himself as a daughter." The LXX (Septuagint) and Megillah 13a (Talmud) both have "he took her to himself for a wife." The problem here clearly lies with the Greek, not the Hebrew, for the latter makes perfectly good sense. Since Esther was taken to the king's harem (2:8), she was obviously regarded by all as a virgin.

Haupt offers the ingenious suggestion that the LXX's translation "for a wife" represents the misreading of *levat,* "for a daughter," as *levayit,* "for a house," which in the Talmud can also mean "for a wife."

ANCHOR

(8) Later on, when the king's edict was promulgated and when many young girls were brought to the acropolis of Susa and placed in Hegai's custody, Esther was also taken to the *palace* and was entrusted to Hegai, who had charge of the women.

Moore

Palace. Literally "the house of the king." Here the phrase does not mean "the king's private apartment (2:13), but rather the entire palace complex....(4:14).

Question _____

Explanation_____

215

ANCHOR

(9) The girl pleased him and gained his support so that he promptly gave her beauty treatment and her delicacies, and he provided her with seven special maids from the palace and transferred her and her maids to the best quarters of the harem.

Moore

Gained his support. The verb used here is *ns*, "to carry, to gain," not *ms*, "to find." *Ns* and *ms* are not exact synonyms in Esther: the former is more active and the latter is more passive....

Question _____

Explanation _____

He promptly gave her. Literally "he hastened to give her." The twelve-month regimen itself (2:12) could not be shortened, but its initiation could be hastened or delayed. The shrewd eyes of Hegai, who knew better than anyone else the king's taste in women, saw in Esther the likely successor to Vashti. Thus, to satisfy the king, and perhaps to gain the potential queen's goodwill, Hegai promptly began Esther's twelve-month program.

CLUE: Notice that this is Moore's opinion; he cites no sources.

Question _____

Explanation _____

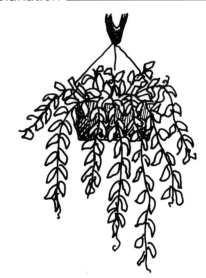

NJV

(9) And the maiden pleased him, and she obtained kindness of him; and he speedily gave her her ointments, with her portions, and the seven maidens who were meant to be given her out of the king's house; and he advanced her and her maidens to the best place in the house of the women.

Rashi

So he hastened her ointments. He was expedient and hurried with her ointments more than all the others.

Koshi: _____

Answer: _____

Lesson: _____

And he advanced her. He changed her. וַיְשַׁנֶּהָ / *vayeshaneha* is a contraction of שִׁנָּה אוֹתָהּ / *shinah otah.*

Koshi: _____

Answer: _____

Lesson: _____

Why does Rashi make this comment?

_____

_____

_____

SJV

(10) Esther had not made known her people nor her kindred; for Mordecai had charged her that she should not tell it.

Rashi

That she should not tell. So that they should say that she is from a common family and would therefore send her away, for, if they knew that she was from the family of King Saul, they would hold on to her.

*Koshi:*_____

Answer: _____

Lesson:_____

ANCHOR

(10)Esther had not said anything about her origins because Mordecai had forbidden her to do so;

ANCHOR

(11) and every day Mordecai used to walk about in front of the court of the harem so as to find out about Esther's well-being and progress.

Moore

To find out. Literally "to know." In the absence of any details in the MT (Masoretic text), many commentators have offered their speculations as to how Mordecai got his information about Esther in the harem.

Some have argued that Mordecai must have been a eunuch; otherwise how could he have had access to her?...Other scholars have suggested that Mordecai may have used a eunuch here as an intermediary, just as he did in 4:2-16....But the best interpretation is that the writer left out details not essential to his main purpose, which was to affirm the fact that Mordecai kept his contact with Esther.

Question_____

Explanation _____

SJV

(11) And Mordecai walked every day before the court of the women's house, to know how Esther did, and what would become of her.

Rashi

And what would become of her. Mordecai is one of two righteous people to whom was given a hint of an impending future. David was the other. We know that David was given a hint (1 Sam. 17:36) because it says: *Both the lion and the bear your servant killed.* David said: *The LORD that delivered me out of the paw of the lion, and out of the paw of the bear, He will deliver me out of the hand of this Philistine.* These incidents happened to me so that I could rely upon them to do battle with Goliath.

In the same way Mordecai said: "This happened to this righteous woman—that she should be taken to the bed of a gentile, only because she is destined to arise and bring salvation to Israel." Therefore, he repeatedly went to find out what would be her fate.

CLUE: In this question, Rashi is asking two levels of questions. One has to do with the specific phrases in this verse; the other is a more global question.

*Koshi:*_____

Answer:_____

Lesson: _____

*Koshi:*_____

Answer:_____

Lesson: _____

BIGGER ANSWERS

As we have seen, the previous commentaries are a verse-by-verse approach to the text. They also deal with larger questions. Reread the comments and answer the following.

ANCHOR

What do we know about the "historic" reality of the text?
What things suggest that it is based on truth?

_____

_____

_____

_____

_____

What did you find to suggest that the "history" is questionable?

_____

_____

_____

_____

_____

RASHI

How can Esther be a "model" for a Jew if she married a non-Jew?

_____

_____

_____

_____

What does this redemption tell us about the final redemption?

_____

_____

_____

Remember, you've only seen a small portion of their comments.

DRAWING SOME CONCLUSIONS

In this module, we have looked at the differences between a "Jewish" rabbinic commentary and a "secular" scientific commentary. Now let's look at some of the similarities.

I. Indicate the comments which were concerned only with "giving meaning" rather than interpretation.

_____

_____

_____

_____

2. Indicate the comments which weren't generated by the text, but rather by knowing someone else's comments on the text.

_____

_____

_____

_____

3. Which comments were included only for the sake of "teaching" and not for the sake of "making a difficulty clear"?

_____

_____

_____

_____

_____

_____

4. In which selections did the commentators acknowledge the work of others?

_____

_____

_____

_____

_____

How does the biblical text create these similarities?

_____

_____

_____

_____

Here are some comments from other Jewish sources. For each, state the question, the answer, and the moral or message.

These are taken from *Me 'am Lo'ez*, a Sephardic commentary written in Ladino by Rabbi Raphael Chiyya Pontremoli around 1864. This was the completion of a project begun by Rabbi Yaakov Culi in 1730. The work is an anthology of midrashim on the biblical text. The following were taken from the volume on Esther.

There was a Jewish man in Shushan, and his name was Mordecai, son of Yair, son of Shimini, son of Kish, of the tribe of Benjamin.

The Megillah says "There was a Jewish man in Shushan," as if Mordecai were the only Jew there. He was given this distinction because he (alone) did not partake in Ahasuerus's feast (even though kosher meat was served).

_____

_____

Mordecai comes from מְרָא דְכָא /mera decha (which is the Aramaic translation of "raw myrrh"; see Exod. 30:23). Raw myrrh has an unpleasant fragrance and only becomes a fine perfume when it is processed by fire. Mordecai, also, attained his status of leadership by being processed through the fire of suffering and exile.

_____

_____

One reason Mordecai was able to deliver Israel was because he came from the tribe of Benjamin. Of all the brothers, Benjamin was the only one who did not participate in the selling of Joseph. Mordecai's ancestor Benjamin therefore had the merit to help him bring about the miracle of Purim.

_____

_____

He had raised his cousin Hadassah, also known as Esther....

Esther's true name was Hadassah, Hebrew for myrtle. She was given this name because she had a deep olive complexion, like a myrtle; and, just as a myrtle has a pleasing fragrance, she had a winning personality.

_____

_____

Most trees have foliage during the rainy season but lose it during the dry season. The myrtle, however, is an evergreen, retaining its foliage all year round. Esther similarly remained virtuous and religious no matter where she was—she was the same in Ahasuerus's palace as she was in Mordecai's house.

_____

_____

The myrtle appears to be without fragrance; its perfume is only evident when its leaves are bruised and crushed. Superficially, Esther seemed to have done wrong in marrying a gentile king and living in his immoral, nonkosher palace. But upon closer examination one sees that everything Esther did was completely virtuous and justified for the benefit of Israel.

_____

_____

221

Hadassah is obviously a Jewish name. Realizing that Esther was destined to marry Ahasuerus and save her people, Mordecai changed her name. Since he was concealing her true name, he called her אֶסְתֵּר /Esther from the root ס־ת־ר /satar, meaning "to conceal." It was almost as if he had named her "Anonymous."

_____

_____

_____

_____

_____

_____

This is your page; use it to draw your own conclusions about this passage from Esther. Think about the most interesting, most beautiful, and most important questions and comments.

TEXT TWO: LEVITICUS 19:1-18 (Part of the Holiness Code)

To understand this passage we will use two JPS translations (NJV and SJV) and two commentaries, the Century Bible and Rashi.

CENTURY BIBLE

This chapter consists of various commandments which parallel those of Exod. 20, 22:18-31, 23:1-19; Deut. 5:6. Their order differs....Sometimes the second person is used and sometimes the third. This is a compilation from many sources.

Question _____

Explanation _____

וַיְדַבֵּר יהוה אֶל־מֹשֶׁה לֵּאמֹר. דַּבֵּר אֶל־כָּל־עֲדַת בְּנֵי־יִשְׂרָאֵל וְאָמַרְתָּ אֲלֵהֶם קְדֹשִׁים תִּהְיוּ כִּי קָדוֹשׁ אֲנִי יהוה אֱלֹהֵיכֶם.

NJV

(1-2) **The Lord spoke to Moses, saying: Speak to the whole Israelite community and say to them: You shall be holy, for I, the Lord your God, am holy.**

SJV

(1-2) **And the Lord spoke to Moses, saying: Speak to all the congregation of the children of Israel, and say to them: You shall be holy; for I the Lord your God am holy.**

CENTURY BIBLE

Verses 2-4. An early set of commandments, involving three injunctions: revere parents, keep the sabbath, shun idolatry. The order is the opposite of that of Exodus 20 (the Ten Commandments).

Question _____

Explanation _____

RASHI

Speak to all the congregation of the children of Israel. The (extra) words "all the congregation" teach us that this section was taught to all of the congregation because most of the fundamental teachings of the Torah are contained in it.

Koshi: _____

Answer: _____

Lesson: _____

You shall be holy. This means to keep away from forbidden sexual relations (taught in Lev. 18). How do we know this?—because every place in the Torah where you find a command to keep yourself away from such things, you also find a mention of holiness. Look at Lev. 21:7 and Lev. 15.

Koshi:_____

Answer: _____

Lesson:_____

אִישׁ אִמּוֹ וְאָבִיו תִּירָאוּ וְאֶת־שַׁבְּתֹתַי תִּשְׁמֹרוּ אֲנִי יְהוָה אֱלֹהֵיכֶם.

NJV

(3) **You shall each revere his mother and his father, and keep My sabbaths: I the Lord am your God.**

SJV

(3) **You shall fear every man his mother, and his father, and you shall keep My sabbaths: I am the Lord your God.**

CENTURY BIBLE

Revere. Hebrew has yare, the usual verb for "fear," used in all connections, including fearing God. Usually the word used of man's attitude to his parents is k-b-d (honor) as in Exod. 20:12 and Deut. 5:16. The word yare is not often used with God's name (about eleven times); see verse 14.

Question _____

Explanation_____

His mother and father. This is not the usual order (cf. Exod. 20:12; Deut. 5:16.). LXX omits the reference to the mother and T (Targum Onkelos) has the usual order.

Question _____

Explanation_____

RASHI

Every one of you shall fear his mother and father. The Torah mentions the mother before the father because it is expected that the child fears the father more than the mother and thereby reversing it the Torah stresses fearing her. In the case of honoring parents (such as in the Ten Commandments) the Torah mentions the father first because it is expected that the child will honor the mother more than the father....

Koshi:_____

Answer: _____

Lesson: _____

אַל־תִּפְנוּ אֶל־הָאֱלִילִם וֵאלֹהֵי מַסֵּכָה לֹא תַעֲשׂוּ לָכֶם אֲנִי יהוה אֱלֹהֵיכֶם.

NJV

(4) **Do not turn to idols or make molten gods for yourselves: I the Lord am your God.**

SJV

(4) **Turn you not to idols, nor make to yourselves molten gods: I am the Lord your God.**

RASHI

Turn you not to idols. **To worship them.** (Sifra) **The word** אֱלִילִם /*elilim* (idols) is related to the word אַל /*al* (not) and means "nothings."

Koshi:_____

Answer:_____

Lesson: _____

וְכִי תִזְבְּחוּ זֶבַח שְׁלָמִים לַיהוה לִרְצֹנְכֶם תִּזְבָּחֻהוּ.

NJV

(5)**When you sacrifice an offering of well-being to the Lord, sacrifice it so that it may be accepted on your behalf.**

SJV

(5)**And when you offer a sacrifice of peace-offering unto the Lord, you shall offer it that you may be accepted.**

CENTURY BIBLE

Offer. This is the normal English translation. This rendering aids the confusion regarding this sacrifice, none of which went to the altar. It is better to keep strictly to the Hebrew and translate "slaughter."

Question _____

Explanation _____

That you will be accepted. The usual assumption is that if the rule is broken the sacrifice will not be acceptable to God, but God did not share in this sacrifice, since none of the flesh went to the altar. The meaning might possibly be to gain favor (peace, good health) for yourselves (cf. 22:19 and 29, 23:11.)

LXX has dekaten (a tenth) but this looks like a scribal error in the Greek for dekten (acceptable).

Question _____

Explanation _____

בְּיוֹם זִבְחֲכֶם יֵאָכֵל וּמִמָּחֳרָת וְהַנּוֹתָר עַד־יוֹם הַשְּׁלִישִׁי בָּאֵשׁ יִשָּׂרֵף. וְאִם הֵאָכֹל יֵאָכֵל בַּיוֹם הַשְּׁלִישִׁי פִּגּוּל הוּא לֹא יֵרָצֶה. וְאֹכְלָיו עֲוֺנוֹ יִשָּׂא כִּי־אֶת־קֹדֶשׁ יהוה חִלֵּל וְנִכְרְתָה הַנֶּפֶשׁ הַהִוא מֵעַמֶּיהָ. וּבְקֻצְרְכֶם אֶת־קְצִיר אַרְצְכֶם לֹא תְכַלֶּה פְּאַת שָׂדְךָ לִקְצֹר וְלֶקֶט קְצִירְךָ לֹא תְלַקֵּט.

NJV

(6-9)**It shall be eaten on the day you sacrifice it, or on the day following; but what is left by the third day must be consumed in fire. If it should be eaten on the third day, it is an offensive thing, it will not be acceptable. And he who eats of it shall bear his guilt, for he has profaned what is sacred to the Lord; that person shall be cut off from his kin. When you reap the harvest of your land, you shall not reap all the way to the edges of your field, or gather the gleanings of your harvest.**

SJV

(6-9)**It shall be eaten the same day you offer it, and on the morrow; and if aught remain until the third day, it shall be burnt with fire. And if it be eaten at all on the third day, it is a vile thing: it shall not be accepted. But everyone that eats it shall bear his iniquity, because he has profaned the holy thing of the Lord; and that soul shall be cut off from his people. And when you reap the harvest of your land, you shall not wholly reap the corner of your field, neither shall you gather the gleaning of your harvest.**

CENTURY BIBLE

Reap...to its very border. Lit. "finish to reap the edge of your field." We must think of the reapers beginning at one end of the strip and moving steadily in a line across the field.

V (Vulgate—the first Latin translation) has "you must not cut down to the very ground." The translation "corners" comes from T.

Question _____

Explanation _____

RASHI

Reap the corners. This means that one must leave a "*peah*," an uncut portion at the end of the field. (Sifra; Peah 1:2; Shab. 23a)

Koshi:_____

Answer: _____

Lesson: _____

The Gleanings. These are ears which are dropped by the harvesters during the reaping. If they drop one or two, it must be left. But if they drop three, it can be picked up. (Peah 4:5; San. 99a)

Koshi:_____

Answer: _____

Lesson: _____

וְכַרְמְךָ לֹא תְעוֹלֵל וּפֶרֶט כַּרְמְךָ לֹא תְלַקֵּט לֶעָנִי וְלַגֵּר תַּעֲזֹב אֹתָם אֲנִי יהוה אֱלֹהֵיכֶם.

NJV

(10) **You shall not pick your vineyard bare, or gather the fallen fruit of your vineyard; you shall leave them for the poor and the stranger: I the Lord am your God.**

SJV

(10) **And you shall not glean your vineyard, neither shall you gather the fallen fruit of your vineyard; you shall leave them for the poor and for the stranger: I am the Lord your God.**

CENTURY BIBLE

Pick bare. Is too weak. Hebrew l-l means "deal severely."...The Arabic alla means to do a thing a second time and probably this is what we have here.

Question _____

Explanation_____

Fallen fruit of your vineyard. The noun peret appears only here (and nowhere else in the Bible). The corresponding Aramaic word means "small change." The word here refers to single grapes which have fallen to the ground and also to grapes which are not part of ordinary clusters. All true grape clusters are to be picked; odd grapes are to be left.

Question _____

Explanation_____

RASHI

And you shall not glean your vineyard. תְעוֹלֵל /te'olel l-l is the verb, which is related to the noun עוֹלֵל /olel, meaning young and tender (see 1 Sam. 15:3). The verb means not to take the tender grapes.

Koshi:_____

Answer: _____

Lesson: _____

I am the Lord your God. I am the judge who will punish you for breaking these rules...as it says in the Torah (Prov. 22:23): *Rob not the poor...for the Lord will plead their cause.*

Koshi:_____

Answer: _____

Lesson: _____

לֹא תִּגְנֹבוּ וְלֹא־תְכַחֲשׁוּ וְלֹא־תְשַׁקְּרוּ אִישׁ בַּעֲמִיתוֹ.

NJV

(11)**You shall not steal; you shall not deal deceitfully or falsely with one another.**

SJV

(11)**You shall not steal; neither shall you deal falsely, nor lie one to the other.**

CENTURY BIBLE

Lie. Cf. Akkadian taskirtu; better than "deal falsely." LXX has "be a sycophant" —literally one who shows figs which normally are hidden by the leaves, and so "informer" in ancient Greece.

Question _____

Explanation_____

RASHI

You shall not steal. This rule forbids stealing property, but the rule found in the Ten Commandments is a warning not to steal people (kidnap). How do we know this? From the context in the Ten Commandments, that of all capital crimes (murder and adultery) that case is clearly about kidnaping and not robbery. Here the crimes are not of that nature. (Mech.; San. 86a)

You shall not steal; neither shall you deal falsely, nor lie one to the other. If you steal, you will come to deny it; then you will lie and ultimately you will swear falsely.

Koshi:_____

Answer:_____

Lesson: _____

וְלֹא־תִשָּׁבְעוּ בִשְׁמִי לַשָּׁקֶר וְחִלַּלְתָּ אֶת־שֵׁם אֱלֹהֶיךָ אֲנִי יהוה. לֹא־תַעֲשֹׁק אֶת־רֵעֲךָ וְלֹא תִגְזֹל לֹא־תָלִין פְּעֻלַּת שָׂכִיר אִתְּךָ עַד־בֹּקֶר.

NJV

(12-13)**You shall not swear falsely by My name, profaning the name of your God: I am the Lord. You shall not defraud your neighbor. You shall not commit robbery. The wages of a laborer shall not remain with you until morning.**

SJV

(12-13)**And you shall not swear falsely by My name, so that you profane the name of your God: I am the Lord. You shall not oppress your neighbor, nor rob him; the wages of a hired servant shall not abide with you all night until the morning.**

CENTURY BIBLE

Oppress. The verb asak is usually used for extortionate, tyrannical behavior, but the Syriac equivalent means "accuse," "slander," whence the "calumniate" of V.

Question _____

Explanation _____

לֹא־תְקַלֵּל חֵרֵשׁ וְלִפְנֵי עִוֵּר לֹא תִתֵּן מִכְשֹׁל וְיָרֵאתָ מֵאֱלֹהֶיךָ אֲנִי יהוה.

NJV

(14)**You shall not insult the deaf, or place a stumbling block before the blind. You shall fear your God: I am the Lord.**

SJV

(14)**You shall not curse the deaf, nor put a stumbling-block before the blind, but you shall fear your God: I am the Lord.**

RASHI

Curse the deaf. While this law states not to curse the deaf, how do I know that one can't curse any person? Because the Torah teaches this in Exod. 22:27: *You shall not curse anyone from your people.* If I have that rule, why do I need this law? The case of the deaf teaches us a new principle. The deaf can't hear the curse. This means that we can't curse a person regardless of whether they can hear about it. This includes the living and the dead. (Sifra; San. 66a)

Koshi:_____

Answer:_____

Lesson: _____

Stumbling block...the blind. This means that one cannot give a person who is "blind" in a situation advice which is wrong for him.

Koshi:_____

Answer:_____

Lesson: _____

לֹא־תַעֲשׂוּ עָוֶל בַּמִּשְׁפָּט לֹא־תִשָּׂא פְנֵי־דָל
וְלֹא תֶהְדַּר פְּנֵי גָדוֹל בְּצֶדֶק תִּשְׁפֹּט
עֲמִיתֶךָ. לֹא־תֵלֵךְ רָכִיל בְּעַמֶּיךָ לֹא תַעֲמֹד
עַל־דַּם רֵעֶךָ אֲנִי יהוה.

NJV

(15-16) **You shall not render an unfair decision: do not favor the poor or show deference to the rich; judge your neighbor fairly. Do not deal basely with your fellows. Do not profit by the blood of your neighbor: I am the Lord.**

SJV

(15-16) **You shall do no unrighteousness in judgment; you shall not respect the person of the poor, nor favor the person of the mighty; but in righteousness shall you judge your neighbor. You shall not go up and down as a talebearer among your people; neither shall you stand idly by the blood of your neighbor: I am the Lord.**

RASHI

As a talebearer. I say this means all the people who sow discord between people by speaking slander, people who go into their friends' houses in order to spy out evil so that they can tell it in the street....

Koshi:_____

Answer:_____

Lesson: _____

Stand idly by the blood of your neighbor. This means that you shall not witness the death of another when you are able to rescue him. (Sifra; San. 73a)

Koshi:_____

Answer:_____

Lesson: _____

I am the Lord. I am the one who rewards those who keep My commandments and I will punish those who break them.

Koshi:_____

Answer:_____

Lesson: _____

לֹא־תִשְׂנָא אֶת־אָחִיךָ בִּלְבָבֶךָ הוֹכֵחַ תּוֹכִיחַ
אֶת־עֲמִיתֶךָ וְלֹא־תִשָּׂא עָלָיו חֵטְא. לֹא־
תִקֹּם וְלֹא־תִטֹּר אֶת־בְּנֵי עַמֶּךָ וְאָהַבְתָּ
לְרֵעֲךָ כָּמוֹךָ אֲנִי יהוה.

NJV

(17-18)You shall not hate your kinsman in your heart. Reprove your neighbor, *but* **incur no guilt because of him. You shall not take vengeance or bear a grudge against your kinsfolk. Love your neighbor as yourself: I am the Lord.**

SVJ

(17-18) You shall not hate your brother in your heart; you shall surely rebuke your neighbor, *and* **not bear sin because of him. You shall not take vengeance, nor bear any grudge against the children of your people, but you shall love your neighbor as yourself: I am the Lord.**

RASHI

Love your neighbor as yourself. Rabbi Akiba said: This is a fundamental principle of the Torah. (Sifra; Ned. 9:3)

*Koshi:*_____

Answer: _____

Lesson: _____

This is your page to draw your own conclusions about the passage from the Holiness Code.

_____
_____
_____
_____
_____
_____
_____
_____
_____
_____
_____
_____
_____
_____
_____
_____
_____
_____
_____
_____
_____
_____
_____
_____
_____
_____
_____
_____
_____
_____
_____
_____
_____

TEXT THREE: DEUTERONOMY 34:1-12 (The Death of Moses)

This time, we're going to look at the last passage in the Torah—the Death of Moses. To understand it, we're going to use:

Two translations (SJV and NJV)
A map
Rashi's commentary
The Ramban's commentary

You'll discover as you work that this passage is more complex than you would expect on first reading.

I. Read the two translations. The *italics* indicate the places where you ought to notice the difference in the translation. The **bold type** indicates the places where Rashi will comment. Make notes on the *kusheyot* you expect to answer.

2. Locate sites on the map. Reading part of the Rashi and the Ramban commentaries will also help you in this task.

3. Work through the rest of the Rashi explication. Identify the problems and the solutions.

4. Write your conclusions.

This text will really show the different elements that can be found in one passage.

וַיַּעַל מֹשֶׁה מֵעַרְבֹת מוֹאָב אֶל־הַר נְבוֹ רֹאשׁ הַפִּסְגָּה אֲשֶׁר עַל־פְּנֵי יְרֵחוֹ   וַיַּרְאֵהוּ יהוה אֶת־כָּל־הָאָרֶץ אֶת־הַגִּלְעָד עַד־דָּן.

NJV

(1)Moses went up from the steppes of Moab to Mount Nebo, to the summit of Pisgah, opposite Jericho, and the Lord showed him ***the whole land:* Gilead as far as Dan;**

SJV

(1)And Moses went up from the plains of Moab unto Mount Nebo, to the top of Pisgah, that is over against Jericho. And the Lord showed him **all the land**, even Gilead **as far as Dan;**

_____

_____

_____

וְאֵת כָּל־נַפְתָּלִי וְאֶת־אֶרֶץ אֶפְרַיִם וּמְנַשֶּׁה וְאֵת כָּל־אֶרֶץ יְהוּדָה עַד הַיָּם הָאַחֲרוֹן.

(2)**all Naphtali; the land of Ephraim and Manasseh; the whole land of Judah as far as the *Western Sea;***

(2)**and all Naphtali, and the land of Ephraim, and Manasseh, and all the land of Judah as far as the *hinder sea;***

_____

_____

_____

וְאֶת־הַנֶּגֶב וְאֶת־הַכִּכָּר בִּקְעַת יְרֵחוֹ עִיר הַתְּמָרִים עַד־צֹעַר.

(3) *the Negeb;* and **the Plain**—the valley of Jericho, the city of palm trees—as far as Zoar.

(3) *and the South,* and **the Plain,** even the valley of Jericho the city of palm trees, as far as Zoar.

MAPPING EXERCISE

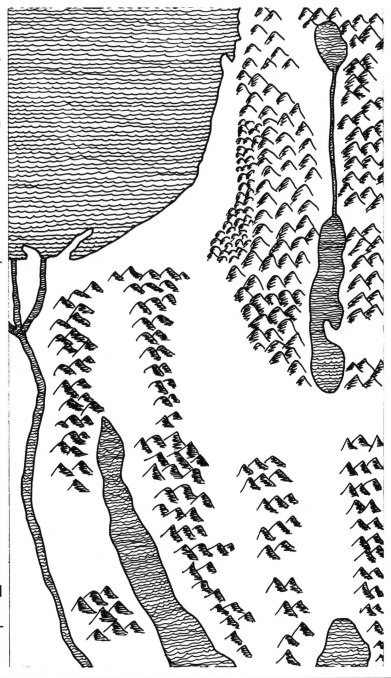

The passage in Deuteronomy is primarily geographical. By using the map and learning about the seven regions of Israel, we will better understand what the biblical author intended to teach us in the description of God showing the land to Moses.

Part One: Geographic Regions

In Deuteronomy the Land of Israel is divided into seven regions. Place these on your map.

1. *The Hill Country*—The central mountain range including the Judean hills and Mt. Ephraim.
2. *The Shefelah*—Low hills running north to south between the Judean hills and the coastal plain.
3. *The Seacoast*—(Also called the *Sharon*).
4. *The Aravah*—The Jordan Riff, the wadi (valley) leading from the Dead Sea to the Gulf of Aqaba.
5. *The Slopes*—The steep descent from the hill country of the Jordan Riff (by the Pisgah).
6. *The Wilderness*—The Judean Desert, which lies between the Judean hills and the Dead Sea.
7. *The Negev*—The Dry Country—The southern region, starting south of the Judean hills.

Part Two: Mapping Our Passage

The above terminology is geographical. The text from Deut. 34:1-3 uses mainly political terms. Put these on your map too.

a. Moab
b. Mt. Nebo
c. Jericho
d. Gilead
e. Dan
f. Naphtali
g. Ephraim
h. Manasseh
i. Judah
j. The last sea
k. Negev
l. The Plain

Part Three: Understanding Our Passage

1. The first time (Deut. 1:7-8) that the Torah describes the Land of Israel, Moses tells the people to conquer the land, and the regions are described in geographical and national terms.

Start out, then, and make your way to the hill country of the Amorites and all their neighbors in the Aravah, the hill country, the Shefelah, the Negev, the seacoast, the land of Canaanites, and the Lebanon, as far as the Great River, the river Euphrates. See, I place the land at your disposal. Go take possession of the land, that the LORD swore to your fathers, Abraham, Isaac, and Jacob, to give to them and to their offspring after them.

The passage at the end of the Book of Deuteronomy describes the way God shows the land to Moses, and many of the areas are labeled with tribal names. Explain this difference.

2. The following sequence is the way the text introduces the land in Deuteronomy 34. Can you make sense of the order or pairings? (It will help you to indicate this progression on your map.) Explain your theory.

   a. from Gilead to Dan
   b. all Naphtali
   c. Ephraim and Manasseh
   d. Judah as far as the Western Sea

e. Negev
f. The Plain
g. The Valley of Jericho
h. Zoar

Part Four: Reading Our Passage with Rashi

The Kusheyot—In Deut. 32:1-3 God shows the land to Moses. This description presents us with two problems.

1. The place names are tribal rather than geographic. This is a change. Why?
2. The order is strange. There doesn't seem to be a logical progression of areas. What are we supposed to learn from this order?

All the land. The Lord showed him all the Land of Israel in its prosperity and the oppressors who in future time would oppress it.

To Dan. He showed him the children of Dan practicing idolatry and he showed him Samson, who would come from Dan.

All of Naphtali. He showed him his land both in its prosperity and in its ruin. He showed him Deborah and Barak of Kedesh-naphtali warring with Sisera and his army.

The land of Ephraim and Manasseh. He showed him their land in both prosperity and in ruin. He showed him Joshua who came from Ephraim warring with the kings of Canaan, and Gideon who came from Manasseh warring with Midian and Amalek.

And all the land of Judah. In its prosperity and in its ruin. He showed him the kings of the House of Judah and their victories.

עַד הַיָּם הָאַחֲרוֹן/**ad hayam ha'acharon (Western Sea)** [understood as the Mediterranean] literally—"the last sea." The seacoast in its prosperity and ruin.

Another explanation: Read it as הַיּוֹם הָאַחֲרוֹן /hayom ha'acharon ("the last day"), meaning the final judgment, rather than הַיָּם הָאַחֲרוֹן /hayam ha'acharon("the last sea"). The Holy One who is to be praised showed him all that will happen to Israel in the future until the "last day," when the dead will live again.

The Negev: This refers to the Cave of Machpelah (where Abraham, Sarah, Isaac, Rebekah, etc., are buried). The Torah teaches (Num. 13:22): *And they went up to the Negeb and came to Hebron* (where the cave was bought).

The Plain: He showed him Solomon casting vessels for the Temple. The Bible teaches (1 Kings 7:46): *The king cast them in thick clay in the plain of the Jordan. (Sifre)*

I. How does Rashi understand this passage? What does he learn from the tribal names?

_____

_____

_____

_____

2. In Rashi's opinion, what does God really want to show Moses?

_____

_____

_____

_____

3. What does Rashi believe is God's central message to Moses? (What idea does he repeat over and over again?)

_____

_____

_____

_____

4. This "future-history" of Israel is designed to prepare us as well as Moses. What should we expect in the future?

_____

_____

_____

_____

Part Five: Reading with the Ramban

Rashi seems to be concerned with the "salvation history" of Israel, with the way the Jewish people will move from slavery to the final redemption. This movement through history is what he finds in the passage.

The רַמְבַּן /Ramban (Rabbi Moses Ben Nachman) finds a different insight. Read his comment and see if you can isolate his concern.

As you work, fill in this chart.

List of Tribes.	Check off the tribes mentioned in Deut. 34:1-3.	Check off the tribes mentioned in Ramban's comments.
Reuben		
Judah		
Levi		
Benjamin		
Ephraim		
Manasseh		
Zebulun		
Issachar		
Gad		
Asher		
Simeon		
Dan		
Naphtali		

And the Lord showed him all the land. That is, all the Land of Israel beyond the Jordan (westward)—and then the verse stated that God showed him **from Gilead to Dan.** Now Moses was in the hill country of Reuben (the far side of the Jordan belonged to Reuben, Gad, and part to Manasseh. This was also called Gilead.)...The passage says **as far as Dan,** which is the far border of the Land of Israel. We learn this in 2 Sam. 24:2: *Go now to and fro through all the tribes of Israel from Dan to Beer-sheba.* Deuteronomy 34 mentions **the land of Ephraim and Manasseh,** which was in the northern part of the Land of Israel, and the **land of Judah,** which was in the south. It mentions **Naphtali,** which was in the east near Judah. But it does not mention Asher and Issachar because they were part of Ephraim and Manasseh. Simeon is not mentioned because we learned in Josh. 19:1: *Their inheritance was in the midst of the inheritance of the children of Judah.* Zebulun is included in the statement **to the Western Sea,** which refers to Zebulun, who lived (Gen. 49:13) *at the shore of the sea.*

236

I. Starting with the uniqueness of the use of tribal names, Ramban found a different *koshi* in this text. What problem was he trying to solve?

_____

_____

_____

2. How does he solve this *koshi?*

_____

_____

_____

3. What "lesson" does the Ramban learn from this passage?

_____

_____

_____

4. Why was there no need to include the tribe of Levi?

_____

_____

_____

NOW LET'S READ THE SECOND HALF OF THIS CHAPTER WITH RASHI

וַיֹּאמֶר יהוה אֵלָיו זֹאת הָאָרֶץ אֲשֶׁר נִשְׁבַּעְתִּי לְאַבְרָהָם לְיִצְחָק וּלְיַעֲקֹב לֵאמֹר לְזַרְעֲךָ אֶתְּנֶנָּה הֶרְאִיתִיךָ בְעֵינֶיךָ וְשָׁמָּה לֹא תַעֲבֹר.

NJV

(4) And the Lord said to him, "This is the land of which I swore to Abraham, Isaac, and Jacob, '**I will give it to your offspring.'** *I have let you see it with your own eyes,* but you shall not cross there."

SJV

(4)And the Lord said to him: "This is the land which I swore unto Abraham, unto Isaac, and unto Jacob, saying: I will give it unto thy seed; *I have caused thee to see it with thine eyes,* but thou shalt not go thither."

Saying, I have let you see it. So that you can tell Abraham, Isaac, and Jacob that the oath which the Holy One who is to be praised swore to you—that oath God has fulfilled. This is why the Torah uses the word לֵאמֹר */lemor* (to say), to teach that I have let you see it so that you can say. But it is a decree from Me that **you shall not cross there.** For were this not so, I would keep you alive until you saw them planted and settled there, and then you would go and tell them (the patriarchs).

Koshi: _____

Answer: _____

Lesson: _____

וַיָּמׇת שָׁם מֹשֶׁה עֶבֶד־יהוה בְּאֶרֶץ מוֹאָב עַל־פִּי יהוה.

(5)So Moses the servant of the Lord died there, in the land of Moab, *at the command of the Lord.*

(5)So Moses the servant of the Lord died there in the land of Moab, *according to the word of the Lord.*

Moses died there. Is it possible that Moses died and then wrote "*And Moses died there*"? Moses wrote up to this point, and Joshua wrote the rest. Rabbi Meir said: It is possible that Torah could have been complete at Deuteronomy 31:26, which says: *Take this book of the law [Torah] and put it by the side of the ark of the covenant of the LORD your God, that it may be there as a witness....*The Holy One who is to be praised dictated the rest, and Moses wrote it with tears in his eyes.
(Sifra; B. Bat. 15a; Menach. 30a)

Koshi: _____

Answer: _____

Lesson: _____

עַל־פִּי יהוה **/al pi Adonai (by the command of the LORD).** [Rashi translates these words as **by the mouth**]—with a kiss. (M. Kat. 28a)

Koshi: _____

Answer: _____

Lesson: _____

וַיִּקְבֹּר אֹתוֹ בַגַּי בְּאֶרֶץ מוֹאָב מוּל בֵּית פְּעוֹר וְלֹא־יָדַע אִישׁ אֶת־קְבֻרָתוֹ עַד הַיּוֹם הַזֶּה.

(6)*He buried him* in the valley in the land of Moab, near Beth-peor; and no one knows his burial place to this day.

(6)*And he was buried* in the valley in the land of Moab over against Beth-peor; and no man knoweth of his sepulchre unto this day.

And H/he buried him. The Holy One who is to be praised buried him. Rabbi Ishmael explained that the word אֹתוֹ */oto* could also mean "He buried himself."

*Koshi:*_____

Answer: _____

Lesson: _____

וּמֹשֶׁה בֶּן־מֵאָה וְעֶשְׂרִים שָׁנָה בְּמֹתוֹ לֹא־כָהֲתָה עֵינוֹ וְלֹא־נָס לֵחֹה.

(7)**Moses was a hundred and twenty years old when he died;** *his eyes were undimmed and his vigor unabated.*

(7)**And Moses was a hundred and twenty years old when he died;** *his eye was not dim, nor was his natural force abated.*

His eye was not dim. Even after he died. [Note: The phrase which we translate as "eyes not dim" may well mean that his color was not faded.] **And his vigor unabated.** Nor did the life-sap that was in him depart; decomposition had no power over him and the appearance of his face did not change.

*Koshi:*_____

Answer: _____

Lesson:_____

וַיִּבְכּוּ בְנֵי יִשְׂרָאֵל אֶת־מֹשֶׁה בְּעַרְבֹת מוֹאָב שְׁלֹשִׁים יוֹם וַיִּתְּמוּ יְמֵי בְכִי אֵבֶל מֹשֶׁה.

(8)**And the Israelites** bewailed Moses in the steppes of Moab for thirty days. The period of wailing and mourning for Moses came to an end.

(8)*And the children of Israel wept* for Moses in the plains of Moab thirty days; so the days of weeping in the mourning for Moses were ended.

The children of Israel wept. Here only the men are mentioned, but, when Aaron died, the Torah says (Num. 20:29), *The whole house of Israel wept*—meaning both the men and the women. This is because Aaron was a pursuer of peace and made peace between people and between husband and wife. (Pirke de-Rabbi Eliezer, ch. 17)

Koshi: _____

Answer: _____

Lesson: _____

וִיהוֹשֻׁעַ בֶּן־נוּן מָלֵא רוּחַ חָכְמָה כִּי־סָמַךְ מֹשֶׁה אֶת־יָדָיו עָלָיו וַיִּשְׁמְעוּ אֵלָיו בְּנֵי־יִשְׂרָאֵל וַיַּעֲשׂוּ כַּאֲשֶׁר צִוָּה יְהוָה אֶת־מֹשֶׁה.

וְלֹא־קָם נָבִיא עוֹד בְּיִשְׂרָאֵל כְּמֹשֶׁה אֲשֶׁר יְדָעוֹ יְהוָה פָּנִים אֶל־פָּנִים.

(9)Now Joshua son of Nun was filled with the spirit of wisdom because Moses had laid his hands upon him; and the Israelites heeded him, doing as the Lord had commanded Moses.

(9)And Joshua the son of Nun was full of the spirit of wisdom: for Moses had laid his hands upon him; and the children of Israel hearkened unto him, and did as the Lord commanded Moses.

(10)Never again did there arise in Israel a prophet like Moses—*whom the Lord singled out, face to face,*

(10)And there hath not arisen a prophet since in Israel like unto Moses, *whom the Lord knew face to face;*

Whom the Lord knew face to face. This means that Moses was familiar with God and used to speak to Him at any time he desired; this is what is learned in Exod. 32:30, *And now I will ascend to the Lord*, and in Num. 9:8, *Stay and I will listen to what God will command regarding you.*

Koshi: _____

Answer: _____

Lesson: _____

לְכָל־הָאֹתֹת וְהַמּוֹפְתִים אֲשֶׁר שְׁלָחוֹ יהוה לַעֲשׂוֹת בְּאֶרֶץ מִצְרָיִם לְפַרְעֹה וּלְכָל־עֲבָדָיו וּלְכָל־אַרְצוֹ. וּלְכֹל הַיָּד הַחֲזָקָה וּלְכֹל הַמּוֹרָא הַגָּדוֹל אֲשֶׁר עָשָׂה מֹשֶׁה לְעֵינֵי כָּל־יִשְׂרָאֵל.

(11)for the various signs and portents that the Lord sent him to display in the land of Egypt, against Pharaoh and all his courtiers and his whole country,

(11)in all the signs and the wonders, which the Lord sent him to do in the land of Egypt, to Pharaoh, and to all his servants, and to all his land;

(12)and for all *the great might* and **awesome power** that Moses displayed before all Israel.

(12)and *in all the mighty hand,* and *in all the great terror,* which Moses wrought in the sight of *all Israel.*

in all the mighty hand. This refers to the fact that he received the Torah and had the strength to carry the tablets in his hands.

in all the great terror. This refers to the miracles and mighty deeds which were made to happen in the great and terrible wilderness. (Sifre)

before [the eyes of] all Israel. This refers to the fact that his heart inspired him to break the tablets before their eyes. This is what the Torah teaches (Deut. 9:7): *And I break them before your eyes.* The Holy One who is to be praised said: *Because you broke them, may your strength be increased.* (Midrashic rereading of Exod. 34:1) (Jeb. 62a; Sab. 87a)

Koshi: _____

Answer: _____

Lesson: _____

The second half of this passage focuses on Moses. What does Rashi teach us about Moses (and how he was a unique leader)? What does Rashi think was Moses' most important quality?

_____

_____

_____

_____

_____

EVALUATION

In this module, you have worked on your own through some very difficult passages. How would you evaluate this experience?

_____

_____

_____

_____

_____

_____

_____

_____

_____

_____

_____

_____

_____

_____

_____

_____

_____

_____

_____

_____

_____

_____

_____

_____

_____

_____

_____

_____

_____

_____

_____

_____

_____

_____

_____

THE MAGIC HAND

"The king I served had an image of a hand," he answered. "The hand had five fingers, and on it were etched all the lines and creases found in the palm of a hand. This hand was in fact a map of all the worlds. On it was marked all that has been since heaven and earth were created and all that will be until the end. Everything in the world was marked on it, down to the last detail, in its lines and creases. It was like a map, and just as on a map there are letters by each mark to show that here is the city and there is that stream, so in the creases of the hand there were special symbols. Every country and city, every stream and river and mountain, in the world and in all the worlds, was marked out in its creases and lines. In the same way, each person in every country and all the events of their lives were marked on the hand.

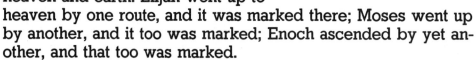

"All the paths from one country to another and from one place to another were shown. That was how I knew how to enter this city, whose fortifications no man could pass. Were you to send me from this city to another, I would know the way. And just as the hand showed the paths between one city and another, it also marked those between the various worlds and those between heaven and earth. Elijah went up to heaven by one route, and it was marked there; Moses went up by another, and it too was marked; Enoch ascended by yet another, and that too was marked.

"Furthermore, everything was engraved on the hand as it had been when the world was created, as it is now, and as it will be. Thus the city of Sodom appeared as it was before it was destroyed, while it was being destroyed, and after its destruction. Everything that ever was, is now, and ever will be was engraved on the hand...."

Rabbi Nachman of Bratzlav, **The Master of Prayer,** retold by Adin Steinsaltz, from **Beggars and Prayers** (New York: Basic Books), 1979.

EPILOGUE

Rabbi Lawrence Kushner frequently teaches that Torah is the "collective unconscious" of the Jewish people—the stuff out of which Jewish dreams are made. For me, I often reflect that the Torah is the DNA of Jewish life, the life-chain of codes and symbols which is uniquely combined in each of us, yet whose passing from generation to generation sustains the process of creation. Talk of Torah, it seems, is talking in metaphors.

Writing this book has taken me more than ten years—it's been a long process filled with constant frustrations, ripped up manuscripts, and revisions of parts that didn't quite work. In writing it, I've been through my own version of a Torah-maze and Torah-thornforest; I've invented my own handles and indeed drunk from the well of Torah. I imagine that the process you will experience in learning Torah from this book will be no easier.

Learning Torah is never easy. Messages come to us slowly, word by word, and take a long time to sink in. When God created people, God put them in the garden and told them to "work it and keep it." A short while later, the Torah echoed the word again, and, with the first murder, we learned to "keep" our brothers and sisters. A few generations passed, and Abraham entered into a relationship with God, and his family became the "keepers" of laws and commandments which became part of the covenant. More generations passed, and we learned to "keep" Shabbat, "keep" the covenant, and slowly "keeper" became a description for being a Jew. But the story didn't end there: in the Psalmist's song, we learned that God is Israel's "Keeper." "Keeping" is an eternal relationship. And that is just one word. Studying Torah requires careful reading and listening and waiting for connections to reveal themselves through the careful examination of clues and insights. It is an adventure, albeit slow and endless.

There are many images of the Torah as being heavy. We saw two stories in Module Two, one about the lifting of the ark, the other about the weight of a Torah scroll. In each case, once they were lifted—they carried the one who had struggled with them. Hopefully that has been your experience in reading this book. It is the same interpretation Rashi brings to the last verse in the Torah—Moses' real strength was in lifting the commandments. These images reflect the reality—that there is a lot of struggle in lifting the Torah. If you've made it this far, climbing so many little technical peaks, then you've had your lifting experience.

Hopefully the study has provided its own reward through insights you're proud of discovering, images which have become meaningful, and friendships which have evolved or strengthened through dialogues over the text.

Turn it and turn it again,
for all is contained in it.

So taught Ben Bag Bag in Pirke Avot. Hopefully you've now begun to find your own meaning, looking into Rabbi Nachman's magic hand.

When He finished speaking *with him* on Mount Sinai, He gave Moses the two tables of the Pact, stone tablets inscribed with the finger of God. Exod. 31:18

RASHI: The words *with him* teach us that Moses first heard Torah from God's mouth, and then they repeated it together. Tanch. Exod. R. 41

The midrash from which this is drawn explains that this is how a good teacher works with students—helping till the students can say the words on their own. I believe you are now ready.

243